Siminoff's
Luthiers
Glossary

FIRST EDITION

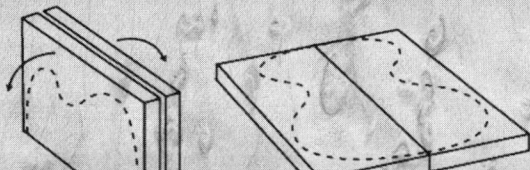

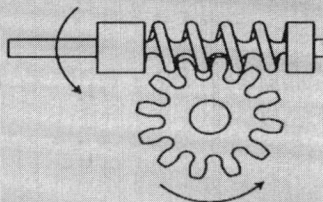

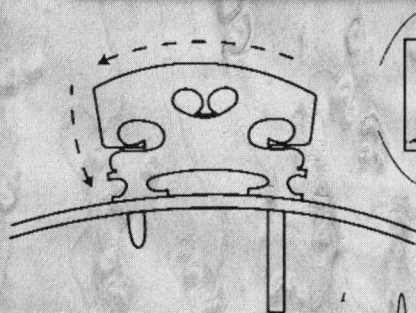

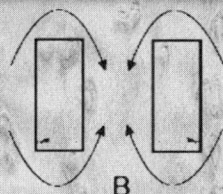

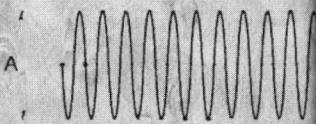

Roger H. Siminoff

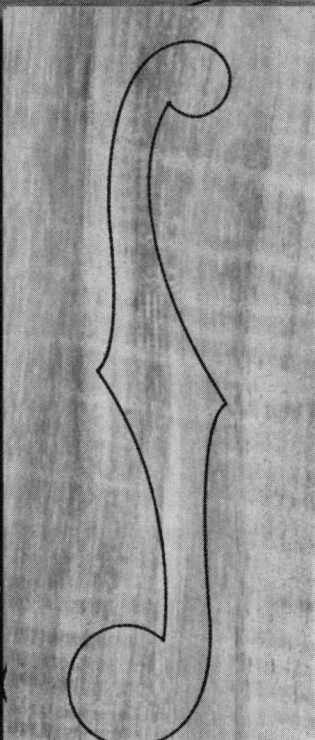

Color plates of wood
courtesy of:

Maderas-Barber, S.L.
Valencia, Spain
www.maderasbarber.com

Siminoff Banjo and Mandolin Parts
Arroyo Grande, California, USA
www.siminoff.net

Also by Roger H. Siminoff:

The Art of Tap Tuning
Constructing a Bluegrass Mandolin
Constructing a 5-String Banjo
Constructing a Solid Body Guitar
How to Set Up the Best Sounding Banjo
The Luthier's Handbook
The Ultimate Bluegrass Mandolin Construction Manual
Publisher: Hal Leonard Corporation

The Physics of Music
Publisher: Roger H. Siminoff

101 Smart Boating Tips
Publisher: McGraw-Hill

Siminoff's
Luthiers Glossary

by
Roger H. Siminoff

Edited by
Rosemary J Wagner

Hal Leonard Books
New York

Published in 2008 by Hal Leonard Books
An Imprint of Hal Leonard Corporation
7777 West Bluemound Road
Milwaukee, WI 53213

Trade Book Division Editorial Offices
19 West 21st Street, New York, NY 10010

Printed in the United States of America

Library of Congress Cataloging-in-Publication Data is available upon request.

ISBN 978-1-4234-4292-9

www.halleonard.com

Siminoff's Luthiers Glossary

by
Roger H. Siminoff

Edited by
Rosemary J Wagner

Hal Leonard Books
New York

Published in 2008 by Hal Leonard Books
An Imprint of Hal Leonard Corporation
7777 West Bluemound Road
Milwaukee, WI 53213

Trade Book Division Editorial Offices
19 West 21st Street, New York, NY 10010

Printed in the United States of America

Library of Congress Cataloging-in-Publication Data is available upon request.

ISBN 978-1-4234-4292-9

www.halleonard.com

CONTENTS

PREFACE

Every trade, art, and hobby has its own language. Sailors use charts, not maps; quilters speak of free-motion quilting; and shooters know that a barrel isn't something that holds rain water.

When I started *Pickin' Magazine* back in the early-1970s, I knew that we were in the business of selling content and that accurate reporting was key to our success. In pursuit of both accuracy and consistency, we developed a "format book" to ensure that our editorial staff spoke the language of the industry – being sure that fingerboards were on violins and fretboards were on guitars, quartered grain was a direction and quarter-sawn was a method. As I brought *Frets Magazine* to life in 1978, our format book grew, and I began to expand my list of luthierie terms from a small set of words and phrases to what has become the content of this book, *Siminoff's Luthiers Glossary*.

About a year before coming to the conclusion that others might benefit from a glossary such as this, a luthier e-mailed me asking for a "face plate." I wrote back and told him that we had three standard woods for peghead veneers and that many other options were available. He wrote back, "No, a face plate, the part that goes under the bridge!" As I sat there thinking about what part he really wanted, it became clear how much easier it would be if we were all reading from the same page (literally and figuratively).

As the words "First Edition" on the front cover imply, this Glossary is neither definitive nor final. There are many manufacturing companies, small enclaves of luthiers, and builders of unique instruments who have their own dialogue or variations of the terms in this Glossary, and new terms and technologies continue to emerge. And, I am sure there are words I have missed. So, it is my hope to expand the content over the coming years to be as rich and all-inclusive as possible.

In addition to the Glossary terms, I have prepared several reference tables that I hope will be helpful to you. And, at the end of the book, there are numerous color plates of both natural and lacquered woods to help you identify the material you are either trying to match or are seeking.

Having laid this groundwork, I would be remiss if I did not recognize the incredible work of my editor, Rosemary Wagner. For her relentless effort and intense focus, I'm deeply indebted to her.

If you are a seasoned luthier, I hope you find a few terms that are new to you. If you are new to the art of luthierie, I hope this Glossary helps facilitate many interesting and valuable dialogues.

Roger H. Siminoff

Glossary

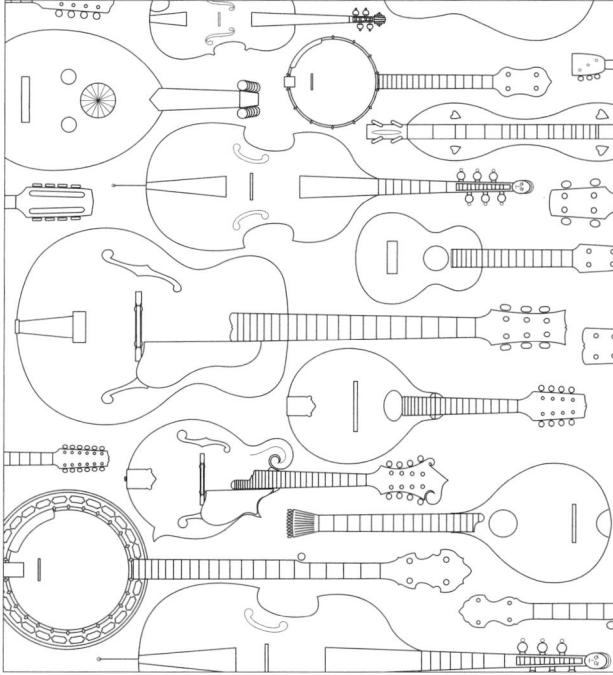

The history of luthierie is profusely populated with builders, manufacturers, marketing expressions, brand names, instrument types, design styles, and specialties, and the diffuse terminologies are magnified by our geographies and our languages. *Siminoff's Luthiers Glossary* contains the most common luthierie terms with the goal of defining the term and its typical usages, and does not suggest that it is the *only* word or description.

The illustrations represent the most common attributes of each item and, except as noted, are not intended to be suggestive of any particular make, model or brand. As a result of the vast individualization in the craft of luthierie, a wide array of design, stringing, and structural variations of these instruments exist, and their unique features are not to be considered incorrect or invalid if they are not listed or are different from the descriptions or illustrations in this Glossary.

All brand names are the property of their respective owners and are provided for reference only. No recommendation or endorsement is implied.

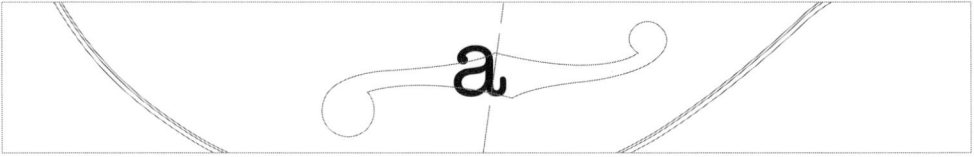

abalone a highly variegated natural mollusk shell that is sawn into small pieces and used for inlays. The extreme curvature of the shell makes it difficult to cut flat pieces larger than about 1″ x 1″. A few large pieces can be taken from the shell's rim for nuts. Various species of abalone provide a wide variety of colors, although red and green are the most popular. (see mother of pearl)

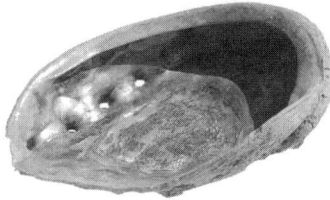

ABALONE SHELL

Acacia koa the botanical name for koa. (see koa)

Acer macrophyllum the botanical name for big leaf maple. (see big leaf maple)

Acer pseudoplantanus the botanical name for sycamore. (see sycamore)

Acer rubrum the botanical name for red maple. (see red maple)

Acer saccharum the botanical name for sugar maple. (see sugar maple)

acoustic bass (see bass viol)

acoustics the science of the production, measurement, enhancement, and sensory perception of sound.

action a description of the height of the strings above the frets. High action signifies excessive space between the frets and the strings; low action signifies limited space between the frets and the strings. Action is usually measured at the 1st and 12th frets. The ideal action at the 1st fret should be the same as the action at the 2nd fret when the string is fretted at the 1st fret. The ideal action at the 12th fret is dependent on the player's or luthier's preference. The action at the 1st fret is the result of the string notch depth in the

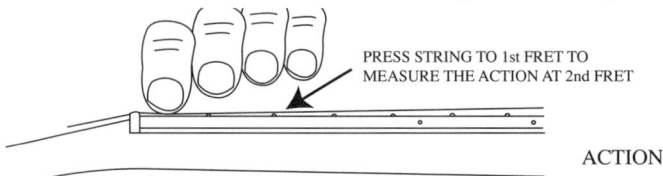

PRESS STRING TO 1st FRET TO
MEASURE THE ACTION AT 2nd FRET

ACTION

nut. The action at the 12th fret is the result of the neck pitch, bridge height, action at the nut or a combination of these. (see zero-fret)

adhesive a compound or material used to secure or bond two or more surfaces together.

Adirondack red spruce a luthierie term for red spruce, named for where the wood is harvested. (see red spruce)

A-Frame "X" a bracing system for stiffening the soundboard of an acoustic guitar. The A-Frame "X" is a modified X-brace system that features a bridgeplate set on an angle. Unlike the standard X-brace pattern, the A-Frame "X" system has only one lower tone bar. The A-Frame "X" bracing system was developed in the mid-1800s by C.F. Martin, Sr.

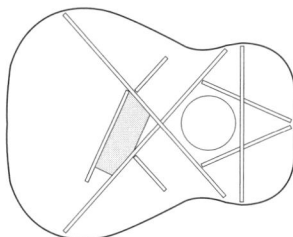

A-FRAME "X" BRACING

African blackwood (*Dalbergia melanoxylon*) a very dark, dense, hardwood from Africa. Blackwood is similar in weight and stiffness to rosewood, but with a very dark grey-brown color. Blackwood can be used for guitar backboards and rims, but it is somewhat rare and difficult to obtain.

African ebony (*Diospyros mespiliformis*) a black wood with some wisps of beige, typically used for bridges, fretboards, fingerboards, and peghead veneers. African ebony has a weight of about 75 pounds per cubic foot. (see Gaboon ebony)

African mahogany (*Khaya ivorensis*) a dark tan wood with mild grain and good dimensional stability. African mahogany is used for backboards and sides and weighs 33 pounds per cubic foot.

African padouk (*Pterocarpus soyauxii*) a dense reddish-brown hardwood used for backboards and sides. Padouk bends well, weighs 48 pounds per cubic foot, and comes from Africa.

African rosewood (see bubinga)

air brush a small spray gun commonly used for photo retouching and small model work. Because of the very fine spray emitted, air brushes are ideal for detail work and shading with dyes and stains. Air brushes can only spray a small amount of a well-thinned liquid and are not recommended for clear-coat finishing (e.g., lacquer or varnish).

air chamber the part of a string acoustic instrument that is enclosed by its body. The size of the air chamber is designed to enhance, support, and resonate with the musical range of the strings. The larger the air chamber, the lower its resonant frequency and vice versa.

air chamber tuning the act of adjusting the resonant frequency of the air chamber by modifying its size, the stiffness of its soundboard and/or backboard, and the size of its aperture(s). (see tap tuning)

air dried a description of wood whose moisture content has been reduced by seasoning it in the open air (vs. kiln dried). While air-dried wood is cured out of doors, it is generally protected from the sun and weather and is well stickered. Occasionally referred to as "air seasoned." (see kiln drying, stickering)

AIR-DRIED WOOD

air pressure 1) as it relates to sound, a measurement in decibels of the force of compressive layers of air against a surface. 2) as it relates to pneumatic systems, the pressure of air per cubic inch or cubic centimeter. (see decibel)

air seasoned (see air dried)

alcohol (see ethanol)

alignment pin a small stud of metal, plastic or wood to help secure a part in place during the gluing process. Alignment pins are used to keep parts such as fretboards, soundboards, backboards, and peghead veneers from sliding when clamping pressure is applied. The alignment pins can become either an integral part of the completed instrument or removed after use, depending on where and how they are used.

aliphatic glue an adhesive comprised of organic compounds that have carbon atoms linked in an open chain (string). Aliphatic glues provide fast curing and excellent bonding when gluing wood to wood. Common aliphatic glues used for luthierie are Titebond® Original Wood Glue and Elmer's® Glue-All (white glue).

Amati, Andrea (ca.1515 - ca.1578) one of the earliest violin luthiers and the founder of the heralded Cremonese School of Violin Makers. He is responsible for defining the basic shape and construction of the violin as we know it today. Andrea had two sons, Antonio and Girolamo. Andrea was less prolific than either of his sons or Stradavari, and only a few of Amati's instruments still exist.

Amati, Antonio (ca. 1550 - ?) the elder son of Andrea Amati. Antonio and brother Girolamo ("the Amati Brothers") are recognized for their development of the violin family's *f*-holes and for crafting the earliest violas.

Amati, Girolamo (1551-1635) the younger son of Andrea Amati. Girolamo and brother Antonio continued their father's craft as "the Amati Brothers." The brothers are recognized for the advancement of the violin family's *f*-holes and for crafting the earliest violas.

Amati, Nicolo (1596-1684) the son of Girolamo Amati, Nicolo continued the family's legacy of violin making. He developed a slightly wider body shape known as the "Grand Pattern" or "Grand Amati" whose size improved the overall power of the violin. It is believed that Nicolo mentored two highly admired apprentices, Antonio Stradivari and Andrea Guarneri.

Amazon rosewood (*Dalbergia spruceana*) a richly colored and figured wood used for backboards, sides, bridges, and fretboards. Amazon rosewood weighs 68 pounds per cubic foot and comes from Brazil. Unlike Brazilian rosewood (*Dalbergia nigra*) which is blocked from exportation by the CITES embargo, Amazon rosewood is available for luthierie. (see CITES)

American black walnut (see black walnut)

amplitude a quantitative measure of sound pressure by a device such as a decibelometer. (see decibel, loudness, sound pressure)

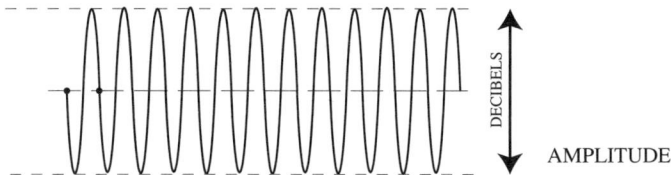

analog 1) data that is continuously varying or comprised of undulating waves. The motion of a vibrating string and the continuous tones it emits are both examples of analog data. 2) as it relates to tools of luthierie, pen and pencil drawings are analog and contrast greatly to digital drawings on a computer, as do analog templates whose use contrasts the work of CNC machines. (see digital)

angle of attack the direction at which a pick, hammer or excitation device contacts a string or vibrating member. The angle of attack is one of the reasons why the two strings of a pair (such as on a mandolin or 12-string guitar) sound different from each other when tuned to the same note. In this case, the player typically picks down on the upper string and up on the lower string of the pair. The picking motion makes the angle of attack different on each of these strings, which sets the strings in motion in correspondingly different orbits that, in turn, transfer energy differently to the bridge feet, braces, tone bars, and soundboard. The result is the same note but with different timbre. Of the five methods of attack, the angle of attack is typically of lesser importance to fretted instruments but of some importance to the violin- and viol-family instruments. (see attack)

aniline dye a fast-drying, deep-penetrating coloring agent that leaves minimal residue on the surface of wood. Aniline dyes are permanent, provide rich color, and come in liquid or powder form. [Rubber gloves should be worn, and care should be taken with aniline dye as the dye is considered to be both permanent and poisonous.]

anisotropic as it relates to acoustics, that property of a material in which sound radiates through the material in different directions at different speeds. An anisotropic material is one in which the cellular or physical structure is different in two or more axes. Wood is anisotropic; metal is isotropic. Wood can also be considered orthotropic. In Sitka spruce, the speed of sound through the longitudinal axis of the wood is approximately four times faster than the speed of sound through the lateral axis of the wood (depending on grain count, density, annular ring shape and alignment, moisture content, etc.) (see isotropic, orthotropic)

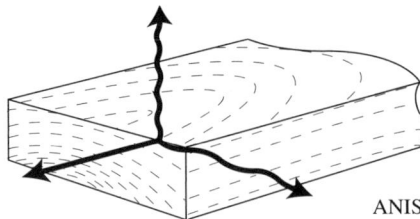

ANISOTROPIC

annular rings, annual rings the circumferential bands (as seen when cutting across a tree or log) that indicate the age of a tree. As the tree grows, one annular ring is added each year to the outside of the previous year's ring. Annular rings vary in width according to the species and growth rate of the species, and can be affected by climatic conditions, environmental events, and nourishment available to the tree during any specific year. Historical research of a tree's growth through the study of its annular rings is called dendrochronology.

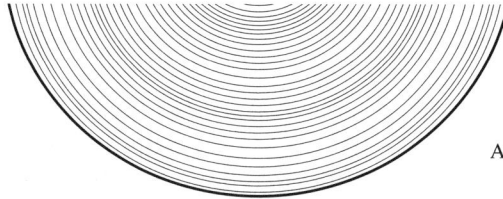

ANNULAR RINGS

aperture in musical instruments, some form of opening in the air chamber to control compression and rarefaction, to voice the instrument, and to connect the air in the instrument's body to the surrounding air. Apertures are typically in the shape of a circle, oval or fancy "*f*". An acoustic musical instrument can have one or more apertures. The aperture on a banjo is the space between the bottom of the rim and the inside face of the resonator.

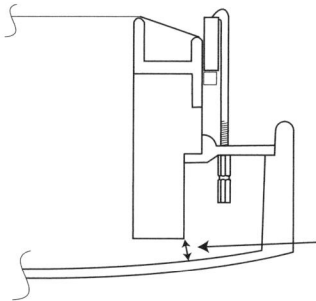

F-HOLE APERTURES OF JAZZ GUITAR, VIOLIN, AND MANDOLIN

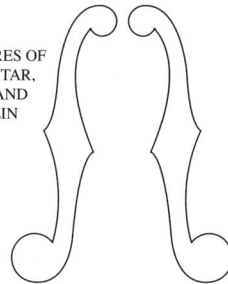

EFFECTIVE APERTURE OF BANJO WITH RESONATOR

APERTURES

arboreal referring to trees.

arched a soundboard or backboard that is higher in the center than along its edges. Arched soundboards and backboards are either carved or laminated. The arched shape is typically strong enough to enable soundboards and backboards to be used without bracing. However, tone bars are often attached to soundboards to control the tuning (stiffness).

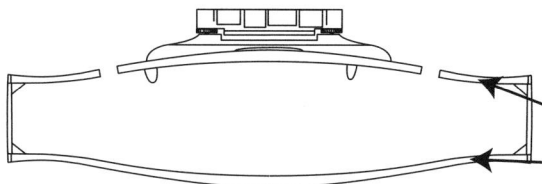

ARCHED SOUNDBOARD

ARCHED BACKBOARD

arched backboard a sound *producing* plate on the back of an instrument whose centermost section is higher than its outermost or perimeter portion. A properly constructed arched backboard is thicker in the center and becomes gradually thinner as it nears the edge. Some inexpensive instruments have arched backboards that are laminated and are the same thickness across the entire width. (see arched, recurve, resonator)

arched fretboard (see radiused fretboard)

arched soundboard a sound *producing* plate on the front of an instrument whose centermost section is higher than its outermost or perimeter portion. A properly prepared arched soundboard is graduated so that it is thicker in the center than it is near its edges. Some inexpensive instruments are made with laminated arched soundboards and are the same thickness across the entire width. (see arched, recurve)

arched tone chamber (see arch-top tone chamber)

arch-top acoustic guitar a wood-bodied, six-string instrument with a contoured (arched) soundboard. Arch-top acoustic guitars typically feature *f*-holes, a movable bridge, and a trapeze tailpiece. Most arch-top acoustic guitars also have an arched backboard. Better arch-top acoustic guitars have soundboards and backboards carved from solid wood (as opposed to being laminated as on some less expensive guitars). (see flat-top acoustic guitar, jazz guitar)

arch-top mandolin an eight-string four-course instrument that features a rasied and contoured (arched) soundboard. Arch-top mandolins can be A-style or F-style and have a movable bridge, a tailpiece, either a single oval soundhole or two *f*-holes, and an arched backboard. (see A-style mandolin, Florentine mandolin)

arch-top tone chamber a banjo head support ring fitted on top of the rim, designed by Gibson in the late-1920s. The "arch-top" is a description of the shape of the head as it fits over the raised innermost lip of the tone chamber. Most arch-top tone chambers are bronze castings. The forerunner of the arch-top tone chamber was the ball-bearing tone chamber that featured a raised inner ring. (see ball-bearing tone chamber, flat-head tone chamber)

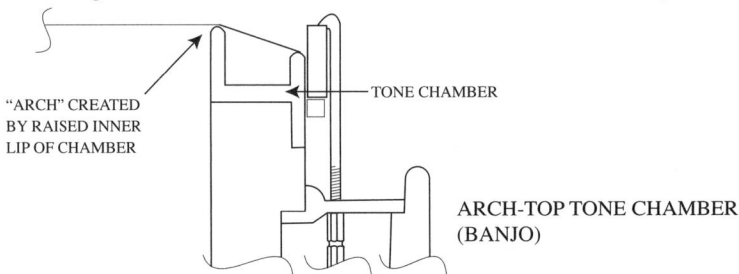

"ARCH" CREATED BY RAISED INNER LIP OF CHAMBER

TONE CHAMBER

ARCH-TOP TONE CHAMBER (BANJO)

Art Deco a design style that was most popular in the 1930s in which multiple curved and nested shapes are the prominent elements. The Art Deco style has a very industrial feel with shapes that overlay or join similar shapes to give the sense of depth. The art influence began around 1925, and in its time was considered to have a "modern" appearance. John Monteleone's Radio City-Blue Deluxe guitar model was influenced by the Art Deco style.

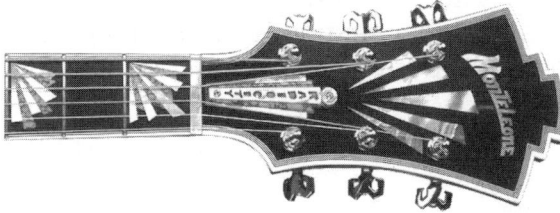

ART DECO DESIGN

A-style mandolin a four-course instrument with two strings per course tuned *E, A, D, G* (high to low). A-style mandolins feature a pear-shaped body, a flat or arched soundboard, a flat or arched backboard, and either a round or oval soundhole or two *f*-holes. The development of the A-style mandolin is attributed to Orville H. Gibson. Numerous similar body styles have been produced, the most popular being those by Gibson, Lyon and Healy, and CF Martin, with each company having its own letter or model designation. (see Florentine mandolin, Neapolitan mandolin)

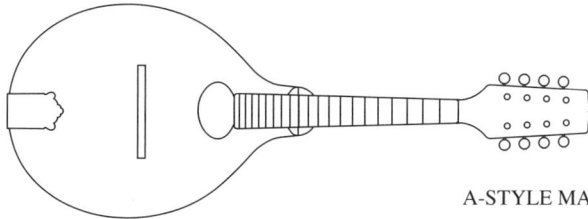

A-STYLE MANDOLIN

attack the act of exciting a string or vibrating member into motion. The overall tone produced is predicated on four primary elements: method of attack (what is used to excite the string; e.g., pick, bow, hammer); location of attack (where along the string's length it is excited); duration of attack (how long the string is excited; e.g., plucked vs. bowed); and intensity of attack (the force or energy of the excitation). A fifth and lesser element is the angle of attack (the direction at which a pick, hammer or bow excites a string or vibrating member).

aural harmonics supplemental tones generated within the ear canal (auditory meadus) that enrich the natural tones we hear.

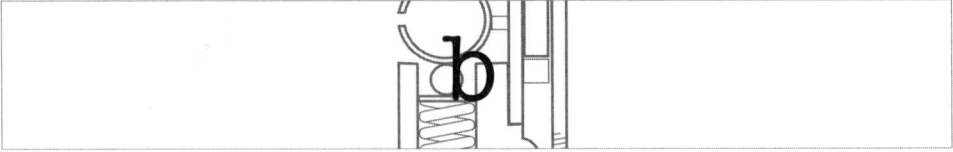

back bow a condition of an instrument's neck in which it is warped backwards such that the center of the fretboard or fingerboard is closer to the strings than it is at either end. Since the strings' tension usually forces the neck into a "hollow," a back bow is caused by either an over-tightened truss rod, by the absorption of too much moisture into the fretboard (causing expansion of its length), by excessive drying of the neck wood (causing shrinkage in the length of the neck) or by a combination of these. The purpose of a double-acting truss rod is to correct a back bow. Sometimes called a "crown." (see double-acting truss rod, hollow, truss rod)

back plate (see backboard)

backboard, back the sound *producing* plate on the back of an instrument. On string acoustic instruments, the backboard is usually made of a dense, rigid wood. (see plate, resonator)

backstrip a decorative piece of laminate, purfling or marquetry inlaid into the center seam or multiple seams of the backboard of a guitar or similar instrument. (see marquetry, purfling)

balalaika a three-string instrument tuned *D, A, D* (high to low) or tuned guitar style to *D, B, G* (high to low). Some balalaikas are three-course instruments with two strings per course. The instrument is a comparatively simple design that features a flat soundboard and backboard and three straight rib pieces that close its triangular body. The balalaika originated in Russia in the late-1600s.

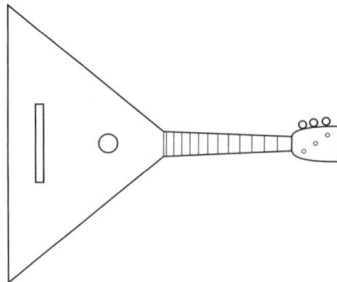

BALALAIKA

ball-bearing tone chamber a banjo structure developed by Gibson in 1918 in which the tone chamber rests on a series of ball bearings. The ball-bearing tone chamber was indented to provide the banjo head with greater resilience for a brighter, more sustained sound. A second version, designed in 1918, features springs beneath the ball bearings to provide even greater resilience. A negative feature of the spring-loaded ball-bearing design was discovered when the skin head expanded and contracted with changes in humidity causing the force of the springs to raise the tone ring and change the action.

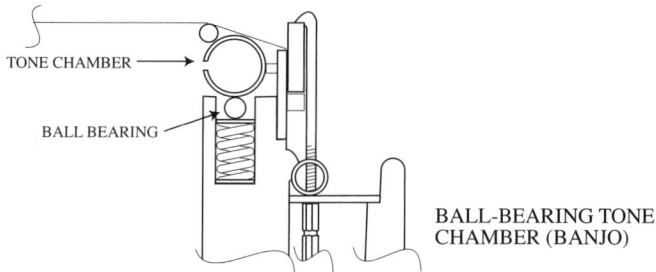

TONE CHAMBER

BALL BEARING

BALL-BEARING TONE CHAMBER (BANJO)

ball-end string a musical string with one end wrapped around a bead-like part to prevent the string from slipping out of the bridge or tailpiece. (see loop-end string)

ball peen hammer a striking tool with a rounded head on one side and a flattened head or face on the opposite side. The name was derived from the hammer having a ball-shaped head to peen (widen and flatten) rivets and similar fittings.

banjo an instrument with four, five, six or eight strings, featuring a round body, a movable bridge, and a membrane-like soundboard (head). The design of the traditional banjo requires one end of the strings be anchored by a tailpiece. The soundboard (head) is typically made of animal skin or Mylar®. The banjo's rim (body) is constructed of either laminated strips or blocks of wood. The sound-producing, neck-connecting, and head-attaching hardware varies with the make and model of the instrument. The rim and hardware combined are often referred to as the "pot assembly." The back of some models of the banjo is fitted with a tone-projecting shell called a "resonator." Banjos without resonators are called "open back" banjos. (see folk banjo, frailing banjo, guitar banjo, mandolin banjo, plectrum banjo, regular banjo, tenor banjo, ukulele banjo)

banjo designation Gibson promoted several abbreviations to refer to its banjo models. These include: GB for guitar banjo, MB for mandolin banjo, PB for plectrum banjo, RB for regular banjo, TB for tenor banjo, and UB for ukulele banjo.

banjo head the soundboard of a banjo. Banjo heads were originally made of animal skin and later replaced by Mylar®. Today, Mylar heads are available in numerous gauges and several versions such as clear, opaque, and white; and sprayed, textured, and plain surfaces.

banjo mandolin (see mandolin banjo)

baritone ukulele (see ukulele)

bass bar a structural element attached to the inside of the soundboard on violin-family instruments. The size and shape of the bass bar establishes the tuning of the soundboard by controlling its stiffness. The bass bar is a longitudinal member located directly beneath the bass foot of the bridge.

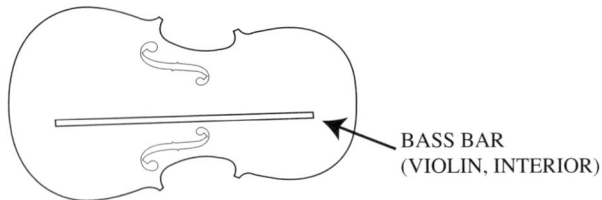

BASS BAR
(VIOLIN, INTERIOR)

bass bout (see bout)

bass viol the largest four-string instrument of the violin family, tuned *G, D, A, E* (high to low). The bass viol features a carved and graduated belly (soundboard) and backboard, one longitudinal bass bar, a soundpost, two *f*-holes, and a pegbox fitted with geared pegs (a necessity to maintain the tension of the heavy strings). While the bass viol has been made in many sizes, there are two basic design styles, the German style with sloping shoulders (related to the viola da gamba), and the Italian style with a traditional rounded violin shape. The bass viol is played with either a bow or pizzicato style (plucked by the fingers) according to the musical score and style of music being played. Also known as acoustic bass. (see viola da gamba)

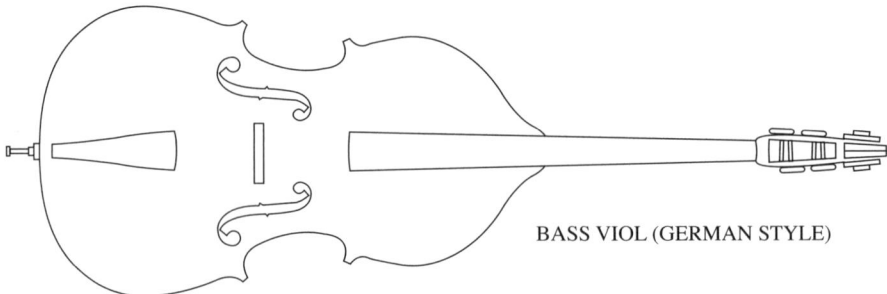

BASS VIOL (GERMAN STYLE)

basswood (*Tilia americana*) a light-colored hardwood of moderate stiffness and strength with great bending ability. Basswood is commonly used for kerfed and unkerfed lining. It is a comparatively weak wood and has a low resistance to breakage. Basswood is found in Eastern Canada and the Great Lakes region of the United States, and it weighs approximately 26 pounds per cubic foot. (see kerfed lining, unkerfed lining)

basswood lining (see kerfed lining, unkerfed lining)

bast the fibrous, soft tissue between the bark of a tree and its inner cell structure.

bastard file a steel tool whose cutting surfaces are covered with two rows of crisscrossed teeth. Bastard files are capable of removing significant amounts of material, but because of the crisscrossed teeth arrangement they leave a rougher surface than single-toothed mill files. Bastard files come in many shapes and sizes and are available in fine, medium, and coarse teeth. (see mill file)

bead 1) a protrusion on the tang of fretwire to help secure it in place. Also called a "barb." 2) a small accumulation of dried glue or finish. (see tang)

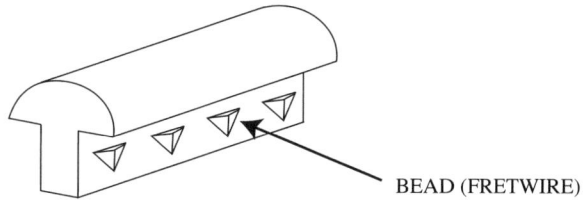

BEAD (FRETWIRE)

bel (see decibel)

bell bronze an alloy comprised of 80% copper and 20% tin and is the purest form of bronze. Because of its rigidity, bell bronze has excellent sustaining (ringing) qualities. Improved sustain comes from the high proportion of tin that does not fully bond with the copper, making the bell stiffer and more brittle. Some builders of more expensive banjo tone chambers use bell bronze. Also known as "bell metal." (see brass, bronze, tone chamber)

belly the soundboard of a violin. Some violin luthiers refer to the belly as just the curved or protruded part of a violin's soundboard.

belly bridge a string support system on acoustic guitars. The belly bridge has a curved lower portion in the area of the bridge pins and was developed by the CF Martin Organisation about 1928. The wider base is more durable than its pyramid bridge predecessor. (see pyramid bridge)

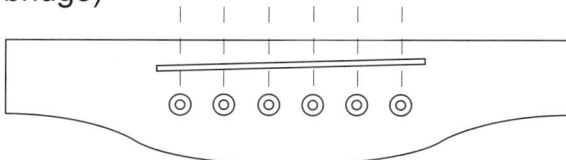

BELLY BRIDGE

bending blanket a thin, heated pad that is placed over wood to be bent. The blanket helps hold the wood evenly against the heating element, and the heat helps to soften the cells of the wood to ease the bending process.

bending iron a heated tube or pipe over which moistened wood can be bent for ribs and sides. The heat causes the cells of the wood to soften, the moisture keeps the wood from burning, and the resulting steam assists in transferring the heat to and through the wood so it can be bent. For improved bending of the wood, an aluminum or stainless steel strap is typically held over the wood to distribute the bending force evenly and to hold the wood against the hot tube. (see bending strap)

BENDING IRON (PIPE)

bending pipe (see bending iron)

bending strap a thin aluminum or stainless steel strip that is held over a piece of wood being bent on a bending iron. In addition to helping to distribute the heat to the side of the wood away from the bending iron, a bending strap also supports the wood over a larger surface to facilitate the shaping of smooth curves and reduce the possibility of cracking or breaking. (see bending iron)

bending tool (see bending iron)

bending tube (see bending iron)

bifurcation the diversion of one element into two elements as in the trunk of a tree that separates into two smaller trunk sections.

big leaf maple (*Acer macrophyllum*) a relatively soft maple that grows in the northwestern part of the United States. Big leaf maple is ideal for mandolin backboards because it is reasonably supple thereby providing "warmth" to the instrument's overall tone. Big leaf maple can also be used for necks and ribs, but harder maples such as red maple or sugar maple are recommended for these purposes. (see red maple, sugar maple)

billet 1) a rectangular or square piece of wood. Billets are of no particular size, shape or form. 2) informally, often used to refer to a shape for a particular use, such as "a billet for necks."

binding a bordering material around the edge of an instrument to protect the wood from being marred or chipped. The binding typically adds a decorative quality as well. While some guitar makers use wood binding, celluloid is the preferred choice because of its hardness, durability, ease of gluing, and strong bonding to lacquers and polyurethanes.

bird's eye a condition in wood caused by insects and birds that results in a decorative figure comprised of small round circles or spots. Bird's eye maple is not a species, but rather a defect. Bird's eye figure most commonly occurs in Eastern United States hard maples such as sugar maple (*Acer saccharum*) but occasionally appears in other woods.

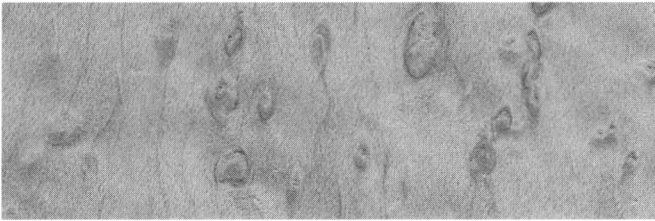

BIRD'S EYE (MAPLE)

black mother of pearl (see mother of pearl)

black walnut (*Juglans nigra*) a dark brown wood, usually with coffee-colored wisps and interesting figure. This wood is often used for instrument necks and has a weight of 38-40 pounds per cubic foot. Black walnut can also be used for rims and backboards. Walnut components contribute to a warmer tone than harder, heavier woods.

blackheart an abnormal black or brown discoloration of a tree's heartwood (innermost portion).

black/white the name given to laminated binding comprised of two layers. Black/white binding (referred to as "b/w") comes in many overall thicknesses as well as in different thicknesses of each laminate layer. If ivoroid is used as one layer, the binding is referred to as "ivoroid/black" or "black/ivoroid." (see ivoroid)

blind hole a hole or recess made with a pilot-less drill bit. A blind hole is typically drilled to accommodate scroll strengtheners in mandolin pegheads. While Forstner bits have a very small pilot, they still produce an acceptable blind hole. (see Forstner bit)

block (see block set)

block set a group of several structural components that help secure the rib or rim pieces to each other. Guitars utilize a headblock and a tailblock; mandolins feature a headblock, a tailblock, and two point blocks; violins have a headblock, a tailblock, and four point blocks.

blushing moisture or tiny air bubbles trapped under a finish coat that causes a milky appearance. Blushing is often the result of excessive moisture encapsulated in the finish during spraying. Blushing can usually be removed by a light sanding of the finish followed by a thinned coat of finish. [To protect against blushing when wet sanding between finish coats, it is important to ensure that the surface is completely dry before the next coat is applied. When spraying finishes, a moisture trap should be used in the air line, and the air compressor should be bled frequently to remove residual water trapped in the tank.]

board foot a unit of lumber predicated on 144 cubic inches of wood. For example, a board 1″ thick by 12″ wide by 12″ long equals one board foot. Some woods are sold by the board foot; others are sold by the linear or running foot. (see linear foot)

bocote (*Cordia gerascanthus*) a Central American hardwood of medium reddish-brown color with prominent grain lines. Bocote is used for guitar sides and backboards, and weighs 55 pounds per cubic foot.

body fixture a device used to secure a rib or side until the soundboard or backboard is glued in place. Violin luthiers call their body fixture a "mold."

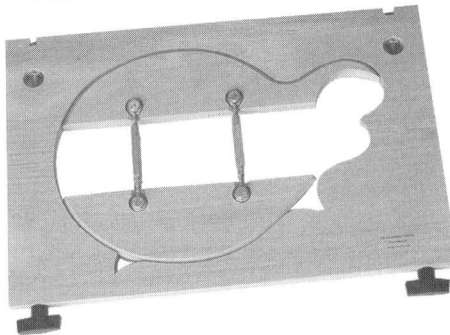

BODY FIXTURE
(H5 MANDOLA)

body point a hard structural element attached to a protruding edge of the instrument to protect the wood from damage. Body points used on Florentine mandolins and mandolas are commonly made of bone, pearl, celluloid or decorative hardwoods.

bole the part of a tree trunk that is above the root butt up to the first branch or limb. Normally refers to tree trunks that are greater than 8" in diameter.

bond strength the load required to break an adhesive joint such that the failure occurs in the joint (i.e., not through the wood itself). Bond strength is the measurement of the structural integrity of the adhesive. The load can be applied in compression, shear, tension, torque, twist, flex or impact.

bone a hard natural substance, usually from a cattle, which is boiled, bleached, dried, sliced, and made into tuning knobs, body points, nuts, and saddles.

bookleafed the result of joining two sawn or sliced adjacent pieces of wood along a common edge. In bookleafing, the grain and figure of the two halves mirror each other since each piece was originally mated. (see bookmatched)

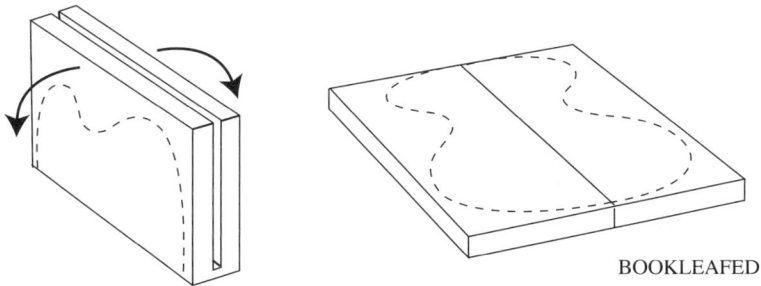

BOOKLEAFED

bookleafing the process of sawing or slicing wood and joining the two adjacent pieces along a common edge.

bookmatched the result of joining two pieces of wood of a flat board along their common edge to make them appear as if they were bookleafed. (see bookleafed)

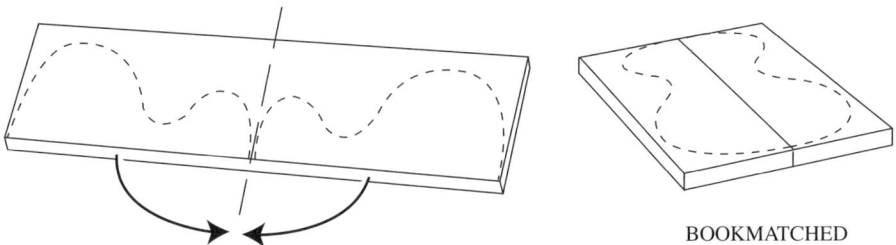

BOOKMATCHED

bookmatching the process of joining two pieces of wood together to make them appear as if they were bookleafed.

bound an edge or corner of an instrument that is protected by binding. In addition to decorating an instrument, the primary purposes of binding are to clean up glued edges and provide a durable edging for the instrument.

bound water the water that is infused within the fibrous structure of wood (compared to free water, the water that is readily available within the wood's pores and cells). Bound water is more difficult to remove during kiln or air drying. (see fiber saturation point)

bout a part of an instrument's body. Segments of the instrument's body are often defined as the "upper bout," "lower bout," and in the case of the violin, the "center bout." Some luthiers refer to left or right halves of an instrument as "bass bout" or "treble bout."

bouzouki a long-neck member of the lute family with three or four courses of strings, two strings per course with several different tunings, such as pairs of *D, A, D* or *E, B, E* (high to low). The bouzouki has a pear-shaped body, a flat soundboard and backboard, 25″ to 26″ string scale, and an unusually-shaped sound hole. The bouzouki has its origin in Greece. (see Irish bouzouki)

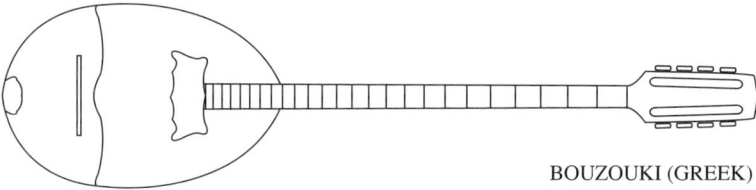

BOUZOUKI (GREEK)

bow 1) a device used to set the strings in motion on instruments of the violin and viol families. 2) a warping of a neck such that the center of the fretboard is closer (higher) to the strings than at either end. The opposite of a "hollow." 3) a reference to a piece of wood that is warped or bent incorrectly as in "this piece has a back bow."

bowl-back mandolin (see Neapolitan mandolin)

box the heart, boxing the heart the process of cutting squarely around the heartwood (innermost) part of a log when sawing it.

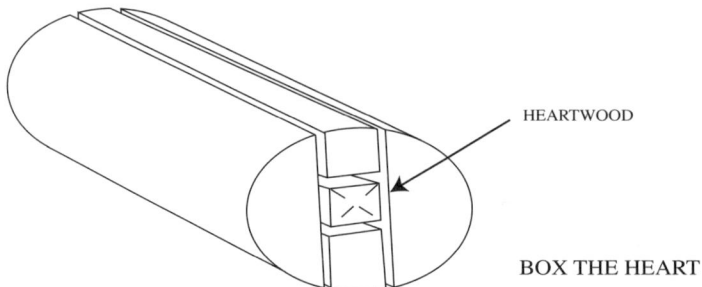

HEARTWOOD

BOX THE HEART

brace a wooden structural element attached to a soundboard or backboard to give it strength. Braces are also used to control stiffness in unsupported areas to reduce low overtones.

bracket hook on a banjo, a long screw-like rod with a J-shaped top used to tighten the stretcher band down to the rim. Most banjos with 11″ heads use 24 bracket hooks.

brass an alloy comprised mainly of copper with zinc being the primary additive. The proportion of copper to zinc determines the alloy's strength and durability. Brass is often inadvertently called "bronze," but the compounds are different. Some inexpensive bells are cast of brass while makers of fine bells use a specific alloy known as "bell bronze." Some makers of inexpensive banjo tone chambers use brass because of the lower cost and availability of the casting resource. (see bell bronze, bronze, tone chamber)

Brazilian rosewood (*Dalbergia nigra*) a highly-figured wood with rich browns, purples, and blacks. This wood is high in resin content and provides a very durable surface when used for fretboards. Brazilian rosewood has a weight of about 63 pounds per cubic foot. While the distribution of Brazilian rosewood is controlled by the CITES embargo of 1992, some guitar makers are able to obtain small quantities for use as peghead veneers, sides, backboards, and fretboards. (see CITES)

break angle the angle, measured in degrees, a string makes when going over a nut or bridge. Also called "string break angle."

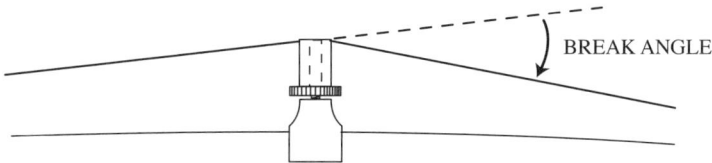

BREAK ANGLE

breaking open the process of cutting a log for the first time as in "breaking open a log." Also referred to as "laying open."

bridge a support that holds the strings in place over the soundboard. The bridge maintains the strings' spacing and enables transmission of the strings' vibrational energy to the soundboard. Bridges attached to the soundboard are called "fixed bridges" and are usually found on instruments that do not use a tailpiece. Instruments with tailpieces typically have bridges that are not attached to the soundboard called "movable bridges." Some bridges feature adjusting wheels or screws to alter the height of the bridge's saddle.

bridge pin a small tapered stud that is placed in the hole of a fixed bridge on a flat-top acoustic guitar to prevent the ball end of the string from pulling out of the hole. Since the bridge pin merely prevents the ball end of the string from going back through the hole, the pin does not need to be *forced* in. Bridge pins are available in many different materials with a variety of decorative features.

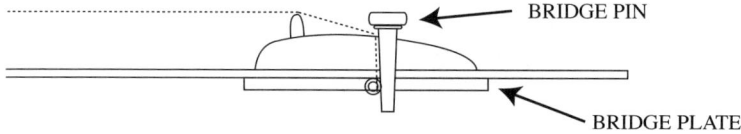

BRIDGE PIN

BRIDGE PLATE

bridge plate, bridgeplate a support inside the soundboard of a flat-top acoustic guitar to reinforce the structure of the soundboard beneath the bridge and to provide a solid bearing place for the ball end of the string.

brittleheart the heartwood (centermost part) of a tree that is so fragile it easily cracks across the grain.

bronze an alloy comprised mainly of copper with a primary additive of tin. Bronze can also include manganese, phosphorus, aluminum, and sometimes silicon. Bronze is used for bushings, hammer heads, and other non-steel parts where durability, friction, and non-oxidation are considerations. Most builders of banjo tone chambers use bronze because of its resilience and tonal properties. Some bell makers who call their material "bell bronze" might add small amounts of phosphorus, silver, and/or gold. (see bell bronze, brass, tone chamber)

bubinga (*Guibourtia tessmannii*) bubinga has similar attributes to Brazilian and Indian rosewood, but is slightly harder, making it more difficult to work. The grain and texture is more consistent than the elaborate grain of Brazilian rosewood. Bubinga weighs about 55 pounds per cubic foot. It is typically used for guitar backs, sides, and peghead veneers. Also known as "African rosewood."

bucked log a short length of wood cut from a segment of a tree in preparation for a subsequent operation such as slicing off layers of veneer.

burl a knotty growth in a tree, often occurring at a bifurcation in the trunk producing figure with a very irregular pattern that is ornately beautiful. Burl most commonly occurs in fruit-bearing trees, and burl-figured walnut is especially beautiful. Burl wood is best used for veneers because the burls are typically neither large nor dimensionally stable.

BURL (WALNUT TREE)

burl figure a swirly figure in wood that is the result of a deformity in the wood's growth. Burls occur at the connecting point of large branches and the trunk or at growths around bifurcations in the trunk. Quarter-section veneers from burls were often used in early furniture to create a floral-like pattern. Also known as a "burr."

burr 1) a small cutting or routing bit used in hand-held motor tools and routers. 2) a rough edge of a piece of metal or plastic. 3) a lay term for burly figure in wood.

bushing a sleeve that provides a smooth surface for a part that turns within it. Bushings are used around string posts to provide a durable, wear-free edge for the string posts to turn against and to conceal the raw edge of the string post's hole.

butt block (see tailblock)

butt peg (see end pin)

butt seam the joint at the end of an instrument where the sides or ribs come together. Butt seams can be a plain joint or can be inlaid with binding, marquetry, purfling or any combination of these elements.

butted seam a joint connection where two pieces are carefully joined edge to edge without overlapping.

button 1) the small covering on the neck heel of a violin. 2) the knob on a tuning machine (especially if it is small as those on a mandolin).

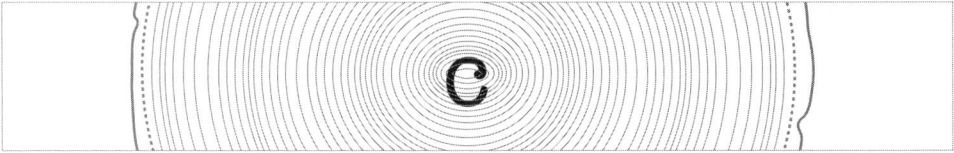

C. G. Conn (Conn-Selmer, Inc.) a manufacturer and distributor of musical instruments and related products. Conn had a line of strobe tuners under the brand names Strobotuner® and Stroboconn®, which was acquired by Peterson Electro-Musical Products, Inc. in 1985. (see strobe tuner)

cabinet scraper (see scraper)

CAD the acronym for "computer aided design" (some refer to it as computer aided drawing). CAD instruction sets prepared on a computer can be used for 3-D modeling or to operate a CNC (computer numerical control) machine. The instructions can include such tasks as the specific cutting tool to pick up, the cutting path to follow, the depth to cut, the speed to turn the tool or move the bed (especially important when cutting with the grain versus across the grain). Many manufacturers use CAD for the rapid production of musical instrument necks, bodies, and other complex parts. The major advantage of using CAD over regular (analog) fixtures, templates, and patterns is that the CAD data is digital and can be kept on storage media and manipulated on a computer. CAD information is easily modified, retrieved, shared, and duplicated. (see analog, CAM, CNC)

Caesalpinia ferra the botanical name for santos rosewood. (see santos rosewood)

CAM the acroynm for "computer aided manufacturing." CAM refers broadly to computer-aided machines that can be controlled by a set of instructions from a computer. Specific CAM devices related to luthierie are CNC routers and CNC milling machines. CAM equipment runs automatically and enables rapid production of parts with a very high degree of reliability and repeatability. Instruction set data for the CAM device is written or drawn on a CAD system. The reference to a CAD-CAM system suggests that computer aided designs are used in conjunction with computer aided manufacturing. (see CAD, CNC)

cam clamp a wood or metal device that closes by an eccentric (off-center) lever forced against one of its jaws (as compared to a clamp that uses a threaded screw for tightening). When the lobe of a cam clamp moves over its center point, it provides a locking action (if the cam is not disturbed).

cambium a very thin layer of new tissue located immediately beneath a tree's bark, from which each new annular ring is formed. The cambium layer provides a main path of nourishment for the tree.

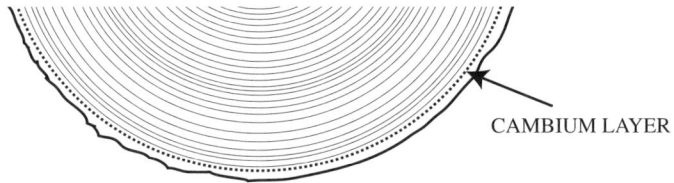

CAMBIUM LAYER

Cameroon ebony (see Gaboon ebony)

cap (see heel cap, peghead veneer)

carbon fiber a material comprised of glass-like strands woven into a cloth. Carbon fiber has the properties of being very dense, hard, light-weight, and strong, and it is typically saturated with epoxy (then referred to as carbon fiber reinforced plastic or CFRP). The material can be formed into custom shapes or into rods, tubes, bar stock, and sheets to make structural parts that are very strong for their size and weight. Often used in bar stock form for structural elements in instrument necks. [Carbon fiber dust is hazardous to breathe. Use a dust collection system and high-quality dust mask when working with carbon fiber.]

Carpathian walnut (see European walnut)

carving 1) the process of chiseling or cutting wood to create a shape in the wood's surface. 2) the decorative result in a piece of wood after having its surface chiseled or cut.

case hardening a result of irregular drying of wood where the neighboring layers of grain are in various degrees of tension or compression. Case hardening becomes obvious when cutting into the wood, and the two cut sections of the board begin to close behind the saw blade or open in diverse paths.

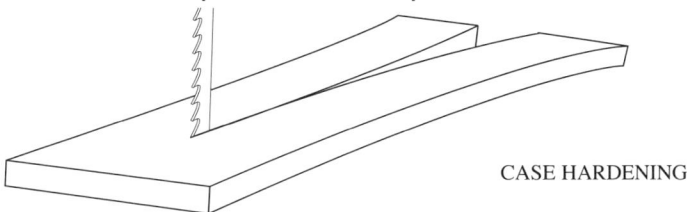

CASE HARDENING

caul protective piece of leather, wood or soft material to prevent marring or denting of a surface being clamped. Cauls are inserted between the clamp and the item being clamped. Also referred to as "clamping caul" or "clamping pad."

cedar (see Western red cedar)

cello the next to largest instrument of the violin family, with four strings tuned *A, D, G, C* (high to low). The cello features a carved and graduated belly (soundboard) and backboard, one longitudinal bass bar, a soundpost, two *f*-holes, and a peg box fitted with geared pegs (a necessity to maintain the tension of the strings). The cello is held in an upright position between the legs and most often played with a bow, but occasionally played pizzicato style (plucked by the fingers).

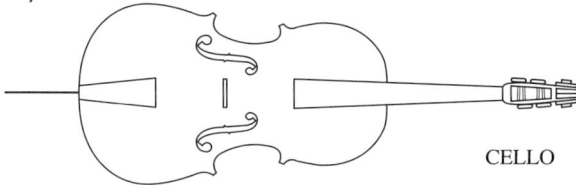

CELLO

celluloid a synthetic material created by Alexander Parkes in 1850, and made commercially available in 1870 by John Wesley Hyatt (a printer from Albany, NY). "Celluloid" (a brand name trademarked in 1872) is a mixture of nitrocellulose and camphor. The development of celluloid was prompted by a New England billiard ball manufacturer who was seeking an alternative to ivory. It was from the initial molding as a substitute for ivory that "grained" white celluloid, sometimes called *ivoroid*, was developed. [Care should be taken in handling and storing celluloid as it is unstable in heat; the material and its dust are highly flammable.] (see Pyralin®)

center bout the narrow center section of a violin's body. (see bout)

center punch a metal shaft with a sharpened point at one end that is used to create a small dent to act as a starting recess for a drill bit.

CFRP the abbreviation for "carbon fiber reinforced plastic." (see carbon fiber)

chalking a glue joint in which the water in the adhesive did not evaporate quickly enough to enable the adhesive particles to join properly, which leaves a chalky residue that is the result of the drying temperature being lower than specified by the manufacturer.

check a separation in the grain of wood, usually occurring across the annular rings. Checks are caused during either the initial kiln drying or natural seasoning process, and are the result of stress or case hardening in the wood that forces a separation to occur at one of the weakest points in the cells. Checks range from a fraction of an inch up to a few feet in length. A check differs from a crack in that a check typically does not go all the way through a board. Cutting off a checked section of a board does not eliminate the possibility of future checks occurring in the seemingly clear part of the board. Wood showing a check should not be used for luthierie. (see shake)

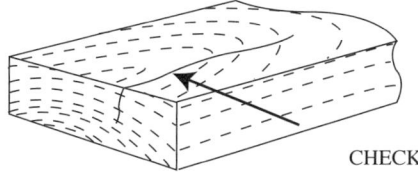

CHECK

checking a piece of wood's propensity to develop checks. For example, "This piece of wood is prone to checking."

chenille a fuzzy fabric covering wound onto the anchoring end of a musical string. Chenille helps to reduce buzzing noises in the tailpiece as well as protect the player's arm or sleeve from the exposed end of the string when the tailpiece or anchoring device does not have a protective cover.

chip out a small breakage at the edge of a piece of wood where a cutting tool has lifted the wood's fibers.

Chladni, Ernst Florenz Friedrich (1756-1827) Chladni was a German physicist, considered the "father of acoustics," who developed a method for visualizing the vibrating modes of acoustical plates. For his tests, Chladni sprinkled fine sand on plates and set the plates vibrating by exciting them with a bow. The array of patterns formed by the sand showed the nodes and anti-notes of the plates. The visual representation of these patterns is often referred to as "Chladni Patterns" or "Chladni Figures."

Circassian walnut (see European walnut)

circulation the movement of refractive and compressive air from one side of an object to another. As the soundboard and backboard of an instrument move in and out, waves of air pressure circulate around the instrument's body to compensate for air that is displaced. Similarly, as the two tines of a tuning fork vibrate back and forth, layers of air circulate from one side to the other.

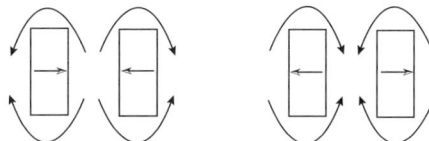

TINES OF TUNING FORK (END VIEW)

CIRCULATION

CITES the acronym for the Convention on International Trade of Endangered Species. The organization is responsible for managing the harvesting and exportation of a wide variety of rare and endangered resources including, but not limited to, ivory, tortoise shell, and Brazilian rosewood.

cittern an instrument similar to the octave mandolin but with five courses, two strings per course tuned *D, A, D, G, A* or *A, D, A, D, G* (high to low). The cittern is constructed with a 20″ to 22″ string scale. The instrument has its roots in Western Europe and the British Isles.

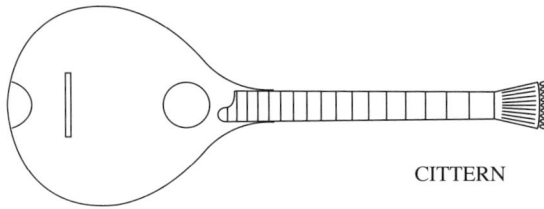

CITTERN

clamp time the time required to keep parts together that are being glued under pressure. The length of clamp time depends on the type of adhesive, ambient temperature, and climatic conditions.

clamping pressure as it relates to adhesives, the amount of squeeze force required to obtain effective penetration and distribution of the adhesive in joints. For most woodworking glues, such as Titebond®, the ideal clamping pressure is 100-150 psi for softwoods, 125-175 psi for medium-hard woods, and 175-250 psi for hardwoods. Clamping pressure varies with the type of adhesive being used.

classical guitar a six-string instrument constructed with a spruce or cedar soundboard and traditionally tuned *E, B, G, D, A, E* (high to low). The features of classical guitars include a flat soundboard and backboard, a wide fretboard, a round soundhole with an elaborate decorative rosette, rearward-facing tuning machines, horizontally-positioned tuning posts, a slotted peghead, nylon strings, and a fixed bridge with an integral harness to which the strings are tied.

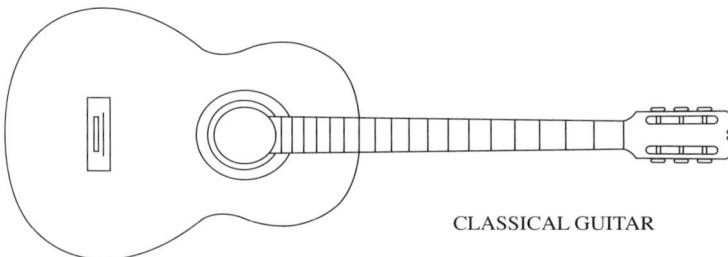

CLASSICAL GUITAR

claw hammer 1) a method of playing the banjo without fingerpicks or plectrum. In the claw-hammer style, the fingernails of the right hand are used to strum down on the strings, followed by the thumb landing on and picking the fifth string. Also called "frailing" or "drop-thumb" style. 2) a hammer with two "fingers" (claws) on the back portion of the head to remove nails.

clean as it relates to lumber, a piece of wood that is free from knots.

clear as it relates to lumber, a piece of wood that is free from checks, cracks, and other defects. (see check, crack)

closed assembly time the time between when glued parts are initially put together and when the clamps are applied. This is typically the time that parts can still be moved or realigned. (see open assembly time).

clothespin spring-loaded wooden clip available as a household commodity that can be used to hold parts together during gluing. Clothespins are typically used for holding kerfed lining in place during gluing. [Clothespins are also available in plastic, but wood is preferred for luthierie.]

CNC the abbreviation for "computer numerical control." A mechanical device that operates from computer instructions. A CNC machine can be a router, a milling machine or similar shaping device that is connected to a computer and provides instructions for a "path" or axis for the tool to follow. Two-dimensional CNC machines (also referred to as "XY" machines) can be controlled to move left/right and forward/backward. Three-dimensional CNC machines (also referred to "XYZ" machines) can be controlled to move left/right, forward/backward, and up/down. The benefit of CNC machines is that instead of working with physical templates and patterns, the CNC machine is given a set of digital instructions that are easily written, modified, copied, duplicated, and stored. The instructions can include, but are not limited to, instructing the machine which path to follow, which cutting tool to pick up, and how fast to go across the grain versus with the grain. Most CNC machines today work from CAD programs. (see CAD, CAM)

cochlea the primary sensory mechanism of hearing in the inner ear. The cochlea is a liquid-filled chamber lined with fine hair fibers (cilia) that sense vibrations transmitted to them from the eardrum (tympanic membrane). The cochlea is the hardest bone in the human body. (see sense of hearing)

cocobolo (*Dalbergia retusa*) a dense, heavy hardwood with vivid colors ranging from deep orange to dark purplish-brown. Cocobolo comes from Nicaragua and the southern part of Mexico. It can be used for peghead veneers, sides, backboards, and fretboards. Cocobolo weighs approximately 65 pounds per cubic foot.

coefficient of expansion the rate at which one piece of wood expands and contracts. Woods used in the same musical instruments should have similar expansion and contraction rates to maintain structural stability.

color in acoustics, the quality of sound described by its richness and sonorous qualities rather than its pitch or amplitude. Also referred to as "timbre" or "tone color."

compensated bridge a string support that has been positioned or adjusted to correct for the intonation anomalies of each string. Because each gauge of string and each combination of core-and-wrap wire requires a minor adjustment in length for true noting at each fret, the string's length needs to be compensated at the bridge. Rather than correcting for each string, an *average* compensation can be made to a straight (non-intonated) bridge by turning either the bridge or the bridge's saddle slightly counterclockwise until each string intonates well at the 12th fret. (see intonation)

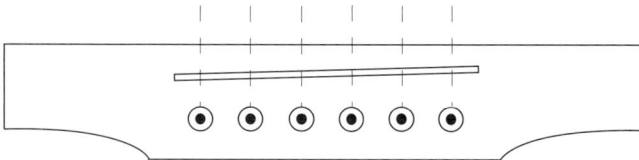

COMPENSATED BRIDGE

compensated saddle the upper part of a bridge that has been notched so that each string's contact point is adjusted for intonation anomalies. Since each gauge of string and each combination of core-and-wrap wire requires a minor correction in length to provide true noting at each fret, the saddle needs to be cut with compensation notches. A compensated saddle can be fitted parallel to the bridge's width. Also referred to as an "intonated saddle." (see intonation)

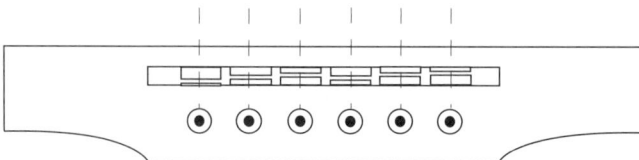

COMPENSATED SADDLE

compression 1) in acoustics, waves of air pressure moving toward the sensing or hearing body (ear). When a soundboard is pressed down as a result of energy being transferred from the bridge, the result is a compressive force on the air inside the air chamber. This air, in turn, is forced out of the instrument through the aperture(s). (The air returning to the air chamber after the compressive force occurs is called "rarefaction.") 2) in a truss rod or mechanical structure, energy exerted from the ends of an object toward its center. 3) the pressure exerted on two or more objects being forced together. (see compression wood, rarefaction)

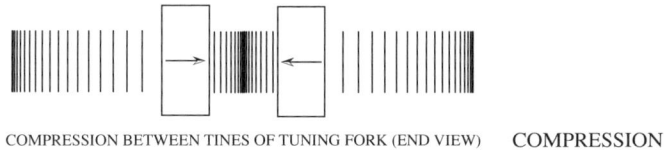

COMPRESSION BETWEEN TINES OF TUNING FORK (END VIEW)   COMPRESSION

compression wood wood from a part of a tree that has been subjected to a severe load, such as the wood directly beneath a branch. Compression wood often has curly figure, crushed cells, dark blemishes or a combination of these defects. Wood that has been in a severe compressive state (such as the burl beneath a branch) is subject to checking and should not be used for the structural parts of musical instruments.

concert pitch the specific frequency used as a reference point for tuning instruments individually or in an ensemble. The note used as a standard to which all other notes on the same instrument are tuned. Today, *A* is typically used as the reference for concert pitch, but *C* has been used as well. (Any note can be used as reference, but common practice is either *A* or *C*). Through the years, many frequencies have been used for *A*, and the earliest reference appears to be to the Halberstadt organ (1361) that featured *A* tuned to 505.8Hz. Hermann Helmholtz (1821-1894) referred to concert pitch as *C*256Hz, which continued through Lloyd Loar's lifetime (1886-1943). Today, *A* is 440Hz (in the scale in which *C* is 256Hz, *A* is 431Hz). In 1971, the European Economic Community (EEC) passed a recommendation to fix international pitch at *A*440Hz. (see *Reference Table: Frequency - A=440Hz*)

condensation an early (and mostly European) usage of the acoustical term "compression" to refer to air pressure being compressed in the pressure phase of sound transmission (the complementary phase being "rarefaction"). (see compression, rarefaction)

cone a formed metal disk with a peaked center that is fitted directly beneath the spider on a resophonic guitar. The cone is the instrument's effective soundboard. (see resophonic guitar, spider)

confidentiality agreement (see non-disclosure agreement)

Conn Strobotuner® a device made by the C. G. Conn Company for measuring the frequencies of musical sounds and their corresponding sharp or flat qualities. Peterson Electro-Musical Products, Inc. acquired C. G. Conn's Strobotuner® and StroboConn® brands in 1985. (see strobe tuner)

coordinator rod a metal bar that connects a banjo's neck to the pot assembly and provides a means of adjusting the neck pitch. A banjo with only one coordinator rod does not have a "coordinator rod system" because two rods are needed to coordinate the angle of the neck. The coordinator rod was developed by Gibson in the early-1920s. (see coordinator rod system)

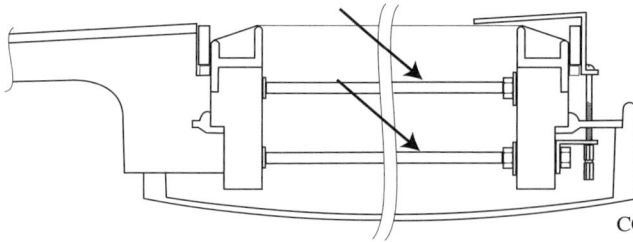

COORDINATOR RODS

coordinator rod system metal bars whose force or counter-force are used to adjust the neck pitch in some banjos. To act as a coordinator rod system, two rods must be present. By tightening the rods counter to each other (i.e., tightening the *inside* nut on the *upper* rod and tightening the *outside* nut on the *lower* rod), the counter-force pulls the neck pitch down. Doing the converse will allow the neck pitch to raise up.

copyright a statement of ownership of a document, piece of music or drawing that expresses the creator's intention to protect his or her rights of copy. Statement of ownership is indicated by the inclusion of the copyright symbol "©" along with the date and originator's name. Example: "© 2008 Bob Smith." For information on copyright declaration of ownership, visit the U.S. Copyright office web site at www.uspto.gov/). [For advanced protection of your rights and to ensure compliance with current law, consult a copyright attorney.]

Cordia dodecandra the botanical name for ziricote. (see ziricote)

Cordia gerascanthus the botanical name for bocote. (see bocote)

core wire in musical strings, the innermost section of a wound string. Most core wires are hexagonal in shape (versus round) to help lock the wrap or cover (outer) wire in place and prevent unraveling. Classical guitar strings have a nylon filament core. (see hex core)

ROUND   HEXAGONAL   FILAMENT   CORE WIRE

Corian® a dense synthetic material made by DuPont® typically used for counters, sinks, and similar household and industrial surfaces. Corian's hard, durable composition, as well as its resistance to stains and dyes, make it an acceptable substitute for bone when used for nuts, mandolin corner points, and guitar saddles.

corner point in mandolin construction, a protector that is attached to the edges of the body's ribs to protect the ribs from damage. Corner points are typically made of bone, but any hard material can be used.

coupled system in acoustics, the whole of the elements that comprise an acoustic device. For example, in a guitar, the soundboard, backboard, sides, braces, neck, bridge, and strings comprise the guitar's coupled system.

course the number of strings on an instrument that are grouped to make up one note, or notes that are an octave apart. For example, a mandolin is a four-course instrument (eight strings, two strings per course.) (Instruments with one string per note are commonly named by the total number of strings as in "six-string guitar" and "five-string banjo." One exception noted is the "12-string guitar.")

CPS (see cycles per second)

crack 1) a tearing of wood *across* its grain at any place other than through one or more of its annular rings. Although a crack can run through a grain line, that type of rupture is usually referred to as a "check." 2) a large radial split in wood caused by the tangential shrinkage being greater than the radial shrinkage. (see check)

cross brace a structural member (strut) that goes across the grain of the wood, typically perpendicular to the length of the soundboard but not necessarily all the way across the instrument as would a transverse brace. (see transverse brace)

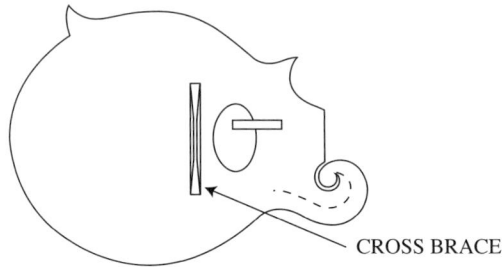

CROSS BRACE

cross patch a small piece of wood glued across the grain of the primary piece of wood to repair a crack.

cross piece a length of binding that goes across the width of the instrument and is attached between the headblock and the fretboard extender to provide a visual termination of the binding at the headblock. Rather than the binding wrapping around the headblock, the binding appears to go through the headblock. The cross piece design feature was typical on many early Gibson instruments including the A1, A2, A3, F4, and F5 mandolins, H5 mandola, and the L5 guitar. On these instruments, it is common to describe the neck length according to which fret is aligned with the cross piece (e.g., "15-fret neck"). (see joins the body)

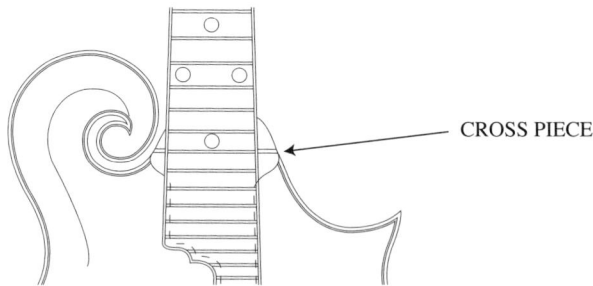

CROSS PIECE

crotch that region of a tree where two trunks are joined or where a large branch adjoins the trunk. Crotch wood typically displays erratic, convoluted burly-grain figure. Crotch wood is very attractive but may have physical defects and is not recommended for structural parts of an instrument.

crown (see back bow)

CRP the abbreviation for carbon reinforced plastic. (see carbon fiber)

cupping a change in the shape of wood as a result of the uneven drying or uneven absorption of moisture. Cupping typically occurs across the width of flat-sawn boards, in a direction that is opposite to the arc of the annular rings.

Cupressus sempervirens the botanical name for cypress. (see cypress)

curls per inch a reference to the number of figure lines (curls) per inch in wood.

curly figure a shimmering striped appearance in any wood that results from the wood being placed in compression during its life cycle. The compressive load forces the wood's grain to buckle longitudinally and presents the appearance of a wavy figure or "curl" across the wood's tangential surface. (see quilted figure)

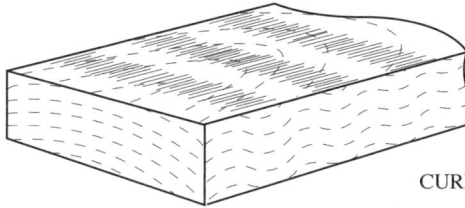

CURLY FIGURE

curly maple a hardwood whose striped figure is caused by the wood being placed in compression during its life cycle. The deformity in the maple appears as shimmering stripes or "curls" and is most readily visible across the tangential grain. Curly maple is not a species, but rather a visually-appealing defect found in maple that also occurs less commonly in other woods. In the lumber industry, "curly maple" typically refers to lumber with more than two curls per inch. (see fiddle maple, flamed maple, quilted maple, tiger maple)

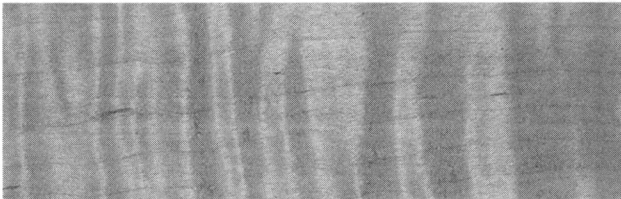

CURLY MAPLE

cut on the quarter wood that is prepared with its grain on an angle, at about 45° to one of its sides. Also known as quartered grain. Wood cut on the quarter is different from "quarter-sawn," which is a log sawing method. (see flat grain, quarter-sawn)

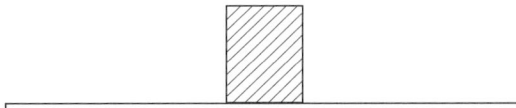

CUT ON THE QUARTER

cutaway a part of an instrument that has been removed by design to enable the musician to have access to a greater portion of the fretboard.

CUTAWAY GUITAR

COURTESY SANTA CRUZ GUITAR COMPANY

cyanoacrylate a fast-drying, durable adhesive that bonds to a wide range of surfaces. Cyanoacrylate provides deep penetration and almost-instant bonding of wood parts. It is also useful in sealing cracks or seams where the thin cyanoacrylate liquid is drawn well into the crack or joint. Setting time can be expedited with the help of a spray-on accelerator, but the resultant joint is somewhat weaker than if allowed to dry on its own. Accelerators can also cause blushing in the adhesive that may present an objectionable white seam. [Accelerator vapors are harmful to breathe. Care should be taken when using cyanoacrylate because it will bond with skin.]

cycles per second (CPS) a reference to the number of complete movements, pulses or orbits an object in motion makes in one second. Today, the common reference for cycle per second is Hertz (Hz). (see Hertz)

cypress *(Cupressus sempervirens)* a light-colored moderately hard wood with attractive grain. Cypress weighs 40 pounds per cubic foot and works well for the backboard and sides of blonde-colored instruments.

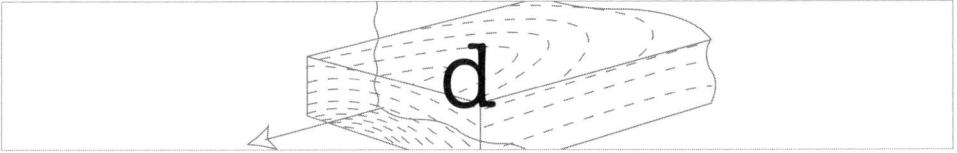

D guitar also known as Dreadnought guitar, with a body size that is typically 39-13/16″ long (overall), a body length of 19-3/8″, a width of 15″, and a depth of 4-1/8″. (see Dreadnought)

Dalbergia baronii the botanical name for Madagascar rosewood. (see Madagascar rosewood)

Dalbergia latifolia the botanical name for Indian rosewood. (see Indian rosewood)

Dalbergia melanoxylon the botanical name for African blackwood. (see African blackwood)

Dalbergia nigra the botanical name for Brazilian rosewood. (see Brazilian rosewood)

Dalbergia retusa the botanical name for cocobolo. (see cocobolo)

Dalbergia spruceana the botanical name for Amazon rosewood. (see Amazon rosewood)

Dalbergia stevensonii the botanical name for Honduras rosewood. (see Honduras rosewood)

damping the process of absorbing vibrational energy through the introduction of a sound deadening or vibration-absorbing material or by interaction with a less dense medium that wicks off energy or inhibits vibration.

dB (see decibel)

decay 1) the reduction in amplitude over time of a musical note immediately following the attack. 2) a deterioration of cells in wood caused by infestation or moisture.

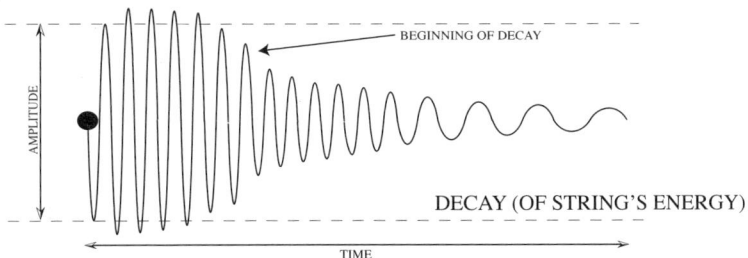

decibel (dB) a measurement of sound pressure. A decibel is one tenth of a bel, a unit of measure devised by engineers at Bell

Telephone Laboratories to describe the loss of power of a standard telephone wire over a distance of 1 mile (1.609 km). Originally called a *transmission unit* (TU), it was renamed in the 1920s in honor of Alexander Graham Bell. A decibel is a logarithmic value in which every three decibels equals twice the sound pressure. (see *Reference Table: Amplitudes in dB*)

decibelometer a device used to measure the amplitude of sound in terms of sound pressure. Measurements are in units of decibels (dB). (see decibel)

deco (see Art Deco)

de-damping the process of mechanically exciting an instrument's body to promote the flexibility of the structural parts and improve the overall tonal qualities. De-damping flexes the fibers of the wood without disrupting the wood's molecular structure. The de-damping process also serves to work-soften new finishes and make them more pliable. De-damping can be presented to the instrument through mechanical strumming, mechanical vibration or external excitation of specific frequencies at great amplitude by which the instrument is set into vibration through sympathetic vibration. (see sympathetic vibration)

deflection tuning the process of adjusting the stiffness of a soundboard or backboard (plate) by measuring how much it deforms under a load. The process begins by using a plate from an instrument that has the desired tone or by tuning a plate to a specific note by using the tap tuning method. Once tuned, a load is placed on the plate, and the amount of deflection is measured with several dial indicators. Then, a fixture is used that can impose the same load and measure the deflection. Tuning subsequent plates is accomplished by removing wood until the same deflections, under

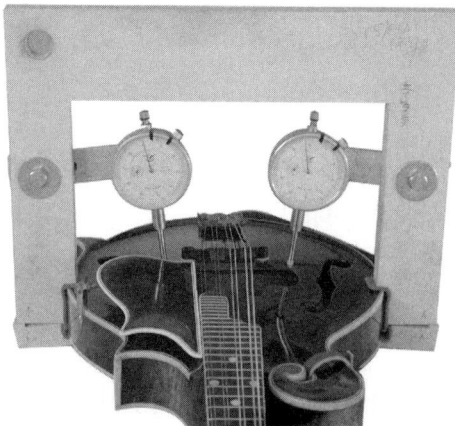

DEFLECTION TUNING
(TAKING DEFLECTION
MEASUREMENTS
FROM F5 MANDOLIN)

the same load, are achieved. Deflection tuning is ideal in locations where tap tuning is desired, but the ambient noise is too great for conventional tap tuning equipment to be used. Deflection tuning was developed by Roger Siminoff in 1978.

dehumidifier a device used to remove moisture from the air and manage the level of humidity. (see desiccant)

delaminate a disruption in the holding power of a glue joint that causes two previously-mated surfaces to separate. (When the natural disruption of a bond in wood occurs between its springwood and summerwood, it is referred to as a "check.")

denatured alcohol ethanol with additives to make it unpalatable and unfit for human consumption (toxic). Denatured alcohol is prepared in many forms and is often colored for identification. The clear version can be used as a thinner, cleaner, and solvent for varnish, shellac, and stain or as a drier for French polish. However, many luthiers prefer pure ethanol because it is less toxic. [Care should be taken when using denatured alcohol because it is also a fuel, which is highly flammable.] (see ethanol)

dendrochronology the scientific study of a tree's annular rings to determine the tree's history, including age, growth rate, life cycle, and environmental influences.

desiccant a non-mechanical compound used to absorb moisture from the air. (see dehumidifier)

detail gun a small spray device used for applying medium-to-light coverage of finishes. Detail guns typically have a small screw-on paint container and are the optimal size for spraying necks and small instruments.

dial indicator a measuring device that has a clock-like gauge with a sweep hand to report measurements that are sensed by a leg or post that extends from the gauge.

digital computer-based information comprised of zeros ("0") and ones ("1"). Digital data is prepared on a computer, which enables the user to manipulate words, numbers, photographs, illustrations, music, audio, and communications through such resources as e-mail. Data created on digital systems can be modified, copied, transferred, stored, and archived. Working drawings of musical instrument parts can be easily and accurately prepared and modified on computers compared to analog drawings that are prepared in pencil or pen and are difficult to draw, modify, reproduce, and store. Digital data prepared in a CAD system can be used to drive CAM and CNC machines in the high-speed production of musical instrument bodies and parts. (see analog, CAD, CAM, CNC)

digital tuner a device to measure the frequency of musical sounds. Digital tuners use solid-state components to interpret the signals, and they feature either digital (numerical) or analog (sweep hand) read outs. Digital tuners look for a sustained note such as the sound of a musical string. Because of the brief time delay in calculating the frequency, digital tuners are typically not suitable for tap tuning.

dimensional lumber wood that is sawn and planed to standard construction sizes and specified in inches. While dimensional lumber is stated in full inch sizes, the actual dimensions are less. Hardwoods and tonewoods sold for musical instrument use are measured by the full quarter of an inch. (see quarter)

dimensional stability that attribute of a piece of wood or material that enables it to keep its shape and size over time and under load. (see plastic deformation)

Diospyros crassiflora hiern the botanical name for Gaboon ebony; also known as Gabon ebony or black ebony. (see Gaboon ebony)

Diospyros macassar the botanical name for Macassar ebony. (see Macassar ebony)

Diospyros mespiliformis the botanical name for African ebony. (see African ebony)

disclosure a statement that validates the date a design or idea was conceived. A disclosure contains a brief description of a design or product, the date the design or product was conceived, and the verification of a witness. While a disclosure does not take the place of a patent, it is an important first step in documenting the date a design was first conceived. [For advanced protection of your rights and to be in compliance with current law, consult a patent attorney.]

Dobro® a brand name of the resophonic guitar originally developed by John Dopyera in the late-1920s. John and brothers Rudy, Robert, Emile, and Louis formed the Dobro Manufacturing Company. The brand name is now owned by the Gibson Guitar Corp. (see resophonic guitar)

double-acting truss rod a structural mechanism placed in the neck of a string musical instrument to help keep the neck straight under the bending force exerted by the strings. The nut on a double-acting truss rod can be tightened clockwise to bend the neck into a positive bow (high in the center) or counterclockwise to bend the neck into a negative bow.

double-cut peghead a peghead shape used on early Gibson banjos beginning in 1929. The double-cut peghead followed the fiddle peghead design, but for a period of time, both were used on different banjo models. The double-cut peghead was named for the two large cuts on either side. (see fiddle peghead)

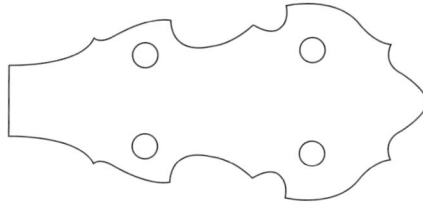

DOUBLE-CUT PEGHEAD

double-lock winding a string winding method in which the fastening of the string around the ball or loop is finished with two sequential turns to ensure a non-slip termination of the string.

DOUBLE-LOCK WINDING

double-O guitar (see OO guitar)

double-X bracing a structural system for steel-string acoustic guitars. The bracing pattern is accompanied by a thin plywood bridge plate. The overly stiff X-braced soundboards require the use of heavy gauge strings to make the instrument perform properly. The double-X bracing system was developed by Gibson to reduce the deformity in soundboards often associated with string tension.

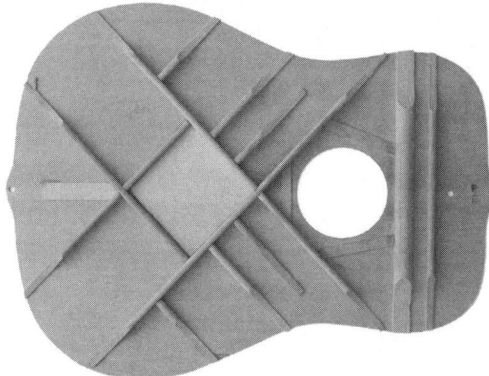

DOUBLE-X BRACING

Douglas fir (*Pseudotsuga taxifolia*) a species of fir with reasonably straight, close grain. At 33 pounds per cubic foot, Douglas fir is about 30% heavier than spruce and can be used for mandolin soundboards with moderate success, providing a bright, cutting tone. Care must be exercised when selecting Douglas fir because it is prone to contain random pockets of resin between its annular rings.

dovetail joint a triangular-shaped male/female connection commonly used to secure an instrument's neck into its headblock. The dovetail joint was introduced in early architecture as a means of locking wood or stone elements together.

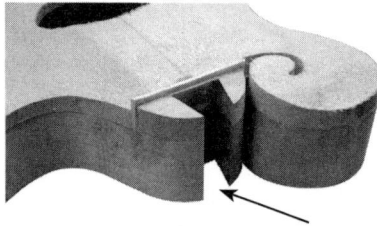

DOVETAIL JOINT
(F5 MANDOLIN)

dowelstick a structural member that attaches to the neck on most open-back banjos to secure the neck in place. Most dowelsticks are square and tapered toward the end nearest the tailpiece.

DOWELSTICK

down pressure a downward force exerted by the strings at the nut or at the bridge. The amount of down pressure at each of these contact points is determined by the tension of the strings and the string break angle (the angle at which the strings go over the contact points). (see string break angle)

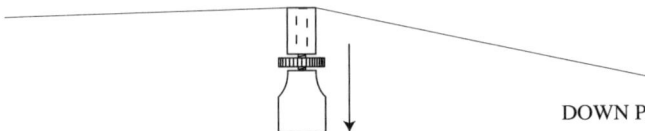

DOWN PRESSURE

Dreadnought a guitar model developed by the CF Martin Organisation. The first instruments were manufactured in 1916 by Martin under a private label for the Oliver Ditson Company, a publishing company in Boston. Because of the large size of these guitars, they were named after a class of World War I British battleships. CF Martin began producing Dreadnoughts under its own label in 1931. (see D guitar)

Dremel® Rotary Tool a small, hand-held router-type device for cutting, routing, and polishing. Many cutters, sanding wheels, router bits, and other attachments are available for this tool.

Dremel® router guide a housing that fits around the end of a Dremel Rotary Tool to act as a height and depth guide; used when routing for binding.

dressing cleaning up or flattening the surfaces of frets to make them square and smooth.

drift a tool of soft metal used as an interface between a driving force (hammer) and the part being driven or hit. A long drift is used to provide greater access to a remote part being driven free. (see punch)

drill guide a fixture used to ensure the accurate placement, alignment, and/or distance apart of drilled holes. The guide should have a means to properly align the fixture's base plate to the peghead or object being drilled. Guides intended for repeated use should be made of steel; guides for limited use can be made of aluminum.

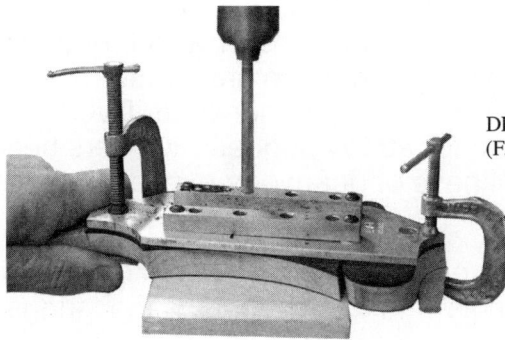

DRILL GUIDE
(F5 MANDOLIN PEGHEAD)

drop-thumb a method of playing the banjo without fingerpicks or plectrum. In the drop-thumb style, the fingernails of the right hand are used to strum down on the strings followed by the thumb landing on and picking the fifth string. More properly referred to as "frailing" and occasionally called "claw hammer" style.

Duco® Cement a nitrocellulose adhesive used to secure binding in place as well as bond other porous and non-porous surfaces. Duco is particularly advantageous for attaching celluloid binding because it attacks the celluloid, creating a better bond of the celluloid, and it seeps into the pores of the wood to which the binding attaches.

dulcimer (mountain) a long and narrow hourglass-shaped instrument with a fretboard attached to the center of the soundboard. The instrument is configured with either three or four strings traditionally tuned *C, C, C* or *C, C, C, G* (high to low). The mountain dulcimer is played on the lap and strummed across with one hand as the other hand presses down on the melody string(s) to fret them. Typically, the two lower strings are used as drones with the upper string(s) used for melody.

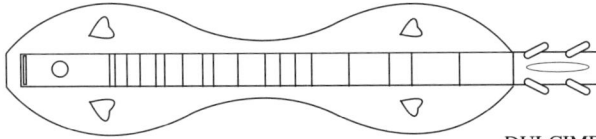

DULCIMER (MOUNTAIN)

duration of attack the period of continuous contact that is received by a string or tone-producing member. The duration of attack of a bowed instrument is far greater than the duration of attack of a picked instrument. This is one of the four main factors that affect the production of tone from a struck object, the other three being location of attack, intensity of attack, and method of attack. (see attack)

dyed pearwood a hardwood that has been saturated with dye and then dried so it resembles some other wood. Pearwood is used because it has a very simple, plain grain pattern with little distinction between its springwood and summerwood. Dyed pearwood is often used as a substitute for ebony peghead veneers because the cost is less, and the softness of pearwood expedites the inlay process.

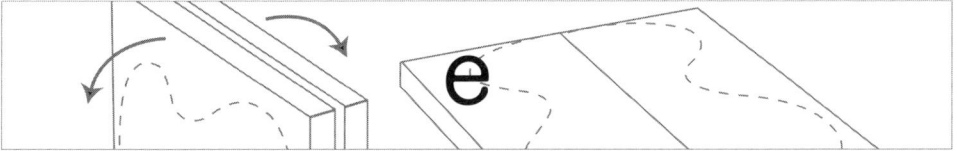

ear an extension added to each side of the neck wood at the peghead to provide sufficient width for shaping the peghead. Ears are added to obtain better yield when cutting a neck blank so that the entire neck does not have to be cut from a billet that is as wide as the peghead. (see billet)

earlywood (see springwood)

ebony (*Diospyros spp.*) a dense black wood with weights ranging from 65 to 75 pounds per cubic foot depending on the species. Typically used for fretboards and peghead veneers, the hardness of ebony provides an excellent surface for holding frets in place and for diminishing fretboard wear. The black color of ebony provides a dark background as a contrast to inlaid designs. Ebony is grown in hot and humid climates and is typically named for its country of origin. (see Gaboon ebony, Macassar ebony)

elastic deformation as it relates to wood, the ability of the material to return to its original shape after it has been distorted. (see plastic deformation)

Elmer's® Glue-All a white aliphatic adhesive. The working and drying qualities of Elmer's make it ideal for mixing with ebony or rosewood dust when making a filler for pearl and abalone inlays. (see aliphatic glue)

EMC (see equilibrium moisture content)

end block (see tailblock)

end check the separation of the grain along the end of a board caused by uneven drying. (see check)

end pin a tapered shaft with a protruding button that extends from the butt seam of an instrument to secure one end of a strap, a tailpiece or both.

energy the capacity of a body to do work or deliver a force. On a string musical instrument, the force of the pick(s) or bow is the initial source of energy that is transferred to the strings. The strings' energy is then transferred to the soundboard which, in conjunction with the air chamber, create compression and rarefaction of the air in and around the instrument, resulting in the sound we hear.

Englemann spruce (*Picea engelmannii*) a wood of the Pineaceae family with moderate "silk" (medullary rays). Englemann spruce is similar to Sitka spruce and is a good selection for soundboards and bracings. The average weight of Englemann spruce is 27 pounds per cubic foot. Englemann spruce was named after George Englemann (1809-1884) who was the first to identify this species.

English walnut (see European walnut)

engraving the process of carving, gouging or cutting thin slivers of material from the surface of an object to leave a pattern or decorative image. (see graver)

Entandrophragma cylindricum the botanical name for sapele. (see sapele)

epoxy a thermosetting polymer that cures when mixed with a hardener (catalyzing agent). Epoxies are available in various setting times and offer strong bonds in wood. Because of the mixing and setting times compared to regular cement (e.g., Titebond®) and the difficulty in re-opening epoxied joints, most luthiers do not use epoxy.

epoxy graphite (see carbon fiber)

equilibrium moisture content (EMC) the point at which wood has acclimated to its environment and is no longer in a state of swelling or shrinkage as when being converted from its initial green state.

ethanol a grain alcohol commonly used for beverages and fuel but can be used as a thinning, cleaning or drying agent. Many luthiers use 190 proof ethanol as a solvent, thinner, and drying agent when French polishing. Ethanol is also helpful in thinning stains when coloring, shading or building grain contrast. Ethanol is mixable with water, lacquer, varnish, shellac, oils, and aniline dyes. [Care should be taken when using near an open flame as ethanol is flammable.] (see French polish)

European walnut (*Juglans regia*) a dark brown wood from Central and Western Europe. European walnut features dramatic grain figure with moderate pores and has an average weight of 40 pounds per cubic foot. Walnut makes attractive guitar backs and sides, and banjo necks. *Juglans regia* is also known as Carpathian walnut, Circassian walnut, English walnut, French walnut, and Persian walnut, depending on its country of origin.

extender (fretboard) a wooden support placed beneath the protruding end of a fretboard to add strength and stability.

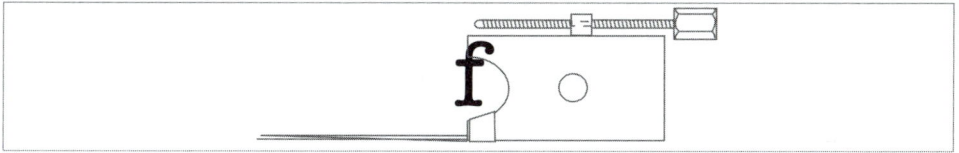

face the soundboard of an instrument. (see soundboard)

fan bracing a method of reinforcing the soundboard of a classical and a flamenco guitar by positioning the braces in a radiating pattern that are close together near the soundhole and spreading wide toward the tailblock. Also called "fan strutting."

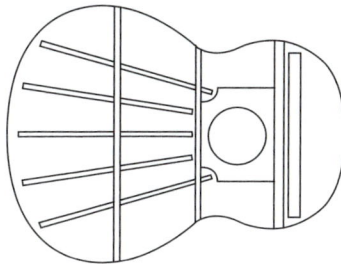

FAN BRACING

fan strutting (see fan bracing)

fence an adjustable side gauge to ensure consistent cutting widths; used on tools such as a bandsaw, table planer or table saw.

ferrule a slip-on collar used to secure or align parts. On a violin bow, a ferrule is used hold the slide in place, which covers the entry slot for the hair into the frog. (see frog)

f-**hole** a decorative aperture in the air chamber of a musical instrument that connects the air in the air chamber to the surrounding air and controls the amount of compression and rarefaction. The size of the *f*-hole(s) determines the tuning of the air chamber: a larger *f*-hole results in a higher pitch; a smaller *f*-hole results in a lower pitch.

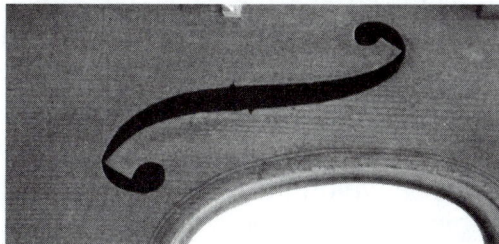

F-HOLE (VIOLIN)

fiber saturation point (FSP) the percentage of wood's moisture content after free water has evaporated leaving the remaining moisture content of the wood to be dependent only on the bound water. The FSP in most species of wood is typically 30% ± 2%. Wood shrinkage occurs when the FSP falls below about 30% moisture content, and bound water is given up from the structure of the cells. (see bound water, free water, moisture content)

fiddle the earliest forerunner of the violin, made in a variety of small sizes and set up in a wide range of stringings and tunings. Today the word "fiddle" is often used to refer to a violin when played in grassroots or traditional music styles (e.g., bluegrass, old-time, country, Irish).

fiddle maple the ripple figure in wood caused by the wood being placed in compression during its life cycle. The compressive load causes the wood's grain to buckle. When cut, the buckling appears as stripes or curls across the wood. Fiddle maple is not a species, but rather an attractive defect that occurs in any species of maple. In the lumber industry, "fiddle maple" typically refers to lumber with more than four figure lines per inch. Also known as "fiddle-back" maple. (see curly maple, tiger maple)

fiddle peghead a peghead shape used on early Gibson banjos. Following the earliest versions of Gibson's banjos, the fiddle peghead made its debut on the full-resonator models that were introduced in 1925. The fiddle peghead was named for the narrow waist and overall shape that resembles a fiddle. (see double-cut peghead)

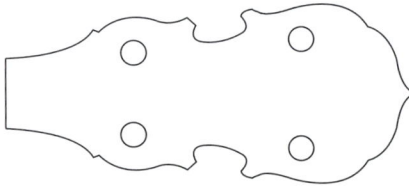

FIDDLE PEGHEAD

fiddle-back maple (see fiddle maple)

Fiebing's® dye an alcohol-based, aniline dye intended for coloring leather. The deep penetrating, fast-drying qualities make this dye ideal for staining wood. Compared to oil-based stains, aniline dyes leave minimal residue on the wood's surface. [Care should be taken because aniline dyes are permanent and poisonous.]

15-fret neck the point at which the 15th fret of an instrument is aligned to the body binding. (see joins the body)

15th fret cross piece (see cross piece)

figure the pattern of a wood's cells caused by some disruption or abnormality in the growth of the tree or portion of the tree. Figure can be caused by rot (spalted), buckling of the grain (curly or quilted), insect infestation (bird's eye) or abnormal growth (burl). Figured wood is typically used for decorative parts of an instrument. Because of its unusual and sometimes wavy grain patterns, figured wood is not as dimensionally stable as non-figured woods of the same species and density. (see bird's eye, burl, curly figure, quilted figure, spalted)

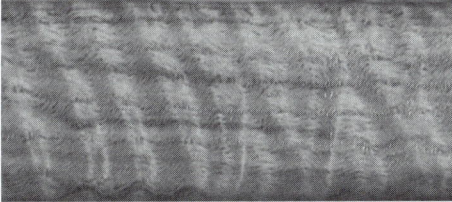

CURLY OAK

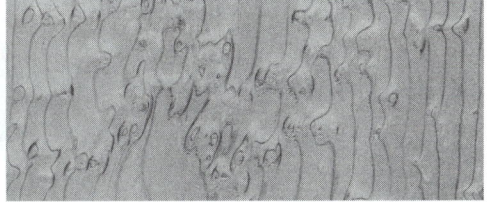

SPALTED PINE

FIGURE

figured maple a common hardwood whose growth has been disrupted such that the alignment of the cells displays an attractive pattern. Figured maple is not a species, but instead a physical condition of the wood. The common figures in maple include bird's eye, burly, curly, quilted, and spalted. (see bird's eye, curly maple, quilted maple, spalted)

file a steel tool whose cutting surfaces are covered with numerous teeth of various configurations. Files come in many shapes and sizes such as flat, round, half round, triangular, and square. According to the use and material to be filed, the teeth are arranged at a single angle (mill files), compound angles (bastard files) or prepared as numerous individual teeth (rasps) for rough cutting and shaping. Files for small, delicate work are called "needle files," and files with curved surfaces and unique cutting shapes are called "rifflers."

filing the process of removing wood or metal with a tool whose cutting surface(s) contains numerous teeth.

filler a thick compound applied to the "whitewood" surface of large-pore, open-cell woods such as mahogany and walnut to fill the pores in preparation for finishing. Closed-cell woods such as maple typically do not need a filler. (see sealer, whitewood)

fillet a small wood (or similar) part used to fill a gap or space.

filling the process of sealing the pores of wood in preparation for finishing.

finger plane a small plane used to shape delicate parts or shape wood in tight places. Finger planes are small enough to be held between the fingers. The bodies of finger planes are made of wood, steel or brass and have curved or flat bases. The steel blades are adjustable to a range of depths. Finger planes are sometimes referred to as "thumb planes."

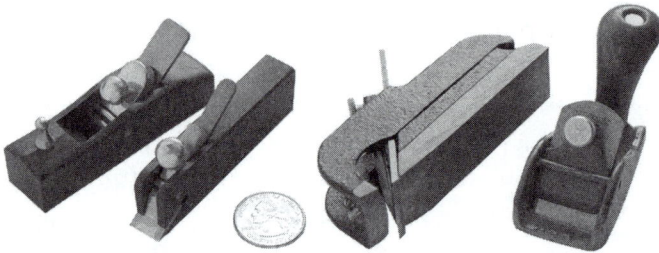

FINGER PLANES

fingerboard a smooth, flat and sometimes plano-convex surface on violin-family instruments to which the strings are held to change their vibrating length, resulting in a change in the strings' pitch. Unlike fretboards, fingerboards do not have frets. (see fretboard)

fingerrest a support raised above the soundboard on which the non-playing fingers rest. While tortoise shell plastic is typical, the material used for a fingerrest is dependent on the luthier's design preference. (see pickguard)

finish the material used to seal wood and provide a protective and cosmetically pleasing appearance to an instrument. Finishes can include, but are not limited to, lacquer, French polish, shellac, varnish, and many super-setting urethane compounds.

five-string banjo, 5-string banjo (see regular banjo)

fixed bridge a string support that is attached to the soundboard. Fixed bridges are fitted with a saddle that is either straight, angled or compensated. Most fixed-bridge systems are also used to secure the ends of the strings on instruments that do not have a tailpiece. (see compensated saddle)

fixture a form that is used to hold parts during gluing, drilling or shaping. The fixture that holds a rib set during gluing of the soundboard and/or backboard is called a "mold" or "body fixture."

flamed maple an informal name used to refer to curly maple. (see curly maple, fiddle maple)

flamenco guitar a six-string instrument constructed with a cedar soundboard and traditionally tuned *E, B, G, D, A, E* (high to low). The features of flamenco guitars include a flat cedar soundboard, a flat hardwood backboard, a wide fretboard, a round soundhole with an elaborate decorative rosette, straight (non-mechanical) wooden friction pegs, nylon strings, a tap plate, and a fixed bridge with an integral harness around which the strings are tied.

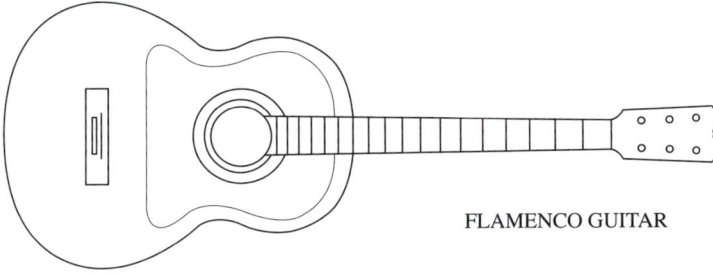

FLAMENCO GUITAR

flange a protrusion used to secure, align, enlarge or cover the connection of two or more parts. On most banjos with resonators, a flange is used to connect the rim assembly to the resonator and to decorate the opening between the rim and the edge of the resonator.

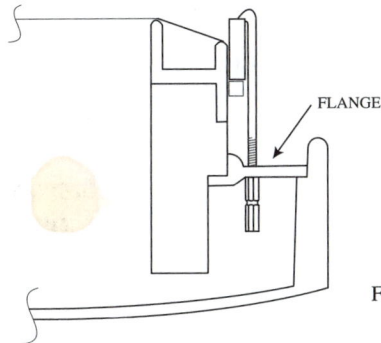

FLANGE

FLANGE (BANJO)

flat file a steel tool whose cutting surfaces are covered with numerous teeth of various configurations. Flat files come in many widths and sizes and are available in fine, medium, and coarse teeth. Files with a single row of angular teeth are called "mill files," those with two rows of crisscrossed teeth are called "bastard files," and tiny versions used for intricate work are called "flat needle files."

flat grain wood that is cut such that its grain lies parallel to the board's width. (see slab-sawn, cut on the quarter)

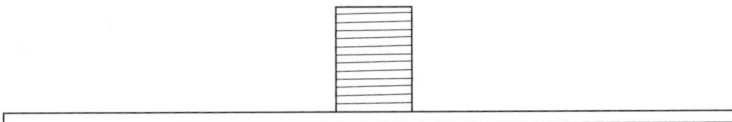

FLAT GRAIN

flat-head tone chamber a bronze support ring inside a banjo designed by Gibson in the mid-1930s. The flat-head or "flat-top" is a description of the shape of the head fitting over the tone chamber in contrast to its arch-top predecessor. Flat-head tone chambers provide the banjo's head with a 33.1% larger area than the same pot assembly with an arch-top tone chamber. Because of the larger size, which provides the head with a lower resonant frequency, flat-head tone chamber banjos have a deeper, richer tone than their arch-top counterparts. (see arch-top tone chamber)

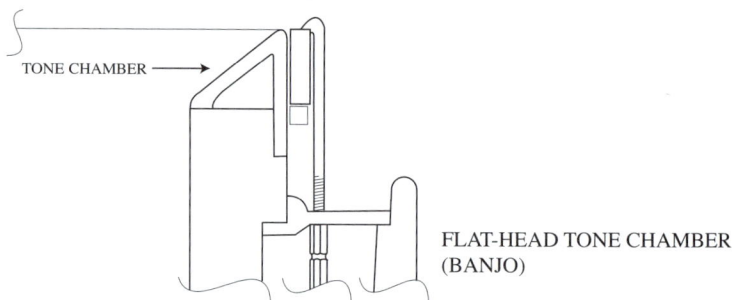

TONE CHAMBER ———→

FLAT-HEAD TONE CHAMBER (BANJO)

flat sawing the process of cutting wood so that the grain through most boards is parallel to the board's width. Flat sawing also expedites cutting by enabling numerous slices to be made without rotating the log.

flat-sawn, flatsawn wood that has been cut so its grain is consistently positioned across the board and oriented somewhat parallel to the board's width. Also known as "plain sawn" or "slab-sawn." (see slab-sawn)

flat-top acoustic guitar a six-course wood-bodied string musical instrument with a non-curved soundboard and backboard. Most flat-top acoustic guitars have a single round soundhole, a fixed bridge, and no tailpiece. For structural and acoustical purposes, the soundboard and backboard are constructed with a slight curvature even though the are referred to as being "flat." (see arch-top acoustic guitar)

flat-top tone chamber (see flat-head tone chamber)

flesh hoop a brass or steel ring on a banjo around which a skin head is folded to lock the skin in place beneath the stretcher band and prevent the skin from slipping when the stretcher band is tightened. The flesh hoop is not visible once it is covered by the skin head. A flesh hoop is not used with today's Mylar® heads because the heads are permanently attached to securing rings that take the place of flesh hoops.

flitch a stack of matched veneers. Technically, flitch refers to a stack or bundle of 500 veneers, but the term is often used loosely to refer to any pile of mated veneers.

floating bridge (see movable bridge)

Florentine a design style with shapes that resemble plants, leaves, vines, and similar patterns found in nature. The Florentine art style has its roots in Italy and dates back to the 13th Century when flowing lines, realism, and depth became important elements of the art form.

Florentine mandolin an elaborately-shaped four-course acoustic string instrument whose body emulates a floral design, with peaks and shaded edges that emphasize perspective and relief. The F-style mandolin ("F" for Florentine) was developed by Orville H. Gibson.

FLORENTINE MANDOLIN

flush-bearing router bit a cutting tool that is designed to trim wood even with its adjoining surface. Most better flush bits are fitted with bearings that roll against the edge of the piece being routed. A flush router bit can have a bearing at the top or at the bottom of the cutting blades.

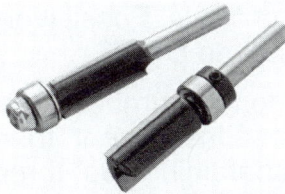

FLUSH-BEARING ROUTER BITS

folk banjo a five-string banjo without a resonator. Folk banjos are commonly tuned *D, B, G, C, G* (high to low, called "C" tuning) and have a string scale of 25″ to 26″ with some long-neck versions reaching scale lengths of 30″. These instruments are usually

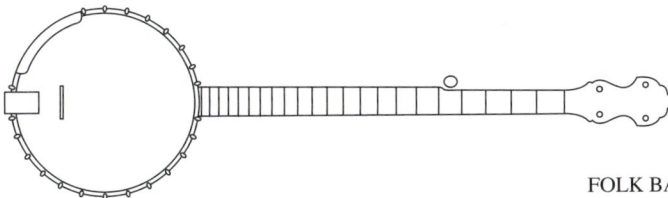

FOLK BANJO

played without fingerpicks in either a frailing, two-finger picking or strumming technique. (see frailing, guitar banjo, mandolin banjo, plectrum banjo, regular banjo, resonator, tenor banjo, ukulele banjo)

force of attack (see intensity of attack)

fork (tuning) (see tuning fork)

Forstner bit a wide drill with a very small pilot used to prepare a "blind" hole. A Forstner bit is helpful when creating the blind hole for the scroll strengthener in a mandolin's peghead.

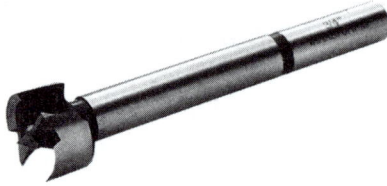

FORSTNER BIT

40-hole archtop a bronze tone chamber that is attached to the uppermost portion of a banjo rim. Early versions of this tone chamber made by Gibson featured 40 holes drilled into the side of the tone chamber (visible only from within the banjo). "Archtop" is a description of the shape of the head as it fits over the raised centermost lip of the tone chamber.

fossil ivory the bone or tusk taken from a dead animal. While fossil ivory is found worldwide, the material recovered in colder climates is less prone to decay and better for cutting and shaping. Fossil ivory typically comes from walrus and mammoth and is exempt from the 1989 CITES worldwide embargo on trading ivory that is taken from hunted animals. Fossil ivory is a suitable material for nuts and corner points. (see CITES)

four course a reference to the number of sets of strings on an instrument. On a four-course instrument, there are four sets of strings with each course containing two, three or four strings.

four-ply rim a banjo rim constructed from four laminates of ¼″ maple. The tube-and-plate flange assembly requires four plies because of the additional lip needed to support the tube. (The one-piece flange utilizes a three-ply rim.) (see one-piece flange, tube-and-plate flange)

four-string banjo, 4-string banjo a general name for any banjo with four strings. (see plectrum banjo, tenor banjo, ukulele banjo)

14-fret neck 1) an instrument whose neck joins the body at the 14th fret. 2) the point at which the 14th fret on an instrument is aligned to the body binding. (see joins the body)

frailing a method of playing the banjo without fingerpicks or plectrum. In the frailing style, the middle finger's nail is used to strum down on the strings, followed by the thumb landing on and picking the fifth string or selectively picking other strings. The nail of the middle finger is also used to pick out the melody. Sometimes referred to as "drop thumb," "drop thumb picking," or "claw hammer banjo" style.

frailing banjo a term given to an open back (non-resonator) five-string banjo. Today, many frailing banjos feature scalloped fretboards that have no frets in the last four to six fret positions nearest to the head. That area of the fretboard is also shaped lower than the neighboring fretboard area to allow ample room for frailing without striking the fretboard. (Attacking the strings near the end of the fretboard provides a warm, mellow tone.) (see frailing, scalloped fretboard)

free water the moisture in lumber that is readily available within the wood's cells (compared to bound water). The free water is more easily removed during kiln or open-air drying. (see bound water, fiber saturation point)

French polish a finishing compound comprised of shellac flakes dissolved in ethanol (alcohol) and, if applied by rag or pad, some linseed or mineral oil (many luthiers prefer walnut or almond oil). The shellac is the solid (finish), the alcohol (preferably 190 proof) is the vehicle (which dissolves quickly), and a small quantity of linseed or other oil is used to prevent the application cloth or pad from sticking. (see pound cut)

French walnut (see European walnut)

frequency the specific rate at which a vibrating medium such as a string makes one complete orbit or cycle, typically measured in vibrations per second or Hz. (see Hertz)

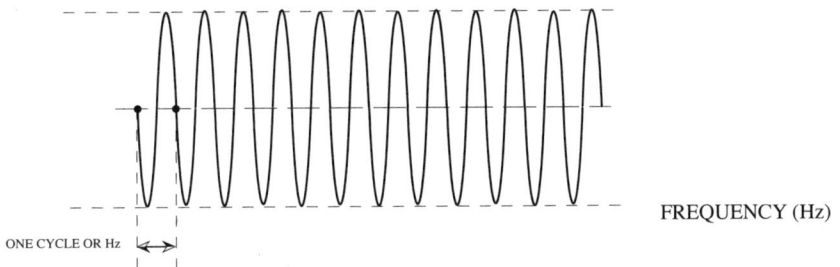

FREQUENCY (Hz)

ONE CYCLE OR Hz

frequency interval the relationship between the vibrational rate of two consecutive notes. The frequency interval can be determined by using an algebraic formula known as the "twelfth root of two." To calculate the frequency of the next lower note, divide the frequency (in Hz) by 17.817. To calculate the frequency of the next higher note, multiply the frequency (in Hz) by 1.05946. (see twelfth root of two)

fret a protrusion above the surface of the fretboard that provides a hard stopping place for the string. Frets are used to ensure an accurate, non-damping string-stop location. Fret locations are determined by using a formula known as the "twelfth root of two." (see twelfth root of two)

fret bead (see bead)

fret buck a heavy metal or wooden support that can be placed beneath a fragile area of the fretboard to absorb the shock when hammering in the frets.

fret file a tool used to shape or flatten frets. Fret files have very fine teeth and can be flat or have a convex cutting edge used to reshape the crown of the fret wire.

fret interval the distance between frets as calculated using a formula known as the "twelfth root of two." (see fret scale calculation)

fret puller a plier-like tool that is used to remove frets. The most common type of fret puller is a pair of end cutters with the outer face ground flush to the cutting edge. The flush outer face helps to prevent the fretboard wood from chipping up as the frets are pulled out of their slots.

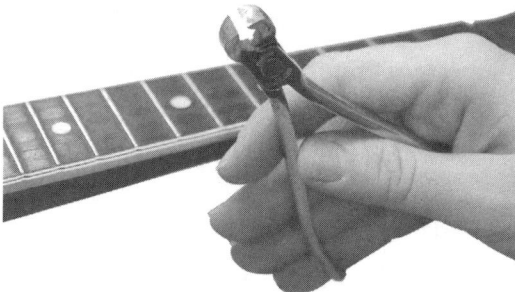

FRET PULLER

fret scale the measurement from the inner edge of the nut to the inner edge of the bridge at the first string. While the overall length of the neck is different from the fret scale, the fret scale is used to determine the length of the playable part of the neck.

fret scale calculation an algebraic formula used to determine the precise location of the frets on a fretboard from the inside face of the nut to the leading edge of the bridge. The fret slot locations are determined by dividing the fret scale (distance from the nut to the bridge) by 17.817. The mathematical *result* is the distance from the nut to the first fret. Then, that result is subtracted from the fret scale to arrive at the distance from the first fret to the bridge (basically, a new fret scale length). That distance is then divided by 17.817 to determine the location of the second fret, and the process of division and subtraction is repeated until all fret locations have been determined. The formula, known as the "twelfth root of two," can also be used to calculate the distance to the next higher fret for those cases where existing fret scales are being lengthened. (see twelfth root of two)

EXAMPLE TO CALCULATE 20" SCALE LENGTH USING 17.817:

DIVIDE: **20"** ÷ **17.817** = **1.123"** (DISTANCE FROM NUT TO FIRST FRET)
  SUBTRACT: **20"** − **1.123"** = **18.877"** (REMAINING SCALE LENGTH)
DIVIDE: **18.877"** ÷ **17.817** = **1.059"** (DISTANCE FROM FIRST FRET TO SECOND FRET)
  SUBTRACT: **18.877"** − **1.059"** = **17.818"** (REMAINING SCALE LENGTH)
DIVIDE: **17.818"** ÷ **17.817** = **1.000"** (DISTANCE FROM SECOND FRET TO THIRD FRET)
  SUBTRACT: **17.818"** − **1.000"** = **16.818"** (REMAINING SCALE LENGTH)
(CONTINUE DIVISION AND SUBTRACTION UNTIL ALL FRET LOCATIONS ARE CALCULATED)

THE MEASUREMENTS ARE THE DISTANCES TO THE CENTER OF EACH FRET SLOT.

TO INCREASE THE SCALE LENGTH (TO ADD A FRET AND CALCULATE THE DISTANCE TO THE NEXT NEW FRET) MULTIPLY THE FRET SCALE BY 1.05946.

FRET SCALE CALCULATION (EXAMPLE)

---

fret scale formula (see fret scale calculation, twelfth root of two)

fret slot a cut across the fretboard into which frets are installed. Fret slots are prepared .023″ wide and are as deep as required to accommodate the tang of the fretwire being installed.

fret slot calculation (see fret scale calculation)

fret tang (see tang)

fretboard a flat surface on a string musical instrument populated by raised ridges against which the strings are pressed to change their pitch. The ridges are called "frets," and they extend across the fretboard's width. The frets act as stopping points to change a string's vibrating length and alter its pitch. Fretboards can be either flat or radiused. (see fingerboard, fret, radiused fretboard).

fretboard extender the element of a string musical instrument that is used to support the free or elevated end of a fretboard.

fretless a string musical instrument whose fretboard does not have frets. Without frets, the musician must have the fingering accuracy to intonate the strings properly. On fretless instruments, some damping occurs where the string is stopped between the finger and the fretboard (compared to the finger holding the string down behind a fret). While violins do not have frets, they are *not* considered "fretless" because no member of the violin family has frets.

friction peg a gearless device used to tension strings. Friction pegs are tapered and fitted to mated tapered holes, and they are commonplace on violins, violas, ukuleles, some old-time banjos, and flamenco guitars. As the name implies, the friction of the peg fitting tightly into a hole keeps the peg from turning.

frog the tensioning and hair-support mechanism of a violin's bow. The frog consists of the frog body, a frog top lining (between frog and stick), a ferrule (secures slide in place), a slide (secures hair and wedge in place), a back lining (support that goes down the back of frog), a wedge, a bow eyelet, and a bow screw.

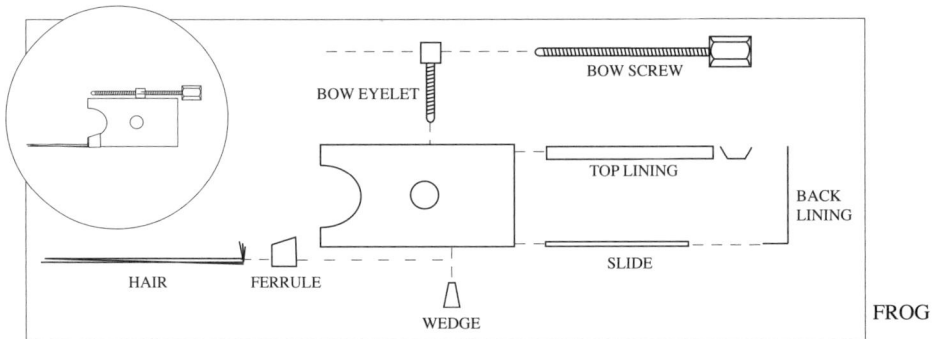

BOW SCREW
BOW EYELET
TOP LINING
BACK LINING
HAIR
FERRULE
SLIDE
WEDGE
FROG

FSP (see fiber saturation point)

fundamental the lowest rate at which a string or object in motion can vibrate. On a string, the fundamental is the lowest note at which it can vibrate at a given tension. When a musical string produces its fundamental, it is vibrating in one full node. In an air chamber, the fundamental is the lowest note an air chamber can produce when excited (referred to as its resonant frequency). (see harmonic, partial)

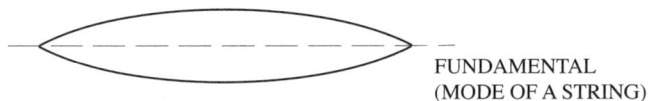

FUNDAMENTAL
(MODE OF A STRING)

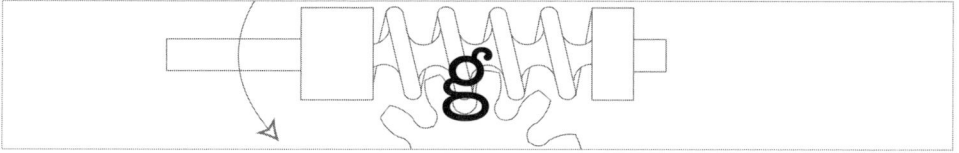

Gaboon ebony (*Diospyros crassiflora hiern*) a dark black wood from Eastern Africa used for fretboards, peghead veneers, and bridges. Depending on its country of origin, Gaboon ebony is also known as Cameroon ebony, Gabon ebony or Madagascar ebony (not to be confused with Macassar ebony). Gaboon ebony weighs approximately 65 pounds per cubic foot.

gauge a measurement of the diameter of metal or wire parts. According to various industry standards, gauges can be numerical (i.e., 12-gauge wire) or measured values (i.e., .010", 12 cm). Mandolin wire is the industry name for the wire used on acoustic string instruments and is gauged in thousandths of an inch.

gauged files a series of files designed for cutting string notches of a specific size in a nut or saddle. Each file is the same width as its corresponding string.

gauze a light-weight, loosely knit fabric glued to the underside of a soundboard to provide strength and stiffness around the soundhole(s). Gauze helps to prevent the soundboard from cracking in cross-grain areas and adds stiffness to the free edge of the soundhole(s) to inhibit damping. Gauze was used on Gibson's Master Model F5, H5, and L5 instruments. (see damping)

gear ratio a numerical reference to the mechanical advantage derived from using two or more gears. The mathematical relationship of the number of teeth on two or more gears. The gear ratio is calculated by dividing the number of teeth of the gear to which the energy is applied into the number of teeth of the gear receiving the energy. For example, if the gear to which the energy is applied has 10 teeth, and the secondary or receiving gear has 20 teeth, the gear ratio is 2:1. If the 20-tooth gear were the powered gear, and the 10-tooth were the receiving or secondary gear, the gear ratio would be 1:2. (see planetary gears, worm and round gear)

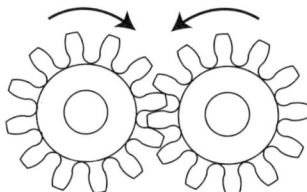

GEAR RATIO

BOTH GEARS HAVE 12 TEETH - RATIO IS 1:1

geared machine, geared tuning machine a geared assembly for improving the mechanical advantage when tightening strings to pitch. Geared machines, especially those that use worm and round gears, serve the purpose of securing the strings when at pitch to prevent them from de-tuning. Also referred to as "machines" and "tuning machines." (see worm and round gear)

German silver spruce (*Picea abies*) a member of the Pineaceae family, generally found in Northern Europe from Germany through Scandinavia. This wood is very light in color, with tight straight grain, and ample silk that gives the wood a shimmering quality. German silver spruce is used for soundboards and bracings and has a weight of 27 pounds per cubic foot.

Gibson, Orville H. (1856-1918) born in Chateaguay, New York, Gibson moved to Kalamazoo, Michigan in 1890 and began building guitars and mandolins with non-traditional features. He was awarded a U.S Patent for an acoustic string instrument (mandolin) made with sides that were cut to their curved shape from one large piece of wood (rather than being bent to shape). His work caught the attention of five local businessmen who bought the rights to his patent and started the Gibson Mandolin-Guitar Mfg. Company in 1902.

gloss a finish or surface in which the reflections of shapes and highlights are well defined. The higher the gloss, the better the definition of the shapes and highlights. (see high-gloss, matte, semi-gloss, semi-matte)

glue pot a container used to hold certain adhesives during the application process. A glue pot heated to 160° is used to prepare and soften hide glue in preparation for use. (see hide glue)

GLUE POT (HOT HIDE GLUE)

gold mother of pearl (see mother of pearl)

Gorilla Glue® an all purpose wood adhesive with excellent qualities for outdoor use. Gorilla Glue is a polyvinyl acetate compound that cleans up well with water. Gorilla Glue has similar hardness characteristics to Titebond® II, expands as it hardens, but is not generally recommended for luthierie.

graduated, graduation the result of progressively altering the thickness of one area to the next on a soundboard or backboard. Graduated soundboards and backboards are usually thinner just a short distance in from their edges and thicker near their centermost region.

grafting the matching, fitting, and inserting of a piece of wood into or next to an existing piece of wood to make a repair.

grain the result of the alignment of the cellular structure of wood. The noticeably visible grain lines are the light springwood and dark summerwood that comprise the annular rings. Each year an annular ring is added to the tree's girth just beneath the bark. (see figure)

grain direction the direction of the cellular structure (not the "figure") through a given piece of wood. The terms "flat grain," "vertical grain," and "quartered grain" refer to the direction of the grain relative to how the board is cut or how the piece is oriented in the instrument. Quartered grain is different from quarter-sawn, which is a method of cutting lumber from logs. (see figure, quarter-sawn)

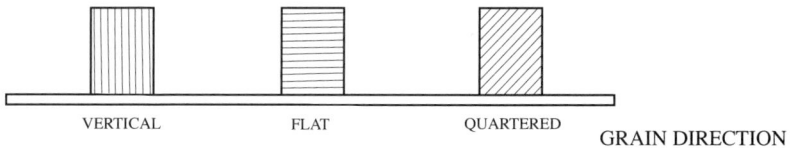

VERTICAL   FLAT   QUARTERED

GRAIN DIRECTION

grain filler (see filler)

grain sealer (see sealer)

graphite epoxy (see carbon fiber)

graver a hardened steel tool with a rounded handle used to engrave wood, metal, pearl, bone, and similar materials. Gravers are made with several different cutting edges.

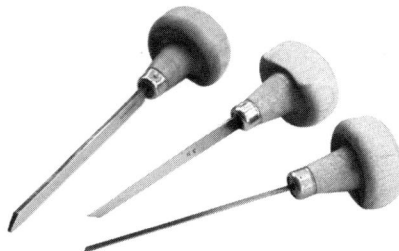

GRAVERS

green lumber wood that has not been dried or seasoned.

growth rings (see annular rings)

Guaiacum officinale the botanical name for lignum vitae. (see lignum vitae)

Guarneri, Andrea (1626-1698) a prominent violin luthier whose instruments imitated the larger "Grand Amati" violins. Guarneri was an apprentice of Nicolo Amati for five years and built violins and violas. Although Guaneri was a fellow student of Antonio Stradivari under Amati, he was not as prolific and his work is not as highly recognized as that of Stradivari. (see Amati [Nicolo], Stradivari)

Guarneri, Bartolomeo Giuseppe (1698-1744) a prominent violin maker who, while not as prolific as Stradivari, is considered to be the finest violin luthier of all time. The grandson of Andrea Guarneri, Giuseppe was more commonly known as Guarnerius del Gesu, a reference gleaned from his labels and marks which bore the initials IHS (the Greek abbreviation for Jesus) beneath a cross. Influenced by Stradivari, Giuseppe's *f*-holes were more elongated and slightly larger, and his finishes bore an orangeish tint. About 150 of his violins exist today. The name Guarnerius is a Latin declension of Guarneri meaning "of [the] man."

Guibourtia ehie the botanical name for ovangkol. (see ovangkol)

Guibourtia tessmannii the botanical name for bubinga. (see bubinga)

guitar a six-course instrument with either a large hollow wooden body or a solid wood body with electric pickups. The guitar is typically tuned *E, B, G, D, A, E* (high to low) in six-string or twelve-string (six courses, two strings per course) versions and is the most popular and widely produced wood-bodied acoustic instrument. Numerous body designs and structural features exist, and the prominent categories are typically considered classical, flamenco, steel-string acoustic, and solid-body electric. While the history of the guitar dates back thousands of years, the traditional shape

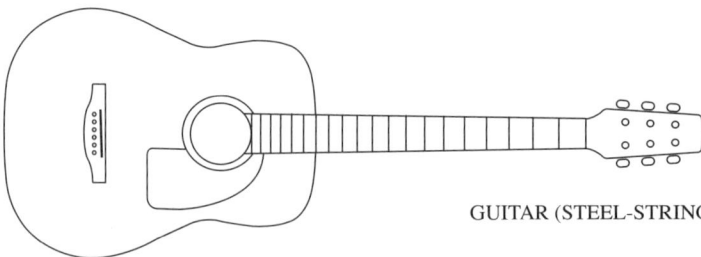

GUITAR (STEEL-STRING ACOUSTIC)

and features of the classical guitar are attributed to Antonio Torres Jurado (1817-1892), and today's steel-string acoustic guitar is attributed to Christian Frederick Martin, Sr. (1796-1873). Debate continues whether Leo Fender (1909-1991) or Les Paul (1915-) created and successfully promoted the first solid-body electric guitar (1940s).

guitar banjo an instrument with six strings, featuring a round body and a membrane-like soundboard (head). The guitar banjo is typically tuned *E, B, G, D, A, E* (high to low) and has a string scale of 25″ to 26″. The instrument has a head made of skin or plastic, and features a movable bridge, a tailpiece, and in-line or straight geared machines. The banjo's body (rim) is usually constructed of either laminated strips or blocks of wood. The sound-producing, neck-connecting, and head-attaching hardware varies with the make and model of the instrument. The back of some models is fitted with a tone-projecting shell called a "resonator." Banjos without resonators are called "open-back banjos." (see folk banjo, mandolin banjo, plectrum banjo, regular banjo, tenor banjo, ukulele banjo)

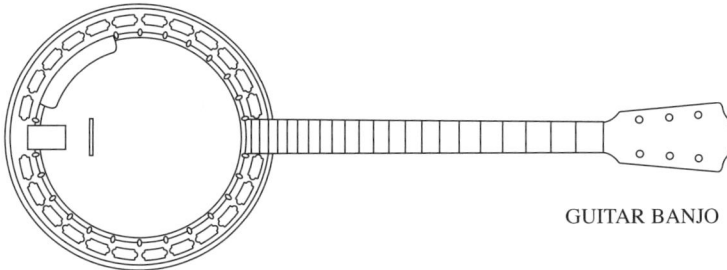

GUITAR BANJO

gut (string) a musical string made from the small intestines of sheep. Gut strings are the earliest known *durable* form of musical strings used. Gut strings are robust but mildly susceptible to changes in weather. While still available today, they have generally been replaced by nylon strings (although some classical performers still prefer gut strings for their rich tonal qualities). (see string)

h

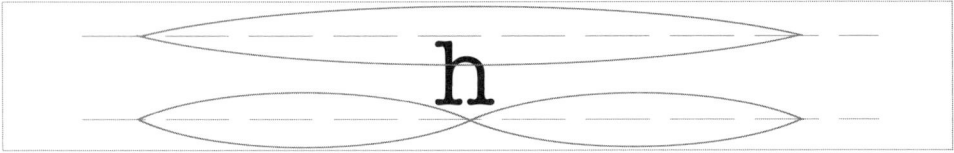

hair 1) the loose fibrous portion of the cells that raise above the surface when wood is wetted or receives its first finish coat. 2) the strands of fiber that make up the active portion of violin- and viol-family bows that are used to excite the strings. The traditional material used is horsehair.

hanger bolt (see neck lag screw, wood screw threaded stud)

hard maple a non-specific name given to any of the more dense species of maple such as sugar maple (*Acer saccharum*) or red maple (*Acer rubrum*). Sometimes referred to as "rock maple." These woods have an average weight of 37 pounds per cubic foot.

hardwood generally considered a type of small-celled wood that loses it leaves each year (deciduous). Most hardwoods are milled in random sizes and not available in conventional quarter-sawn sizes.

harmonic the tone produced by a string that is forced to vibrate in a way such that it cancels the fundamental. A harmonic is created by placing a finger lightly at a specific position on the string to promote a node and stop the fundamental from vibrating. The creation of the node causes the harmonic to be predominant. The word "harmonic" – often used interchangeably with "overtone" – refers to a sound; a "partial" is the numbered order of the harmonic. Harmonics are the components of the overtone series. (see fundamental, overtone, overtone series, partial)

harness a block on the rear portion of a fixed bridge on a classical or flamenco guitar around which the strings are tied.

harp guitar a six-string, guitar-like instrument with numerous additional bass strings. The main strings are tuned *E, B, G, D, A, E* (high to low, like a guitar) and the bass course is usually comprised of ten drone bass strings tuned *G#, G, F#, F, D#, D, C#, C, B, A#* (high to low). The bass course is commonly positioned at an angle across the face of the harp guitar with no fretboard beneath it, and a traditional fretboard is used under the regular guitar strings. The structure of the instrument must be sufficient to support the compressive load of the instrument's 16 strings which, depending on string gauges selected, could approach 450 pounds of compressive force. Harp guitars have been made in several designs, with either a flat or arched soundboard and backboard;

a round, oval or *f*-hole aperture(s); a movable bridge; as well as a fixed tailpiece to anchor the strings and support the load.

HARP GUITAR

head 1) the soundboard of a banjo. 2) the part of the instrument where the strings are connected to the tuning machines. More properly referred to as the "peghead."

headblock, head block a structural member inside an acoustic string instrument body for the purpose of securing the neck to the rib/rim assembly and distributing the load and bending force of the neck to the soundboard, backboard, and rib/rim assembly.

headplate a thin, wood covering for the peghead. Also referred to as a peghead veneer. (see peghead veneer)

heart the portion of a natural shell (e.g., snail, abalone, mother of pearl) nearest to the central muscle that yields the most elaborate wavy-grain patterns. (see abalone, mother of pearl)

heartwood the innermost portion of a tree in which growth no longer occurs. Although heartwood is the hardest and most durable part of the timber, it is not suitable for luthierie because of its discoloration and tendency to deteriorate and check. (see check, sapwood)

heated bending tube (see bending iron)

heavy gauge string a general description of string gauge that presents a higher than normal tension when tuned to the instrument's intended pitch. Heavy gauge strings are harder to play (be pulled to the fret or choked sideways) and present a substantial load to the instrument's structure. Ideally, the gauge of the strings should be relative to the stiffness and bracing of the soundboard (e.g., heavy gauge strings for heavily-braced soundboards). Since string sets come in many different gauges and are produced by several manufacturers, there is no standard set of string gauges designated as "heavy." Some manufacturers provide the string tensions for the various strings in each set; comparisons must be made to other sets to determine the relative gauges and loads. The intended string gauges that best suit the instrument's design should be designated by the luthier.

heel the end of a string instrument's neck that attaches to the body.

heel cap a decorative or protective piece of wood, shell or plastic used to cover the lower end of the neck heel.

Helmholtz, Heinrich (Hermann) (1821-1894) a highly respected German physician and physicist who, among other studies, devoted a great deal of attention to musical acoustics and authored the book *On the Sensations of Tone as a Physiological Basis for the Theory of Music* (written in 1863 and translated in 1885). Helmholtz experimented with a series of small glass balls with an opening at two ends; one end which was placed to the ear and sealed from the surrounding air with wax. These "Helmholtz resonators" aided him in studying the effects of resonant frequencies of various tone-producing systems. Helmholtz determined that every given size air chamber has a specific pitch or resonant frequency. Further, he determined that for every given size of air chamber, there is an aperture (opening) that most ideally tunes the air chamber and makes it resonate with the greatest amplitude.

herringbone the name given to a style of purfling whose center-most design meets at opposing angles in a style that resembles the spine of a herring (fish).

HERRINGBONE

COURTESY DARRYL WOLFE

Hertz (Hz) a reference to the number of complete movements or orbits an object in motion makes in one second. Named for the work done by Heinrich Rudolf Hertz, a German physicist (1857-1894) who furthered the study of the production and reception of radio waves. Among his studies, Hertz discovered that the velocity of radio waves was the same as the velocity of light. Hertz studied under Heinrich Helmholtz.

hex core, hex core string, hex core wire in musical strings, a special shaping of the core wire to help lock the wrap wire in place and prevent it from loosening or unraveling. The core wire is drawn through dies by the wire manufacturer to achieve its hexagon-like shape. (The actual shape approximates, but is not a perfect hexagon.) On this type of string, the wrap wire is wound around the core (hex) wire. (see core wire)

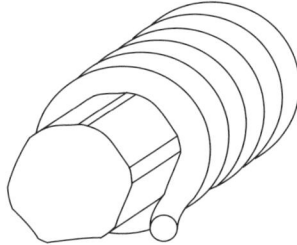

HEX CORE WIRE

hide glue a compound made of dried, ground horse hooves, skin, bones, and tendons that is mixed with water, heated to 160° to melt into a workable adhesive. Hide glue was the traditional gluing medium used by luthiers before modern-day adhesives were available. Since hide glue is worked hot and begins to harden quickly as it cools, it has a shorter open assembly time than Titebond® Original Glue or other non-heated wood glues. Hide glue has an open assembly time of one to two minutes depending on the temperature of the part being glued. Hide glue dries to a very hard and durable set. [Working in a warm room with warm parts will extend open assembly time.] (see open assembly time)

Hide Glue® a natural protein emulsion adhesive made by Franklin International that is darkish in color and is used out of the tube without being heated. Franklin's liquid "Hide Glue" brand has a similar appearance to hot hide glue and may be softened with water, but it is not to be confused with the hot hide glue used for instrument work. While the open assembly time of Franklin's Hide Glue is ten minutes, the resultant bond is somewhat weaker than that derived from traditional hot hide glue and is not recommended for luthierie

high-gloss, hi-gloss a glass-like finish or surface in which the reflections of shapes and highlights are clearly and brilliantly defined. (see gloss, matte, semi-gloss, semi-matte)

hole drilling fixture (see drill guide)

hollow a warped condition of a neck such that the center of the fretboard or fingerboard is further from the strings than it is at either end. The hollow causes a high-action problem in the center of the fretboard that can usually be cured by tightening the truss rod. On a neck without a truss rod, the playing surface must be straightened by squaring and refretting the fretboard. Also referred to as a "warp."

holly (*Ilex opaca*) a very light colored (almost white) wood with subdued annular rings such that the wood's grain is nearly invisible. Holly is an ideal selection where whitish highlights are desired in purfling, wood inlays, and marquetry. Holly weighs approximately 50 pounds per cubic foot.

Honduras mahogany (*Swietenia macrophylla*) a hardwood with an orange-brown color and an attractive but delicate figure. The shimmering grain appearance of Honduras mahogany is the result of the overlapping cellular structure caused by the unusual growth of the annular rings. Each year's new wood is added at a different angle of about one degree per year, first growing clockwise up the tree for about ten years and then reversing its direction for the next ten years. The result of the overlapping grain structure gives this wood an attractive fiberglass-like appearance as well as a dimensionally stable structure, making it an ideal choice for necks, sides, block sets, and backboards. Honduras mahogany machines and sands well, is excellent for making patterns, and has an average weight of 36 pounds per cubic foot.

Honduras rosewood (*Dalbergia stevensonii*) a dense hardwood with colors ranging from orange-brown to dark purplish-brown. Honduras rosewood is denser than Brazilian rosewood, weighs 60 pounds per cubic foot, and is ideal for backboards, sides, fretboards, bridge bases, and peghead veneers.

honeycombing checks that cannot be seen from the outside of a log or in a piece of lumber.

horsehair the string-excitation component of a violin- or viol-famly bow. Natural horsehair is used for its durability as well as the rough follicles that populate the sides of the hair and provide for a positive grip of the strings. Horsehair also offers an excellent bonding surface for rosin, which adds further to the drag-and-release function of the bow hair.

hot knife a heated knife or blade used to soften the glue in seams during the disassembly of parts.

hygrometer a device that measures the relative humidity, used to monitor proper storage conditions for wood (and other materials).

Hz the abbreviation for Hertz, a reference to vibrations in terms of their complete cycles per second. (see Hertz)

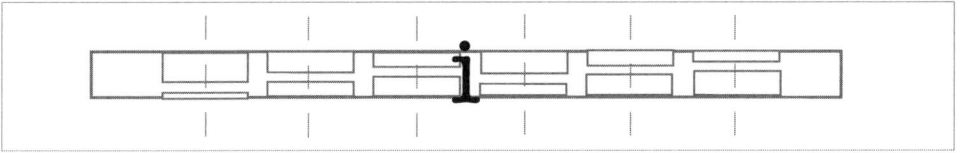

Ilex opaca the botanical name for holly. (see holly)

Indian rosewood (*Dalbergia latifolia*) a hardwood commonly used for guitar backs, sides, and veneers. Indian rosewood is slightly less dense and hard as Brazilian rosewood, and has more consistent grain and color. Indian rosewood is readily available and not hampered by the export embargo that impacts the availability of Brazilian rosewood. Indian rosewood weights about 53 pounds per cubic foot.

inlay 1) the act of placing decorative components into the wood's surface. 2) a piece of pearl, abalone, wood or metal cut to shape and placed into the wood's surface for decorative or position-indicating purposes.

in-line machines a set of geared tuners mounted on a metal strip for use on guitars and mandolins. In-line machines use worm and round gears. (see worm and round gear).

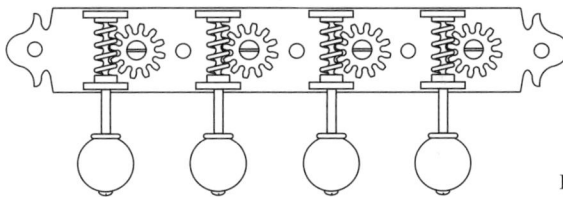

IN-LINE MACHINES

intellectual property (IP) any unique technique, method, process, patent, copyright or design an individual or organization uses in the pursuit of its business. For example, a special tool or custom method of preparing a glue joint, carving wood or applying a finish may be considered as a luthier's intellectual property.

intensity of attack the amount of impact delivered to a string or tone-producing member. One of the four main factors that affect the production of tone from a struck object, the other three being location of attack, duration of attack, and method of attack. Sometimes referred to as the "strength of attack" or "force of attack." (see attack)

interlocked grain wood grain that is comprised of changes in the direction of its fibers, often producing a ribbon-like figure as in Honduras mahogany.

intonated saddle a bridge support (saddle) that has staggered string-contact points to correct for various string gauges and core/wrap wire combinations. The intonation notches compensate for the anomalies in various string gauges that require slightly different scale lengths.

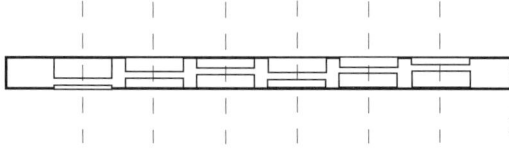

INTONATED SADDLE

intonation in musical strings, the attribute that causes one string gauge or core/wrap combination to change pitch at a different rate from another gauge when fretted (stopped) at the same length. Thicker gauges tend to note sharper than thinner gauges because of the heavier gauge's greater resistance to being stretched.

intonation correction the adjustment made to a bridge or saddle to correct the scale length of a musical string to compensate for different gauges and windings. Because of the increased tension when a string is "choked" and pulled to the fretboard, a scale-length correction must be made for each string's core/wrap wire combination to have it note correctly. (see compensated bridge, compensated saddle)

inverted machine a geared tuning machine in which the worm gear is above the round gear. Inverted machines provide better meshing of the round gear to the worm gear because the string's tension on the top of the post forces the round gear on the bottom of the post into the worm gear. (see worm and round gear)

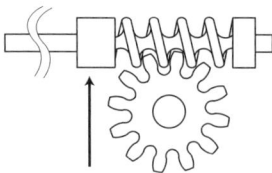
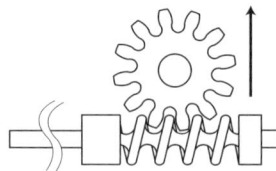

INVERTED   NON-INVERTED   INVERTED MACHINES
                                       (GEARS)

Irish bouzouki an instrument with four courses, two strings per course tuned *D, A, D, G* (high to low). Some Irish bouzoukis are tuned *E, A, D, G,* an octave below the mandolin and the same as the octave mandolin. The Irish bouzouki has a roundish pear-shaped body, a flat soundboard and backboard, 22″ to 24″ string scale, and a modified oval soundhole. In essence, the instrument is an octave mandolin. The Irish bouzouki was developed in the mid-1900s and, as the name implies, had its origin in Ireland as a local folk music instrument. (see bouzouki)

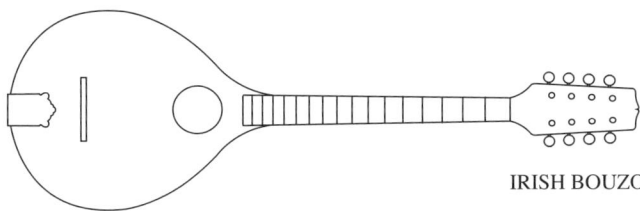

IRISH BOUZOUKI

isotropic as it relates to acoustics, that property of a material in which sound radiates through it in all directions at an identical speed. An isotropic material is one in which the cellular or physical structure is identical in all axes. Metal is isotropic; wood is anisotropic. (see anisotropic, orthotropic)

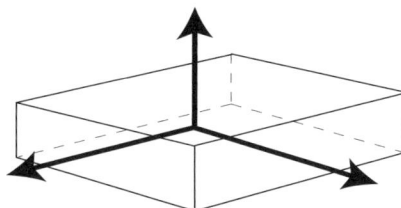

ISOTROPIC

ivoroid a white celluloid material made with a grained pattern to simulate ivory. The name was derived from combining the words "ivory" and "celluloid." Ivoroid is commonly used for the binding that decorates and protects the corners and edges of an instrument. (see celluloid)

ivory a natural material from the teeth of mammals and from walrus tusks. Ivory is similar to bone but has no blood vessels so it is more dense. Before the 1989 CITES embargo on tusks from certain animals, ivory was used to make nuts and bridge saddles and was originally used for billiard balls and the covering of white piano keys. Today, it is more common in luthierie to use bone, pearl or any of several synthetic materials. (see CITES)

jack a tool that helps to force or hold parts in place. A jack is used when gluing braces or repairing soundboard/backboard cracks on finished instruments. The jack can be L-shaped, curved or a threaded turnbuckle-like mechanism, but must be small enough to fit through the soundhole.

jazz guitar a six-string instrument tuned *E, B, G, D, A, E* (high to low). The features of jazz guitars include an arched and graduated soundboard and backboard, a radiused fretboard, geared tuning machines, *f*-holes, an adjustable two-footed bridge, and a trapeze tailpiece. The end of the fretboard on a jazz guitar is elevated over the soundboard.

JAZZ GUITAR

jeweler's saw a small, hand-held cutting frame that holds a thin blade and is used for cutting pearl and small parts. Jeweler's saw blades are available in sizes ranging from .018″ to .025″ thick.

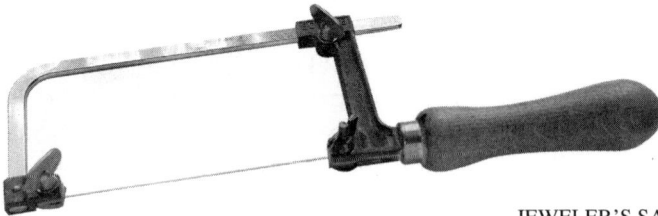

JEWELER'S SAW

jigsaw (see scroll saw)

joins the body a description of where the neck connects to the body of the instrument. This expression refers to the fret that is aligned to the body binding immediately alongside the neck's connecting point. On most acoustic guitars, the neck is connected so that either the 12th or 14th fret aligns with the binding. On A-style and early F-style mandolins, the neck is connected so that the 12ᵗʰ fret aligns with the binding. On the F5 mandolin, the neck is made a bit longer so that the 15ᵗʰ fret aligns with the binding. Note that on arched-soundboard mandolins, the binding connects to a crosspiece that appears to go through the headblock, and the fret that joins the body is actually further into the body than at the soundboard's edge as on guitars. The connecting point where the neck joins the body is not a set standard and varies according to model and maker. (see cross piece)

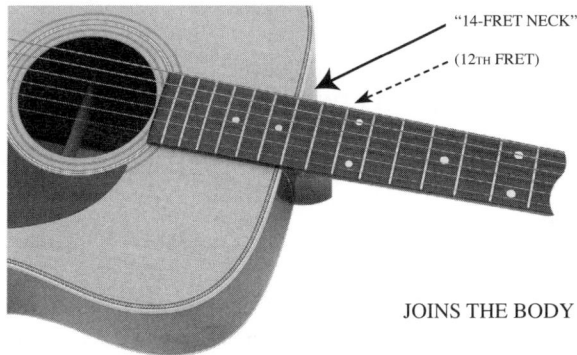

"14-FRET NECK"

(12ᴛʜ FRET)

JOINS THE BODY

Juglans nigra the botanical name for black walnut. (see black walnut)

Juglans regia the botanical name for European walnut. (see European walnut)

k

kerf the width of a saw blade's teeth.

kerfed lining an edge beading that has shallow saw cuts at close intervals to enable the beading to be bent. Kerfed lining is used at the intersection of the rim and soundboard or backboard. The saw cuts in the beading are referred to as "kerfs." Some acoustic string instruments use plain, unkerfed lining. Mahogany, maple, and basswood are typical wood choices for kerfed lining.

kerfs small cuts made partially through a piece of wood to facilitate bending. (see kerfed lining)

Kershner tailpiece a popular early brand of tailpiece used on banjos. The Kershner tailpiece is made of heavy, bent brass and has no cover over the ends of the strings. The greater length of the Kershner tailpiece provides excellent down pressure at the bridge.

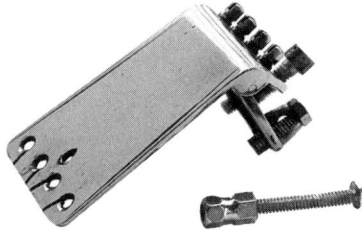

KERSHNER TAILPIECE

Khaya ivorensis the botanical name for African mahogany. (see African mahogany)

kiln drying the process of physically removing water from lumber that is sawn from freshly cut ("green") logs. Boards to be kiln dried are placed in heated chambers, and the temperature is carefully maintained for a set period of time to accelerate the evaporation of "free water." The lumber is removed when it reaches the desired moisture content. (see air dried, bound water, free water, moisture content)

koa (*Acacia koa*) a beautifully colored and patterned wood from Hawaii. Koa features colors ranging from ochre to brown and has elaborate grain patterns. It is an excellent choice for guitar backs and sides, and can be used successfully for mandolin backs and sides. Koa also can be used for binding and peghead veneers.

Krazy Glue® (see cyanoacrylate)

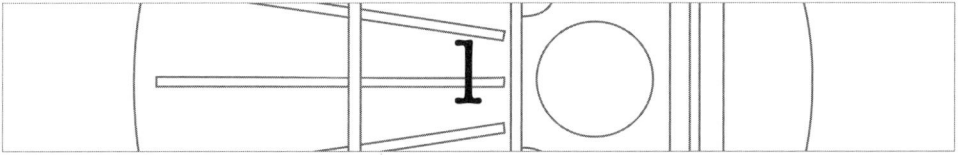

lac a gummy substance collected from the *coccus lacca* (an insect from Southern Asia and India). After feeding, the insect produces lac through its pores that hardens into a protective covering. The lac is collected, crushed, washed, and dried. When mixed with alcohol, it forms shellac. Lac is also used to make items such as electrical insulators, sealing wax, and fireworks. (see French polish, lacquer, pound cut, shellac, varnish)

lacquer a hard, glossy, clear or colored finish made from resins or cellulose derivatives and a plasticizer, dissolved in a volatile fast-drying solvent. Lacquer has a short set-up time and cures quickly. It can be polished to a high gloss, and its surface is quite durable.

ladder strutting the placement of numerous cross braces that run perpendicular to the center axis of the instrument. Ladder strutting is the common bracing pattern used in ukuleles.

laminate 1) the process of gluing two layers of material together. 2) a hard, durable plastic-like covering affixed to wood or particle board to protect and decorate its surface.

lateral vibrations on a musical string, those vibrations that go side to side (as opposed to going longitudinally) and are the result of the initial attack from a pick, hammer or bow. Mandolins, banjos, and other movable-bridge instruments are driven primarily by lateral vibrations compared to fixed-bridge instruments that are driven primarily by longitudinal vibrations. (see longitudinal vibrations)

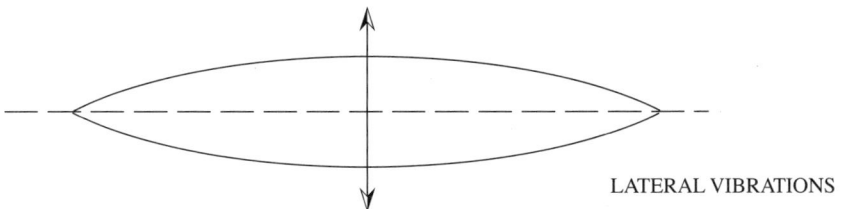

LATERAL VIBRATIONS

latewood (see summerwood)

leather dye aniline dye typically used for coloring animal skins. The deep penetrating, fast-drying qualities make these dyes ideal for coloring wood. Compared to oil-based stains, aniline dyes leave minimal residue on the wood's surface. (see aniline dye)

light gauge string a general description of string gauge that can be tuned to the instrument's designed pitch with reasonably low tension. Light gauge strings are easy to play (be pulled to the fret or choked) and present a light load to the instrument's soundboard or head. Ideally, the gauge of the string should be balanced to the stiffness and bracing of the soundboard (e.g., light gauge strings for lightly-braced soundboards). Since string sets come in many different gauges from several manufacturers, there is no one standard gauge of strings designated as "light." Comparisons must be made to other sets to determine the relative gauges and loads. The intended string gauges that best suit the instrument's design should be designated by the luthier. Some manufacturers provide the string tensions for the various strings in each set.

lignometer a device that measures moisture content. Most lignometers determine the moisture content by measuring the resistance between the meter's two electrodes. Greater moisture content results in a higher reading. (see moisture content)

lignum vitae (*Guaiacum officinale*) a very dense hardwood from Central America. Lignum vitae has great durability and is highly resistant to checking. The high saturation of guaiac gum (which comprises about 30% of the wood's weight) gives it a very slippery, oily feeling and provides the wood with excellent qualities making it ideal for chisel handles and mallet heads. Used more in the tools of luthierie than in the instruments themselves. Lignum vitae has an approximate weight of 77 pounds per cubic foot.

linear foot a measurement of lumber based on one running foot of wood, regardless of the board's thickness or width. Some woods are sold by the linear (running) foot; others are sold by the board foot. (see board foot)

lining an edge beading to extend the thickness of a rim or rib to provide a larger gluing surface for attaching the soundboard and backboard. Some linings are plain (as in a violin) while others have kerfs (as in a guitar or mandolin). (see kerfed lining)

linseed oil an extract from flax seed. Linseed oil is used by cabinet and furniture makers as a lubricating agent when French polishing. However, because linseed oil leaves a slightly tacky residue, most luthiers prefer to use walnut or almond oil in conjunction with French polishing. (see French polish)

Liriodendron tulipifera the botanical name for poplar. (see poplar)

load the amount of pressure exerted on the soundboard by the bridge as a result of tightening the strings up to pitch.

loading the act of the bridge exerting a downward or twisting pressure on the soundboard when the strings are brought up to tension. The amount of loading is dependent on the string break angle over the bridge, height of bridge, position of tailpiece, neck angle or a combination of these factors. The amount of resistance to the load is based on the soundboard's wood type, grain density, thickness, shaping (graduated or flat), and bracing method. (see soundboard loading)

Loar, Lloyd Allayre (1886-1943) a musician, college professor, and acoustical engineer who worked for Gibson intermittently from 1918 to 1925. Among his contributions were the development of Gibson's "Master" line of instruments including the Master Model F5 mandolin, L5 guitar, H5 mandola, and the Mastertone banjo line. Master Model acoustic instruments feature a graduated soundboard and backboard, longitudinal tone bars, *f*-holes, an elevated fretboard, a 6° neck pitch, and a tuned and voiced air chamber. Loar founded the Acoustic-Lectic Company with former Gibson executive Lewis Williams. Loar went on to teach music theory and acoustics at Northwestern University's School of Music from 1930 until his death in 1943. One of his last contributions to the world of acoustics was the development of an air raid whistle – a design whose patent rights he gave to the U.S. Government.

location of attack the point of impact on a string or tone-producing member. The location of the attack determines which partials become prominent. One of the four major factors that affect the production of tone from a struck object, the other three being duration of attack, intensity of attack, and method of attack. (see attack, partial)

log a section of a tree from either its trunk or from a large branch.

longitudinal brace a supporting brace positioned parallel or nearly parallel to the centerline of the instrument.

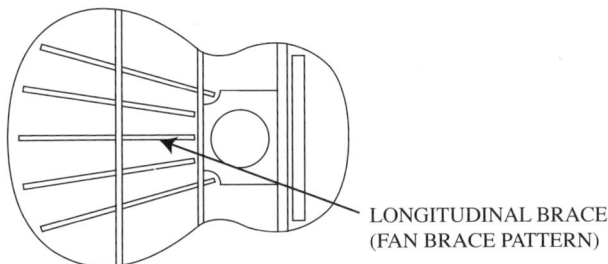

LONGITUDINAL BRACE
(FAN BRACE PATTERN)

longitudinal vibrations on a musical string, those vibrations that go lengthwise through or along a string and are the result of the string's response to loading and unloading of its tension. Longitudinal vibrations occur in response to the lateral (side to side) movements whose pull increases and decreases the longitudinal tension of the string. Instruments with fixed bridges are driven primarily by longitudinal vibrations whereas movable-bridge instruments such as mandolins and banjos are driven primarily by lateral vibrations. (see lateral vibrations)

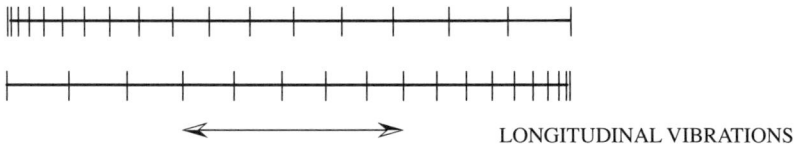

LONGITUDINAL VIBRATIONS

loop-end string a musical string that is finished at one end with the string bent back and wound onto itself. The loop that is created enables the string to be placed over a pin or hook in the tailpiece. Some makers of loop-end strings apply a yarn covering called "chenille" around the wound part of the loop to help eliminate buzzing or rattling of the string in the tailpiece and to prevent the open end of the string winding from catching on the player's sleeve when the tailpiece does not have a cover. (see ball-end string)

loudness the human *perception* of how much sound is coming from an object based on ambient sound conditions (e.g., a dropped coin in dead silence could be perceived as loud whereas the same dropped coin in a noisy factory would not be heard even though the actual amplitude of the dropped coin did not change). Sometimes referred to as volume. (see amplitude)

lower bout (see bout)

luthier a builder of string musical instruments; originally someone who built lutes.

luthierie the art of building string musical instruments.

m

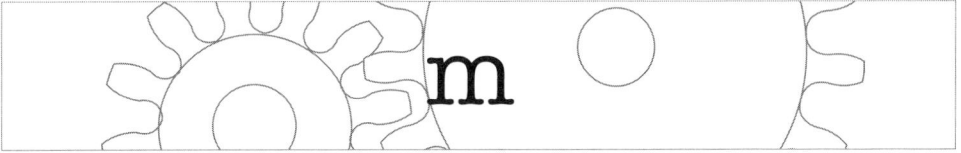

M guitar a guitar with a body size that is typically 40-5/8″ long with a body length of 20-1/8″, width of 16″ and a depth of 4-1/8″.

Macassar ebony (*Diospyros macassar*) a dark black wood from Southern India. Macassar ebony usually has light tan wisps, and some luthiers prefer its non-black appearance for fretboards and peghead veneers. It is sometimes called "golden ebony" for its grey to yellow sapwood. Macassar ebony machines and carves well but tends to dull tools, and it is difficult to glue. Macassar ebony (not to be confused with Madagascar ebony) weighs approximately 69 pounds per cubic foot. (see Gaboon ebony)

machine head (see geared machine)

machines (see geared machine)

Madagascar ebony (see Gaboon ebony)

Madagascar rosewood (*Dalbergia baronii*) a heavily-figured hardwood with deep purplish-brown color. Madagascar rosewood weighs 40 pounds per cubic foot and has very similar features to Brazilian rosewood, and is a good choice for backboards, sides, fretboards, bridge bases, and peghead veneers.

mallet a hammer with a large head made of wood, hardened leather, plastic or rubber. Mallets are used to drive chisels or to hit directly on work. The head style imparts a lighter blow than a steel-headed hammer, and the softer heads do not tend to damage the part being struck.

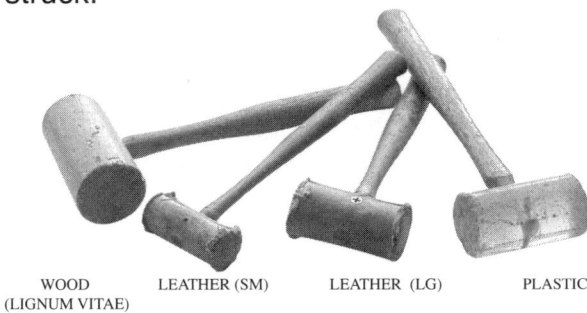

MALLETS

WOOD
(LIGNUM VITAE)   LEATHER (SM)   LEATHER (LG)   PLASTIC

mando-bass a four-string instrument tuned *G, D, A, E* (high to low) and the largest of the mandolin-family instruments. While Gibson named their product a "mando-bass," it was more of a fretted upright bass viol played pizzacato style. Mando-basses are made with a tear-drop shaped body, an oval soundhole, an arched soundboard and backboard, a movable bridge, and a trapeze tailpiece. While very few are made today, the Style-J mando-bass was offered by Gibson during the 1920s and 1930s when mandolin orchestras were in style.

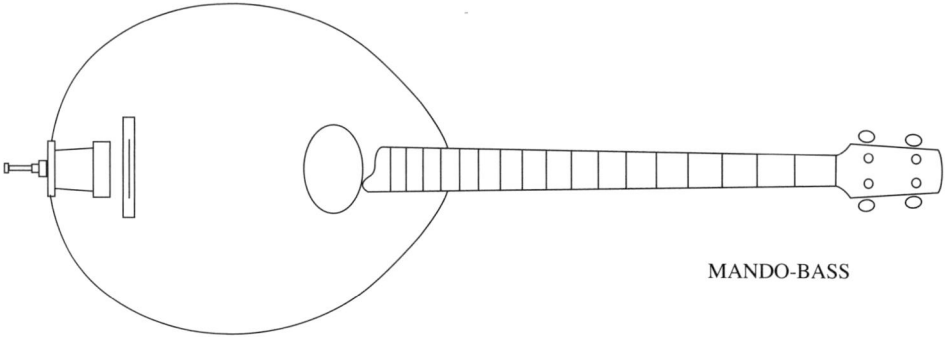

MANDO-BASS

mando-cello a four-course instrument with two strings per course tuned *A, D, G, C* (high to low), an octave below the mandola. Mando-cellos are constructed similar to jazz guitars with a 25″ to 26″ string scale, an arched soundboard and backboard, a flat or radiused fretboard, geared tuning machines, *f*-holes, an adjustable two-footed bridge, and a trapeze tailpiece.

MANDO-CELLO

mandola a four-course instrument with two strings per course tuned *A, D, G, C* (high to low). Mandolas feature a 15″ to 16″ string scale and can be either pair shaped or Florentine design. Typically,

MANDOLA (FLORENTINE)

mandolas feature an arched and graduated soundboard and backboard, a movable bridge, and a tailpiece. (see Florentine)

mandolin a four-course instrument with two strings per course tuned *E, A, D, G* (high to low). Mandolins feature a 13″ to 14″ string scale and have been produced in many body styles. F-style mandolins feature an elaborate Florentine body shape, two *f*-holes, a movable bridge, two longitudinal tone bars (although some versions have been made with X-bracing), an arched and graduated soundboard and backboard, and a tailpiece. A-style and Neapolitan mandolins feature a pear-shaped body, an oval soundhole, a movable bridge, a singular cross brace below the soundhole, and a tailpiece. A-model mandolins of the Western-world are made with various combinations of flat and arched soundboards and backboards. Neapolitan mandolins – sometimes called "bowl back mandolins" – are made with a flat soundboard (some of which have a slight bend across the soundboard, below the bridge) and a rounded back made of many sections. (see Florentine mandolin, Neapolitan mandolin, octave mandolin)

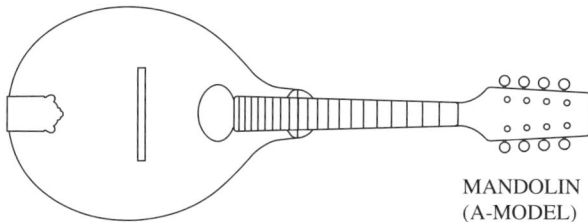

MANDOLIN
(A-MODEL)

mandolin banjo an instrument with four courses of strings, two strings per course. The mandolin banjo has a round body and a membrane-like soundboard (head). The mandolin banjo is tuned *E, A, D, G* (high to low) like its mandolin counterpart and typically has a string scale of about 14″. The instrument has a skin or plastic head, a movable bridge, a tailpiece, and geared machines. The body (rim) is constructed of either laminated strips or blocks of wood. The sound-producing, neck-connecting, and head-attaching

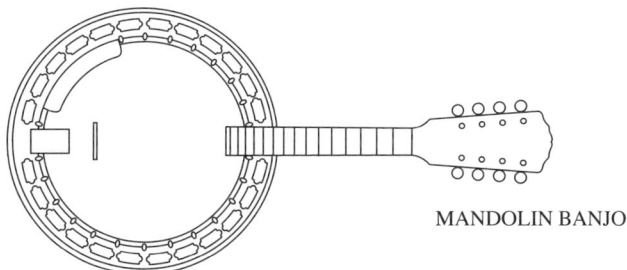

MANDOLIN BANJO

hardware varies with the make and model of the instrument. The back of some models of the mandolin banjo is fitted with a tone-projecting shell called a "resonator." (see folk banjo, frailing banjo, plectrum banjo, regular banjo, tenor banjo, ukulele banjo)

mandolin wire the term used in the wire industry to describe the composition, sizing, and spooling of wire used for musical instrument strings. Heavier gauges of this wire (larger than .050″ [1.27mm] diameter) are referred to as "piano wire."

maple (*Acer* spp.) a blond wood that is easily worked, reasonably strong, and subject to many anomalies that often provide it with interesting figure variations. The intensity of maple figure varies with each tree but falls into the general categories of curly, bird's eye, burl, quilted, and spalted. Figured maple is not a species, but rather a growth defect that provides an attractive attribute.

marquetry a design or ornamentation created from inlaid wood veneers. Marquetry usually is comprised of many wood species to take advantage of the wide variety of Mother Nature's colors, figures, and grains.

Martin, Christian Frederick, Sr. (1796-1873) an innovative designer of the acoustic guitar who developed structural features that are still prominent today. Martin was born in Germany and became a student of Vienna guitar maker Johann Stauffer. Martin moved to the United States in 1833 and set up a shop in Manhattan, later moving to Nazareth, Pennsylvania where the company still exists today as a family business under the name CF Martin & Company.

mass a description of the weight and size of an object when taken as a whole. (Scientifically, the amount of energy required to make an object overcome inertia, relative to the object's size and weight.)

matte a finish or surface in which there is minimal or no reflection of shapes and highlights. A matte finish will show some highlights but is less reflective than a semi-matte or semi-gloss finish and much less reflective than a high-gloss finish. (see gloss, high-gloss, semi-gloss, semi-matte)

MC (see moisture content)

medium gauge string a general description of string gauge that can be tuned to the instrument's designed pitch with moderate tension. Medium gauge strings are easy to play (be pulled to the fret or choked) and present a moderate load to the instrument's soundboard or head. Ideally, the gauge of the string should be balanced to the stiffness and bracing of the soundboard (e.g., medium gauge strings for modestly-braced soundboards). Since string sets come in many different gauges from several manufacturers, there is no one set of strings designated as "medium" that refers to a standard gauge. Comparisons must be made to other sets to determine the relative gauges and loads. The intended string gauges that best suit the instrument's design should be designated by the luthier. Some manufacturers provide the string tensions for the various strings in each set.

medullary rays flat, ribbon-like cells of connective tissue in a tree that radiate from the pith to the bark. Since the direction of osmosis is predominantly along the length of trunks and branches, medullary rays support the trees growth by providing cross-grain nourishment. Medullary rays are readily visible in oak, moderately visible in other woods, and miniscule rays appear as "silk" in spruce.

method of attack the type or nature of impact delivered to a string or tone-producing member. For example, the attack of a flatpick versus a padded hammer of the hammered dulcimer. One of the four primary factors that affect the production of tone from a struck object, the other three being location of attack, duration of attack, and intensity of attack. (see attack)

Micarta® a composition of paper layers emulsified in a thermoset plastic to produce a hard, durable material. Micarta was developed in 1910 and primarily intended for use in electrical insulators. Micarta is prepared in many forms, and when manufactured in black, it is an excellent substitute for ebony for fretboards and peghead veneers. When sanded or steel-wooled, it takes on a similar appearance to ebony, and Micarta machines like ebony.

Microberlinia brazzavillensis the botanical name for zebrano. (see zebrano)

mill file a steel tool whose cutting surfaces have a single row of angular teeth. Mill files remove comparatively small amounts of material, but their single row of straight teeth leave a smoother surface than the crisscrossed teeth of bastard files. Mill files come in many shapes and sizes and are available in fine, medium, and coarse teeth. (see bastard file)

minimum area the area of least (minimum) thickness that runs around the edge, or just near the edge, of a carved and graduated soundboard or backboard. (see recurve)

miter gauge a sliding tool that fits into a track on a bandsaw or table saw against which stock can be held to cut wood at a right angle. Most miter gauges can be set to a range of angles, and better miter gauges have preset stops at 45° and 90°.

modes of vibration the various patterns a string or plate (i.e., soundboard, backboard) exhibits when it is excited. Strings and plates vibrate in many different patterns according how and where they are struck, and plates vibrate in many different patterns according to their shape. On plates, the modes of vibration can be demonstrated through Chladni patterns. (see Chladni)

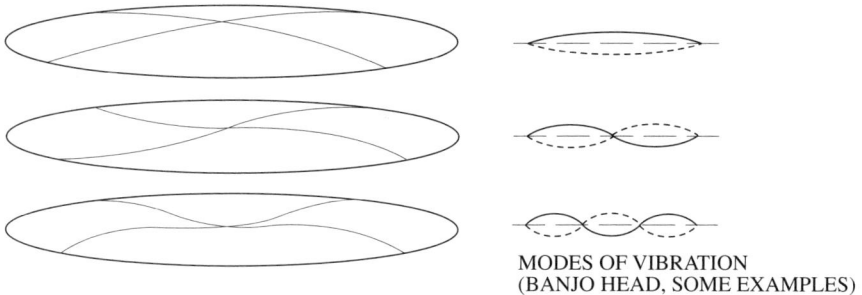

MODES OF VIBRATION
(BANJO HEAD, SOME EXAMPLES)

moisture content (MC) the amount of water contained in wood stated as a percentage of the wood's dry weight. Moisture content can vary from about 20% to about 250% depending on when a tree is harvested (having greatest moisture content at the moment it is felled), the species of wood, how the wood is dried, and whether the wood is heartwood or sapwood. Dried wood in normal storage conditions has a moisture content of 18% to 20%. (see bound water, fiber saturation point, free water)

moisture trap a device used in the air line between a compressor and a spray gun to capture water vapor that is a by-product of the compressed air in the tank. Most moisture traps have a bleed valve to remove the collected water. The use of a moisture trap helps prevent blushing when spraying finishes.

mold the name used by violin luthiers to describe a body assembly fixture. (see body fixture)

monel an anti-corrosive wire used for musical strings. Monel is an alloy comprised primarily of nickel (65%-70%), copper (20%-25%), and other metals. Monel wire was introduced for musical strings by Gibson.

mortise (see mortise and tenon)

mortise and tenon a straight-slotted joining method. In a mortise and tenon joint, a straight male connection (tenon) is fitted into a similarly sized and shaped female connection (mortise).

mother of pearl a hard, durable, iridescent, decorative material sawn from a natural sea shell (mollusk) and used for inlays. Pearl is harvested in a range of colors including black, yellow, and white, with white being the most popular. Pearl shells are larger and flatter than abalone shells, which enables the yield of larger flat pieces. The shells are also thick enough so tuning machine knobs and nut stock can be prepared from the thickest part. (see abalone)

MOTHER OF PEARL (SHELL)

mother-of-toilet-seat a pejorative name given to an early pearlescent celluloid material used on the peghead and back of some banjos to give a glitzy, mother-of-pearl appearance. (see Pyralin)

movable bridge a string support on a musical instrument over which the strings pass. As the name implies, a movable bridge is not secured in place, and a tailpiece is required to hold the butt end of the strings.

movement ratio the relationship between the radial and tangential movement of wood as it experiences a change in its moisture content.

music in acoustical terms, sounds that are chordant, harmonic, pleasant, not over-bearing, and have a cadence. (see noise)

musical acoustics the science of the production, measurement, reflection, absorption, enhancement, and sensory perception of musical sounds.

Mylar® a polyester film developed by DuPont in the 1950s. Mylar has played a major role in musical instrument development as a replacement for the natural skin heads used on banjos. Mylar is strong, dimensionally stable, durable, heat resistant, and has excellent tensile strength that can resist the heavy loads imposed on banjo heads. One of the earliest developers of Mylar for use in musical instruments was Remo Belli, a drummer who began manufacturing drum heads made of Mylar under the Remo® brand.

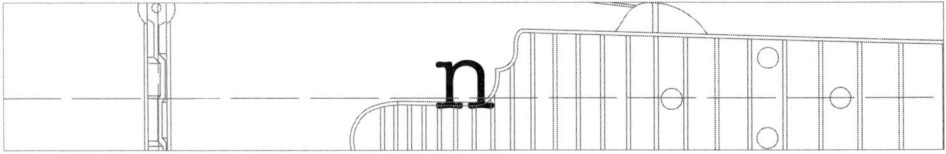

narrow grain a reference to the number of annular rings per inch in wood. Narrow grain refers to wood that has more than 12-14 grain lines per inch.

NDA (see non-disclosure agreement)

Neapolitan mandolin a four-course instrument with a rounded bowl-like back comprised of numerous strips of wood. The basic configuration has two strings per course, tuned *E, A, D, G* (high to low). Variants include six-string, twelve-string (three strings per course), and sixteen-string (four strings per course) configurations. Soundboards are either flat or have a slight arch below the bridge. The instrument has a round or oval soundhole that is open (i.e., no lattice work). A descendant of the mandora, the design of the Neapolitan mandolin originated in Naples, Italy. Also known as a "bowl-back" mandolin. (see Florentine mandolin)

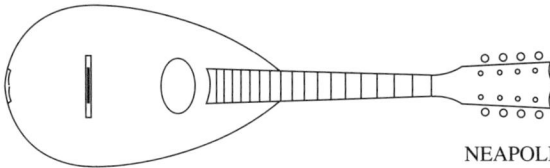

NEAPOLITAN MANDOLIN

neck that part of an instrument to which the fretboard is attached. The neck typically has a peghead at one end with tensioning devices to tighten and secure the strings. The neck gives the musician access to the strings to manipulate their vibrating length thereby changing their pitch.

neck angle (see neck pitch)

neck block that part of the instrument's body to which the neck is connected. The neck block distributes the bending load of the neck to the soundboard, backboard, and rim. Also referred to as a "headblock."

neck lag screw a rod with a wood thread at one end and a machine thread at the other end. Neck lag screws are used to secure a banjo's coordinator rod(s) to the neck. (see wood screw threaded stud)

neck pitch the angle the fretboard plane makes relative to the top edge of the rib or rim. Sometimes referred to as "neck angle."

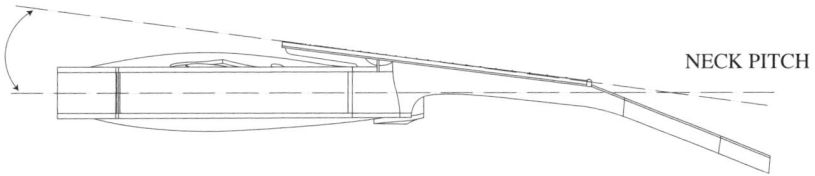

NECK PITCH

neck re-set the process of removing a neck from its connection or joint so that it can be re-installed at the proper alignment. Neck re-sets are often required due to poorly made neck joints, settling of the wood, movement of the glue or similar structural failures.

needle file a small steel tool whose cutting surfaces are covered with numerous teeth of various configurations. Needle files are designed for small, intricate work and come in many shapes and sizes, including flat, round, half round, triangular, and square. Needle files are used for filing the string notches in bridges, for shaping the edges of pearl and abalone pieces, as well as shaping and cleaning up other small parts.

noise 1) in acoustical terms, sounds that are dischordant, overbearing, and of uneven cadence. 2) in electrical terms, unwanted signals that come from poorly shielded cables or electronic assemblies. (see music)

non-disclosure agreement (NDA) a document that confirms the confidential nature of information shared or discovered between parties. In order to protect designs or intellectual property, a non-disclosure agreement should be signed, which states that secrets, designs or processes that are disclosed during a meeting will be kept confidential and not disclosed to another party. A one-way non-disclosure agreement protects one party. A two-way non-disclosure agreement protects both parties. Also known as a "confidentiality agreement." [For advanced protection of your rights, consult a patent attorney.] (see intellectual property)

non-porous substrate a surface that is not penetrable by air, water, adhesives, etc.

nut the contact and alignment point at the peghead for the strings of a string musical instrument. The nut is made of a hard, dense, and durable material such as bone, mother of pearl, abalone or Corean®.

nylon (string) a synthetic polymer used for musical strings. Nylon was developed by DuPont in 1935, and the stranded version is very strong and durable. Nylon fiber has excellent tensile properties and, while it stretches, it reaches a point of elongation where it cannot be stretched further without rupturing. String manufacturers select the gauges for their classical strings to permit the string to be tuned to its intended pitch at a tension that is well below the rupture point. Nylon strings for classical and flamenco guitars are available in plain and wound varieties. (see core wire, gut string)

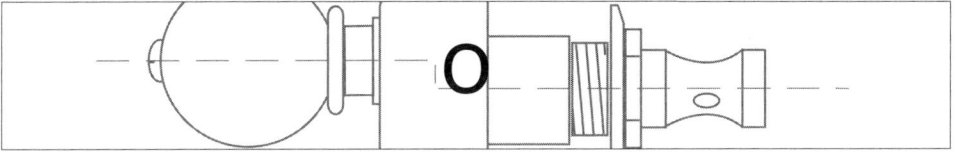

oak (*Quercus* spp.) a wide-grained, large-pored hardwood, consisting of more than 30 species. Oak is populated with large medullary rays and is occasionally found with curls and other figure. Because of its large pores and generally unattractive grain, oak is not used for exterior instrument work but is a great material for truss rod filler strips, peghead scroll strengthener plugs, forms, and fixtures. Oak weighs 48 pounds per cubic foot.

octave mandolin a four-course instrument with two strings per course tuned *E, A, D, G* (high to low), one octave below a standard mandolin. Octave mandolins feature a 19″ to 20″ string scale and can be either pear shaped or Florentine style. The instrument is strung with a plain first string and wound 2nd, 3rd, and 4th strings. Octave mandolins have a tailpiece and a movable bridge.

OCTAVE MANDOLIN

offset tuner a geared machine used on some banjos in which the tuning post is not aligned with the tuning knob. Offset tuners are designed with a modified planetary gear system. It has one small central gear to which the tuning knob is attached that turns a larger female gear to which the string post is attached. (see planetary gears)

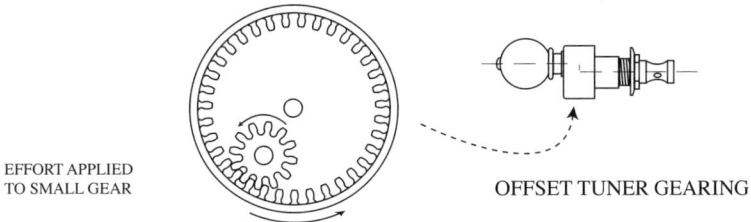

EFFORT APPLIED TO SMALL GEAR

OFFSET TUNER GEARING

old-time banjo a term given to an open-back (no resonator) banjo. (see resonator)

OM guitar a guitar that is 39-13/16″ long (overall) with a body length of 19-3/8″, a width of 15″, and a depth of 4-1/8″.

one-piece bridge a string support (typically wood) that does not have adjustment posts or a separate saddle and base.

one-piece flange a hardware design for a banjo rim developed by Gibson in the early-1930s to replace the previous tube-and-plate system. The one-piece flange is a casting that fits snugly to a wood lip on the rim. Threaded hooks pass through the flange and connect to the stretcher band in order to tighten the banjo's head. (The hooks pull the stretcher band down to the one-piece flange.) The flange acts as a decorative cover for the space between the open edge of the resonator and the side of the banjo's rim. Two advantages of the one-piece flange over the previous tube-and-plate system are the one-piece flange is a comparatively easy-to-manufacture single-part casting, and it requires only a three-ply rim instead of the four-ply rim needed for the tube-and-plate system. (see tube-and-plate flange)

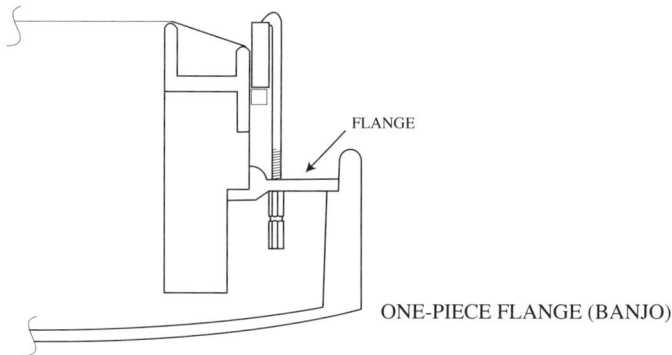

FLANGE

ONE-PIECE FLANGE (BANJO)

OO guitar called a "double oh," the name refers to a guitar that is 38-5/8″ long (overall) with a body length of 18-7/8″, a width of 14-5/16″, and a depth of 4-1/8″.

OOO guitar called a "triple oh," the name refers to a guitar that is 39-13/16″ long (overall) with a body length of 19-3/8″, a width of 15″, and a depth of 4-1/8″.

open assembly time the time between the initial application of an adhesive and when the two surfaces are joined together.

open-back banjo a banjo without a resonator. (see resonator)

orthotropic as it relates to acoustics, that property of a material in which sound radiates through a material at different speeds according to the resistance it meets in each direction. An orthotropic material is one that has two or three orthogonal (right angle) axes of rotational symmetry. Although wood is orthotropic, it is more properly categorized as anisotropic. By contrast, metal is isotropic. (see anisotropic, isotropic)

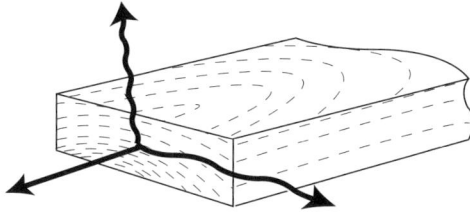

ORTHOTROPIC

oscillating spindle sander a table-mounted machine with a constantly moving vertical shaft to which sanding drums are mounted for various shaping and finishing procedures. The oscillating (up and down) shaft prevents the same part of the sanding drum to continuously contact the work during sanding thus yielding a smoother and more consistently dressed surface. Having the sanding drum set at a right angle to the table is an advantage for many sanding applications. Some oscillating spindle sanders feature a tilting table. (see spindle sander)

oud an instrument with eleven strings, ten of which are in five courses, two strings per course with numerous Arabic and Turkish tuning variations. The instrument features a pear-shaped soundboard with two or three latticed soundholes and a rounded bowl back made of laminated strip construction. The peghead is set at a severe 45° to 90° pitch, and the strings are secured with friction pegs. The fingerboard is not fretted, the bridge is fixed, and the instrument does not have a tailpiece. Ouds date back to the 1100s, and it is believed that the instrument has its origin in Egypt, possibly having been influenced by the Greek or Roman pandura.

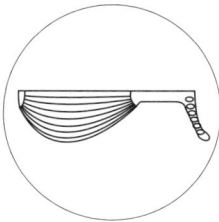

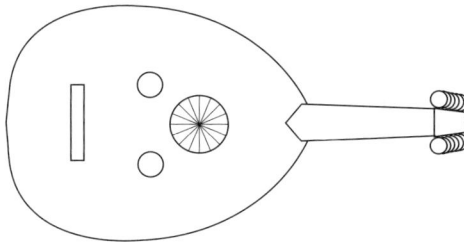

OUD

oval fingerboard, oval fretboard (see radiused fretboard)

ovangkol (*Guibourtia ehie*) a rich brown hardwood with pronounced dark grain. Ovangkol has an attractive figure ranging from straight to swirly dark lines. It weighs 50 pounds per cubic foot and can be used for backboards, sides, fretboards, bridges, and peghead veneers.

overtone a sound produced by a string, by a component of an instrument or a combination of both that is higher than the fundamental. The word "overtone" – which is often used interchangeably with "harmonic" – refers to a sound; a "partial" is the numbered order of the overtone series. (see fundamental, overtone series, partial)

overtone series the whole tone created by a string, a set of strings, a part of a musical instrument or strings and the components of the musical instrument. The overtone series is comprised of the fundamental and all of its partials, each at various intensities according to the design and acoustical attributes of the instrument. For example, an overtone series might be comprised of the fundamental (1st partial) producing 30% of the amplitude, the 2nd partial producing 22% of the amplitude, the 3rd partial producing 20% of the amplitude, the 4th partial producing 12% of the amplitude, the 5th partial producing 9% of the amplitude, and so on until 100% of the tone is accounted for. (see amplitude, fundamental, partial)

p

padouk (*Pterocarpus spp.*) a dense reddish-brown wood with attractive grain. There are six prominent species of padouk, ranging in weight from 41 to 53 pounds per cubic foot. (see African padouk)

pandura an early lute-like string instrument with three or four strings. The pandura was the predecessor of many string instruments including the balalaika, bouzouki, mandolin, and oud. The pandura is made in many shapes, sizes, and stringings and is the instrument featured in numerous ancient sculptures.

partial one component in the numbered series of vibrational modes a string can produce. The 1st partial is the fundamental in which the string vibrates in one complete arc. The 2nd partial is the string vibrating in two equal parts (the octave). The 3rd partial is the string vibrating in three equal parts and so on. The *sounds* produced by partials are called "harmonics" or "overtones." All of the tones created by a string (or other vibrating medium) are called the "overtone series." For example, on an *A440* string, *A440* is the fundamental, vibrating 440 times per second. The second partial is 880Hz (440+440), which is the octave above *A440*. The third partial is 1,320Hz (440+440+440), an *E*, and so on. (see fundamental, harmonic, overtone series).

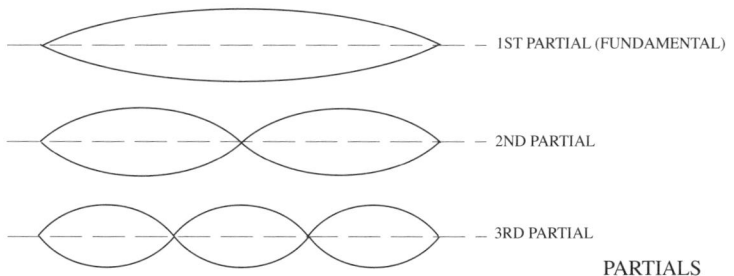

— 1ST PARTIAL (FUNDAMENTAL)

— 2ND PARTIAL

— 3RD PARTIAL

PARTIALS

patent a government-issued certification of the attributes of a design, the date it was filed, references to similar prior filings, and the claims that clarify the features of the design with the objective of establishing the patentee's exclusive rights to make, use or sell the design. Patent applications can be made by individuals (not recommended), patent filing services or patent attorneys. To capture the date a design is first conceived, the creator should prepare a disclosure statement. For more information, consult the government Patent and Trademark office at www.uspto.gov. [For advanced protection of your rights, clarification of the law, and to be in compliance with current law, consult a patent attorney.] (see disclosure)

patent search the process of looking for previous design validation documents (patents) that may have been issued by the government for a similar idea. The process of looking for "prior art." A patent search can be performed by a patent attorney, a patent search service or by an individual looking through previous patents at www.uspto.gov.

pattern a master template, sketch, drawing or sample part used as a guide for making additional parts.

paua a multi-colored natural shell (mollusk) and member of the abalone family, typically with good figure and rich in blue, turquoise, red, and purple coloration. (see abalone)

PB a model designation for a plectrum banjo. (see plectrum banjo)

pearl (see mother of pearl)

pearloid a simulated pearl material made from celluloid and used as an inexpensive replacement for mother of pearl. Pearloid was often used to decorate a large area such as a fretboard or the back of a banjo resonator. (see Pyralin)

pearwood (*Pyrus communis*) a light-colored wood with subdued annular rings such that the wood's grain is almost invisible. Pearwood is easily dyed or stained black and used as a substitute for ebony peghead veneer. The cost and softness of pearwood versus ebony or rosewood for use in peghead veneers greatly reduces material costs and facilitates the inlay process.

peg a tensioning device used to tighten the string. Pegs can be mechanical (geared) or plain (friction). Also referred to as "tuning pegs."

peg board a term used by some European luthiers when referring to a peghead.

peg box the box-like section at the end of the neck of violin- and viol-family instruments that holds the tuning pegs.

peg bushing a small collar support that acts as a bearing surface for a tuning post and prevents the tuning post from resting directly against the peghead wood. Also called "post bushing."

peg hole the opening in a peghead into which the tuning peg fits. The size of the peg hole is dependent on the size of the tuning machine's shaft and/or bushing or eyelet size. [When using peg bushings, it is ideal to counter-drill the entire peg hole to the size of the bushing so that the pegs only bear against the bushings and backstrap of the tuning machines and not against the peghead wood.]

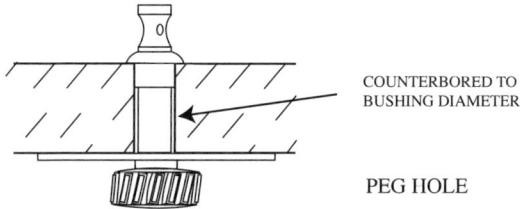

COUNTERBORED TO BUSHING DIAMETER

PEG HOLE

peghead that part of the instrument that holds the tuning pegs. The peghead is usually at the opposite end of the neck from the body.

peghead back veneer a covering over the back of the peghead, common on better-quality instruments. Peghead back veneers are used for cosmetic purposes to cover up the peghead ears. If properly applied, a peghead back veneer can also add some strength to the peghead's structure.

peghead veneer a covering over the face of the peghead around the tuning pegs. Peghead veneers are used for cosmetic purposes to cover up the peghead ears and the truss rod filler strip, and to provide a contrasting background for decorations or inlays. Peghead veneers add a moderate amount of strength to the peghead's structure. Also called a "headplate."

Peltogyne porphyrocardia the botanical name for purple heart. (see purple heart)

phloem a layer of a tree's inner bark that transports the nourishment for a growing tree.

phosphor bronze a type of bronze alloy used to make wrap wire for musical strings (as well as bushings and other wear-resistant parts). Phosphor bronze for musical strings is 90% copper alloy, 9.4% tin, and .6% phosphorous. The term "Phosphor Bronze Strings" was a creative brand name coined by Jim D'Addario to market his company's strings.

photosynthesis the nourishment process by which a plant or tree produces simple carbohydrates from carbon dioxide and hydrogen. Photosynthesis uses the energy of the sun or other radiant sources to generate nutrients through the use of chlorophyll. Photosynthesis takes place in the leaves.

Picea abies the botanical name for German silver spruce. (see German silver spruce)

Picea engelmannii the botanical name for Englemann spruce. (see Englemann spruce)

Picea glauca the botanical name for white spruce. (see white spruce)

Picea rubens sarg. the botanical name for red spruce. (see red spruce)

Picea sitchensis the botanical name for Sitka spruce. (see Sitka spruce)

pickguard a protective covering attached flush to the face of an instrument to prevent fingers, fingernails or picks from gouging or marking the soundboard. Pickguards can be made of wood, shell, celluloid or other plastics. (see fingerrest)

pie-cut a method of cutting logs in which the log is split, rotated slightly, split, rotated slightly, and so on. The pie-cut or pie-sawn method is often used for tonewoods to provide for matched bookleafed sets of arched soundboards and backboards. An advantage of the pie-cut method is that nearly 100% of the yield has vertical grain. (see bookleafed, quarter-sawn, slab-sawn, tonewood)

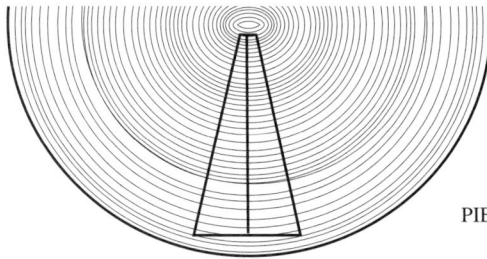

PIE-CUT LUMBER

pie-sawn (see pie-cut)

piezo transducer, piezoelectric transducer the core of some pickup devices. Piezo transducers are comprised of a piece of polarized ceramic-like material in which some parts of the molecule are positively charged and other parts are negatively charged. The transducer has electrodes (leads) that are attached to the opposite faces. When the piezo transducer is deformed (bent or squeezed), the electrical current running through the transducer senses a change in resistance. Because the piezo transducer is a solid-state component that does not require the windings of traditional coil-wound pickups, they can be made very small and placed into or under bridge saddles or attached to bridge plates.

pin router a device with a router mounted in an overhead support, and a round steel stud mounted in a table directly below and centered on the router's collet. Pin routers require the use of a fixture that is prepared with a female pattern attached to the fixture's underside and a means of securing the part to be cut to the fixture's upper side. When the fixture is placed over the pin and moved around, the pin follows the female pattern below, and the router mimics the shape of the pattern to cut the work above.

pin vise a small hand tool used to hold a drill bit. A pin vise is helpful when drilling holes for fretboard side position dots.

PIN VISE

pitch 1) a specific note or frequency. 2) the angle at which a neck is tilted relative to the axis of the body. 3) a tar-like substance found in small pockets between the annular rings of firs and pines.

pizzicato the technique of playing an acoustic string instrument by plucking the strings with the fingers (as opposed to using a bow, plectrum or hammer).

plain sawn (see flat-sawn)

planer a machine used to dress the face of wood and to make it square (smooth and flat). Planers are commonly used to dress the fretboard plane of necks and to square the edges of wood to be joined. (see thickness planer)

planetary gears an assembly of toothed wheels in which a small toothed wheel has one or more toothed wheels rotating around its axis. In planetary gears, there is one central (sun) gear with two, three or four gears (planets) rotating between the central gear and an outer ring gear. The force is applied to the smaller center gear, which forces the planetary gears to rotate in the opposite direction. However, as the planetary gears rotate, their centermost points move in the same direction as the center gear. Another shaft (like the string post of in-line banjo tuners) is connected to the center of

THE STRING POST IS ATTACHED TO THE TWO PLANETARY GEARS (AT BLACK DOTS). TURNING EFFORT APPLIED TO CENTER GEAR CAUSES PLANETARY GEARS (AND POST) TO ROTATE.

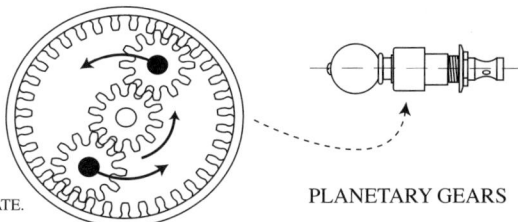

PLANETARY GEARS

the planetary gears, and the shaft turns in the same direction as the center gear but at a slower speed. (see offset tuner)

planetary pegs another name given to straight tuning machines used on banjos. (see planetary gears)

plastic deformation as it relates to wood, an attribute that describes the wood's propensity to change shape under load. Some woods that take a set under load and stay deformed are said to have the quality of being plastic (not suggesting they are plastic material, but rather possessing the properties of plastic). A common example of plastic deformation is the dent made in a peghead by excessively tightened machines. Plastic deformation is non-reversible. Some woods are resilient and will come back to their original shape after a load has been removed; these woods are said to experience *elastic* deformation. (see elastic deformation)

plate in acoustics, the name of a vibrating surface. Soundboards and backboards are often referred to as "plates" or as "top plates" and "back plates." (see bridge plate)

playing action (see action)

plectrum 1) a flat, hard object used to pick the strings of an instrument; also referred to as a pick or flat pick. 2) a style of four-string banjo. (see plectrum banjo)

plectrum banjo an instrument with four strings, featuring a round body and a membrane-like soundboard (head). The plectrum banjo is tuned *D, B, G, C* (high to low) and features a string scale of 25″ to 26″. The instrument has a head made of skin or plastic and has a movable bridge, a tailpiece, and geared machines. The banjo's body (rim) is constructed of laminated strips or blocks of wood. The sound-producing, neck-connecting, and head-attaching hardware varies with the make and model of the instrument. The back of most models of the plectrum banjo is fitted with a tone-projecting shell called a "resonator." Banjos without resonators are called "open-back banjos." (see folk banjo, frailing banjo, guitar banjo, mandolin banjo, regular banjo, tenor banjo, ukulele banjo)

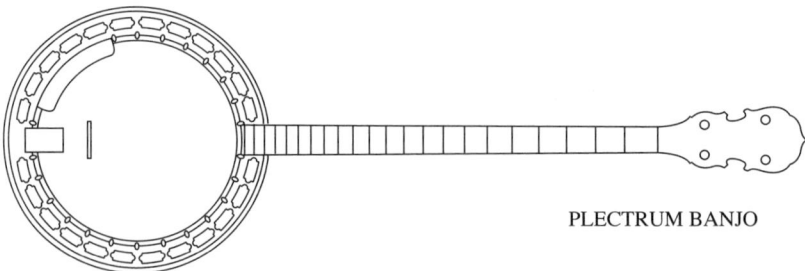

PLECTRUM BANJO

point block in violin or mandolin construction, a solid piece of wood that supports the intersection of two rib pieces.

points (see corner point)

poplar (*Liriodendron tulipifera*) a hardwood similar in appearance to maple but lighter in weight. Poplar has a yellowish cast and is typically void of figure. Unlike maple, poplar has low bending strength and a low resistance to shock loads. Poplar is often used for turning and carving, has excellent gluing properties, and weighs about 28 pounds per cubic foot. Most poplar comes from Eastern Canada and Eastern United States. While poplar is not generally attractive enough for rims or backboards, it is occasionally used for purfling strips. Also known as "American whitewood."

porous substrate a surface that is permeable and can absorb or pass air, water, adhesives, etc.

position marker a dot placed in the binding to mark a specific interval along the side of a fretboard to aid the musician in finding the fret position from the musician's view. Pearl dots placed on the fretboard are also considered position markers.

post bushing a small collar support that acts as a bearing surface for the tuning shaft. Post bushings prevent the tuning posts from resting directly against the peghead wood thus avoiding unwanted friction. Also called "peg bushing."

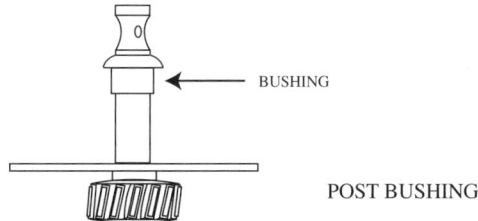

BUSHING

POST BUSHING

post-tensioning an engineering and architectural method of increasing the strength of a structural member by adding steel rods or bars beneath it. By tightening the rods or bars (called "tendons"), a lifting force is exerted near the center of the member. Post-tensioning is the technology by which single-rod (as opposed to double-acting) compressive truss rods work. (Double-acting rods impose a bending moment independent of the member to which they are attached and therefore are not true post-tensioning devices.) (see truss rod)

pot assembly an informal name used to define the banjo's rim and its hardware. (see arch-top tone chamber, ball-bearing tone chamber, flat-head tone chamber)

pound cut a reference to the composition of shellac that describes how many pounds of shellac flakes are dissolved in a gallon of ethanol (alcohol) in the preparation of French polish. The reference to pound cut is often made with the pound sign as in "1# cut," "2# cut." (see French polish)

pressure the transfer of force from one object to another object. (see clamping pressure, sound pressure, soundboard loading)

Presto tailpiece a popular string-attaching device with a hinged cover used on banjos. Many early Gibson banjo models featured a Presto tailpiece.

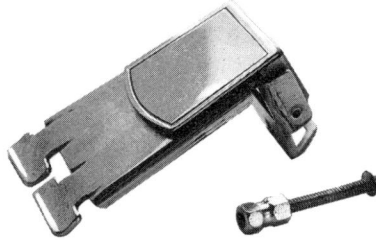

PRESTO TAILPIECE (BANJO)

proper action (see action)

proud an esoteric woodworking term that refers to oversize material. For example, "If the neck wood is proud at the fretboard, you can file it down flush to the binding."

Pseudotsuga taxifolia the botanical name for Douglas fir. (see Douglas fir)

Pterocarpus soyauxii the botanical name for African padouk. (see African padouk)

punch a metal shaft used to tap, dent, peen or drive another part. A center punch has a sharp point and is used to make a starting dent for drilling. (see ball peen hammer, drift)

purfling a strip of wood that decorates or protects the edge of a soundboard or soundhole. Purfling can consist of a single strip of wood or many strips of colored wood (dyed or natural) arranged

PURFLING

in a decorative pattern. Purfling is often placed next to binding and in some cases is used instead of binding. Elaborate purfling can also consist of inset abalone or pearl pieces. (see herringbone)

purple heart (*Peltogyne porphyrocardia*) a hardwood of a bluish-magenta color. Purple heart can be used for center laminates and strips of binding. It is not commonly used for structural or tonewood parts of the instrument. Purple heart is very hard and dense, tough on tools, and weighs approximately 54 pounds per cubic foot.

Pyralin® the trade name for a decorative celluloid. Pyralin is a material that is the result of coloring or reflective agents (such as ground fish scales) embedded in celluloid to produce products that are both durable and attractive. In the early-1900s, Pyralin was popular for its decorative use on banjo resonators and fretboards. Sometimes referred to as "mother-of-toilet-seat" or "MOTS" (named for its original use in bathroom and cosmetic products). Pyralin is a trade name of E.I. duPont de Nemours.

PYRALIN RESONATOR

pyramid bridge the name given to the bridge design on some flat-top acoustic guitars in which each wing of the bridge is shaped to a four-sided peak. The pyramid bridge was one of the earliest bridge designs developed by the CF Martin Organisation (ca. 1900), prior to the development of the "belly" bridge (ca. 1928). (see belly bridge)

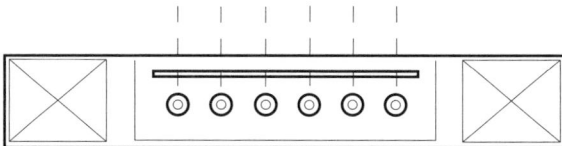

PYRAMID BRIDGE

Pyrus communis the botanical name for pearwood. (see pearwood)

q

quarter a measurement of lumber thickness based on true fourths of an inch. The use of the term "quarter" specifies that the wood is a minimum of full quarter-inch measurements and not undersized as in dimensional (construction-grade) lumber. For example, the reference to 8/4 x 16/4 ("eight quarter by sixteen quarter") specifies wood that is a full 2″ thick and 4″ wide. (Although construction-grade lumber is purchased in inch sizes [e.g., 2″ x 4″] referred to as dimensional lumber, the actual measurement of these woods is less than the referenced inch size.)

quarter-sawn a method of cutting logs in which the log is first split down the center and then each half is split down its center, creating four equal sections. Quarter-sawn lumber provides a consistent yield of specific sizes and is the common method in the United States of sawing wood for construction (dimensional) lumber. (see cut on the quarter, pie-cut, quartered grain, slab-sawn)

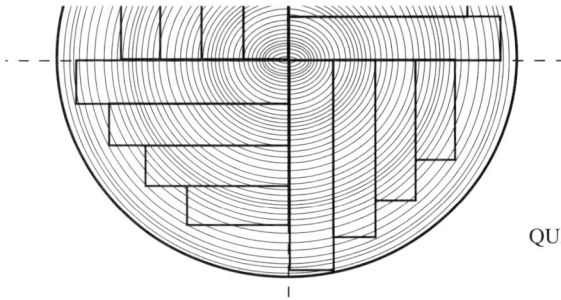

QUARTER-SAWN

quartered grain, quarter grain wood that is prepared with its grain on an angle, typically at about 45° to one of its sides. Quarter grain is different from "quarter-sawn." Also known as a "cut on the quarter." (see flat-grain, quarter-sawn)

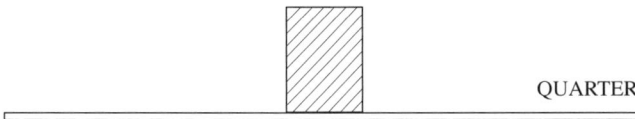

QUARTERED GRAIN

quilted figure a bubble-like appearance in wood that results from anomalies in the wood's growth or from the wood being placed in compression during its life cycle. The compressive load forces the wood's grain to buckle in both radial and tangential directions, which results in the appearance of a bubble-like figure in the wood's tangential surface. (see curly figure)

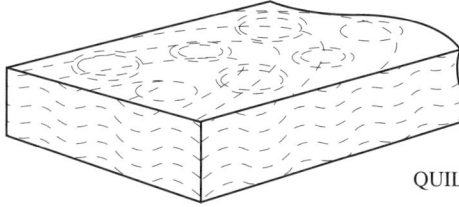

QUILTED FIGURE

quilted maple a hardwood whose bubble-like figure is caused by the wood being placed in compression during its life cycle. The bubble-like or "quilted" figure is exposed on the tangential surface and is the result of the confluence of both radial and tangential buckling of the wood's grain. Quilted maple is not a species, but rather a visually pleasing defect that occurs mostly in big leaf maple. (see curly maple, radial, tangential)

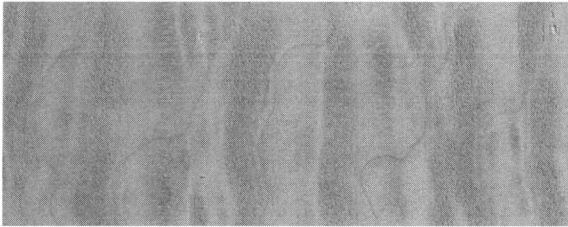

QUILTED MAPLE

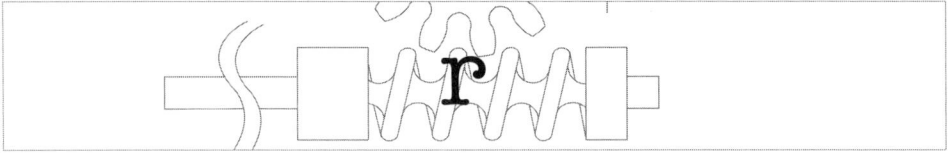

radial as it relates to the preparation of wood, the direction that is perpendicular to the center core of the log and in a plane from the center core through the annular rings. (see annular rings, tangential, transverse)

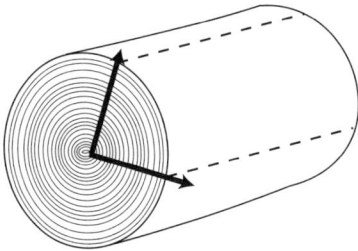

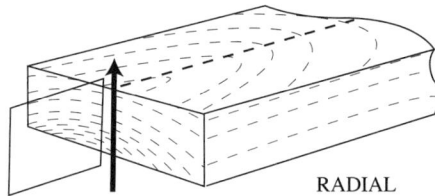

RADIAL

radiused fretboard a convex playing surface whose crosswise shape has been curved for ergonomics. The radius used is dependent on the design of the instrument but typically ranges from 14″ (mild) to 6″ (severe). If the instrument is constructed with a radiused fretboard, the bridge should be fitted with a radiused saddle whose arc takes into consideration the string action and complements the arc of the fretboard. The nut should be likewise radiused to match the radius of the fretboard. (see radiused saddle)

radiused nut a string support at the upper end of the fretboard whose string-contact points have been matched to the height of the fretboard's curvature. The upper edge of a radiused nut can be straight as long as the action (depth of cut) of each string slot conforms to the curvature of the fretboard. (see action, radiused fretboard)

radiused saddle the upper portion of a bridge that has been curved to match the arc of the accompanying fretboard. While not ideal, the upper edge of a radiused saddle can be flat as long as the depth of the notch for each string is matched to the curvature of the fretboard. (see radiused fretboard)

rarefaction in acoustics, waves of air pressure receding from a sensing or hearing body (ear). The motion of air that is the opposite or aftermath of compression. When a soundboard is pressed down as a result of energy being transferred from the bridge, the result is a compressive force on the air inside the air chamber. For a fraction of a second, this air is compressed out of the instrument through the aperture(s). The air returning to fill the void in the air chamber after compression is the rarefaction. (see compression)

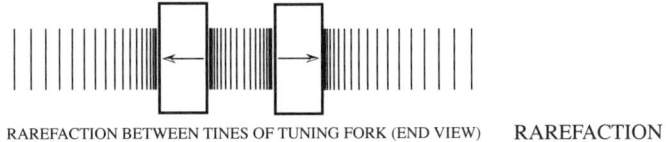

RAREFACTION BETWEEN TINES OF TUNING FORK (END VIEW)   RAREFACTION

rat-tail file a round steel tool with a tapered end, covered with numerous teeth of various configurations. Rat-tail files come in many sizes and are available with fine, medium or coarse teeth. Tiny versions of the rat-tail file that are used for intricate work are called "rat-tail needle files."

rays (see medullary rays)

RB a model designation for a five-string banjo. (see regular banjo)

recurve the name given to the curvature of an arched soundboard or backboard where the convex shape reverses as it curves back up to the binding edge. The recurve is the "minimum area" of the soundboard or backboard (the area of minimum thickness). (see minimum area)

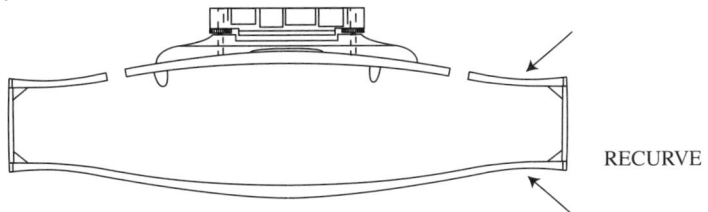

RECURVE

red cedar (see Western red cedar)

red maple (*Acer rubrum*) a common blond-colored hardwood that grows in the northeastern part of the United States. Red maple is among the hardest of maples, weighs an average of 37 pounds per cubic foot, and is ideal for necks and banjo rims. Also known as "rock maple" or "swamp maple." (see big leaf maple, sugar maple)

red spruce (*Picea rubens sarg.*) a member of the Pineaceae family, this wood typically is light in color, has moderate "silk," good strength-to-weight ratio, and weighs about 28 pounds per cubic foot. Known to luthiers as "Adirondack red spruce" because of where it is harvested, red spruce is widely used for soundboards and bracings, and provides a richer, warmer tone than Sitka spruce or Englemann spruce. (see silk, white spruce)

redwood (*Sequoia sempervirens*) a durable, light-weight softwood that is reasonably resistant to checking and cracking with a weight of 25 pounds per cubic foot. If properly braced, redwood makes excellent soundboards for archtop mandolins and has similar tonal properties to Western red cedar. Also known as "California redwood," "Californian redwood" or "coast redwood."

reflection in acoustics, the transfer of sound waves from one direction to another caused by the sound waves striking and bouncing off of an interfering surface.

refraction in acoustics, the altering of a sound wave's shape and speed when it passes from one medium to another.

regular banjo an instrument with five strings, featuring a round body and a membrane-like soundboard (head). The regular banjo, also known as the five-string banjo, is typically tuned *D, B, G, D, G* (high to low, called "G" tuning) and has a string scale of 25″ to 26″ with the fifth string attached so that its nut is in alignment with the instrument's 5th fret. The instrument's head is made of skin or plastic, and it has a movable bridge, a tailpiece, and geared machines. The banjo's body (rim) is constructed of either laminated strips or blocks of wood. The sound-producing, neck-connecting, and head-attaching hardware varies with the make and model of the instrument. The back of some models of the regular banjo is fitted with a tone-projecting shell called a "resonator." Regular banjos without resonators are called "open-back banjos" or "folk banjos." (see folk banjo, frailing banjo, guitar banjo, mandolin banjo, plectrum banjo, tenor banjo, ukulele banjo)

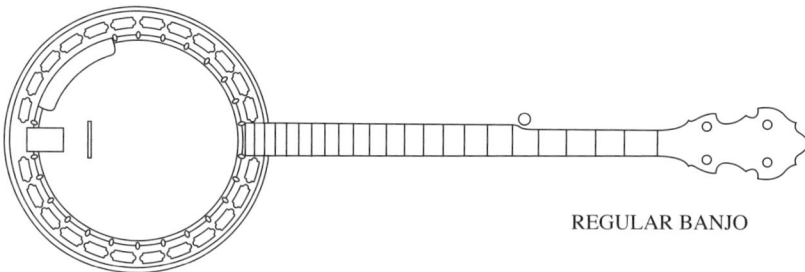

REGULAR BANJO

reinforced neck an instrument neck with a structural center component to help stiffen the wood. Reinforcements can be adjustable truss rods (one-way or two-way), carbon fiber, wood center laminates, steel or aluminum T-bars, steel square tubing or any similar structure. The reinforcement is glued into a channel cut into the centerline of the neck. If adjustable, the access to the truss rod nut can be at either the peghead or heel end of the neck.

re-set to disassemble and reassemble the fitting of an existing part to correct its alignment. (see neck re-set)

resonance in musical acoustics, the tone emitted from an air chamber or component of the instrument when it is excited.

resonant frequency the lowest rate at which a plate, string or air within an air chamber can vibrate. The lowest natural frequency (i.e., a note not imposed by some other device or object) that is produced by a space, string or element when it is excited.

resonator 1) an air chamber, plate or membrane that vibrates most intensely at a specific frequency. 2) a sound *reflecting* plate on the back of an instrument such as the resonator on the back of a banjo. (see backboard)

resonator bracket a small angle bracket attached to the side of a banjo rim to provide an attachment means for the resonator. The resonator bracket is slotted to receive the thumb screw. (see resonator stud, resonator thumb screw)

resonator stud a hexagonal or round lug that fits into the inner side wall of a banjo resonator to provide an attachment means for the resonator to the banjo's body. The resonator stud is threaded into a blind hole in the resonator's rim. (see resonator bracket, resonator thumb screw)

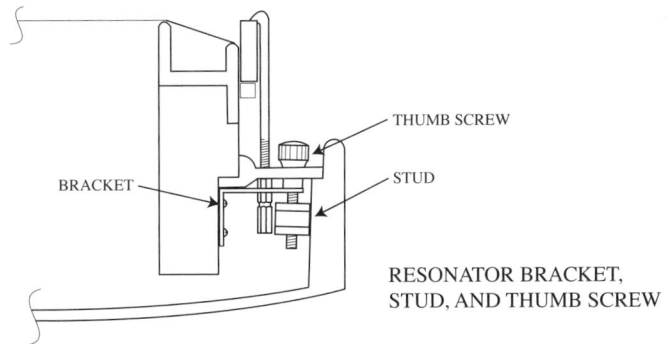

THUMB SCREW

BRACKET

STUD

RESONATOR BRACKET,
STUD, AND THUMB SCREW

resonator thumb screw a knurled fastener that is threaded into the resonator stud on a banjo's resonator to secure the resonator to the body. The resonator thumb screw goes through the bracket and into the resonator stud. (see resonator bracket, resonator stud)

resophonic guitar a six-string instrument shaped like an acoustic guitar, constructed of a wood body with a metallic sound-producing diaphragm. Resophonic guitars are traditionally tuned *D, B, G, D, G, D* (high to low) in an open *G* tuning. The features of resophonic guitars include a flat soundboard and backboard, a round metallic sound-producing "cone," a structural web-shaped "spider" that supports the bridge over the cone, a raised nut, a flat fretboard, round soundholes of various sizes, geared tuning machines, steel strings, and a trapeze tailpiece. The action on most resophonic guitars is set very high so that the strings can be stopped ("fretted") with a bar. Some resophonic guitars use standard guitar action and are played and fretted in a traditional manner.

RESOPHONIC GUITAR

restoring force the energy that is absorbed and stored by some component of an acoustical system and then transferred back to the strings or to some other component of the acoustical system to help sustain and continue the initial energy.

retarder a compound added to lacquer or a finishing medium to slow down the drying process.

reverse gear machine a geared tuning machine whose knob turns in the opposite direction of a conventional tuning machine. The knobs on reverse gear machines turn clockwise to increase the pitch. (see inverted machine)

rib the proper name for the rim of a mandolin, violin- or viol-family instrument. While the words rib, rim, and sides refer to the parts of specific instruments, the words are often used interchangeably. (see rim, sides)

riffler a steel tool whose ends are covered with numerous teeth used to remove wood from unusually-shaped and hard-to-reach parts. Rifflers are basically files with atypical cutting surfaces that are prepared in many shapes and sizes for filing round, hollow, concave, and curved parts.

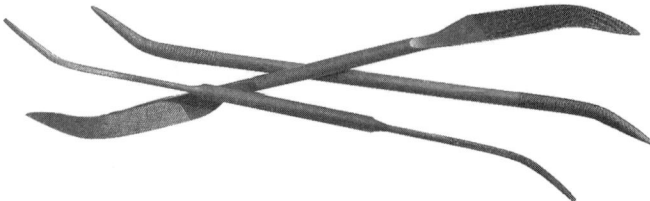

RIFFLERS

rim the laminated wooden center element of a banjo. Luthiers use the words rib, rim, and sides interchangeably when referring to the perimeter of an instrument. (see rib, sides)

rock maple a lay term that suggests a particular hard wood. Sugar maple (*Acer saccharum*) and red maple (*Acer rubrum*) are often called "rock maple." While rock maple is often thought to be a better grade of wood, it is not an ideal choice for all uses. Its stiffness may be preferable for necks, but it is too stiff for backboards. Rock maple is not a species but rather a generic reference to hard maples. (see red maple, sugar maple)

Rogers head a brand name of skin banjo heads made by the Joseph Rogers Company (founded in 1849). Rogers' skin heads were available in four models: Union Brand, Minstrel Brand, One Star, and Three Star. Skin heads were used on banjos until they were replaced by the more durable Mylar® heads in the early-1950s. (see Mylar)

rosette a ring of wood or pearl strips or pieces inlaid around the soundhole of an instrument. The rosette serves a decorative function and also provides some structural support to the cross grain edges of the soundhole.

ROSETTE

rosewood (*Dalbergia spp.*) a genus of trees high in natural resin content with wood of deep red/brown coloration and occasional black and purple stripes. Species of rosewood range in weight from 40 to 63 pounds per cubic foot. Rosewood is an excellent material for guitar backs and sides, fretboards, peghead veneers, and other decorative and structural uses.

round gear a wheel with teeth around its perimeter. Round gears are a common component of geared tuning machines. The number

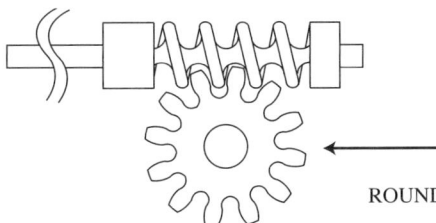

ROUND GEAR

of teeth on a series of gears determines the gear ratio. (see gear ratio, planetary gears, worm and round gear)

router guide a device that fits onto the end of a router to control the depth and/or height of the cutting bit.

running foot the measurement of wood based only on its length, regardless of its width and thickness. Some wood is sold by the running (linear) foot; some is sold by volume (board foot). (see board foot)

runout a description of a cut that leaves the wood's cells *not* positioned parallel to the edge or face of the board. Wood that is glued on its runout edge often results in a weak bond.

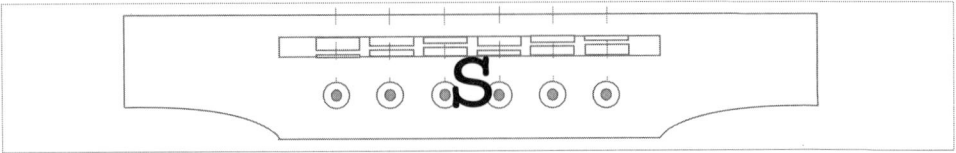

saddle that portion of a bridge on which the strings rest. The saddle fits into or sits on the base of the bridge. A one-piece bridge has an integral saddle. (see radiused saddle)

santos rosewood (*Caesalpinia ferrea*) a richly colored and figured hardwood. Santos rosewood weighs 59 pounds per cubic foot and is among the heavier rosewoods. Ideal for backboards, sides, bridge bases, fretboards, and peghead veneers. Santos rosewood comes from Brazil.

sap pocket a space between the grain of the wood where sap collects due to either the clogging of cells or the accumulation of sap from some other natural phenomenon. Sap pockets, which range from small specks to large masses, are found in all woods and are especially prominent in Douglas fir and pine.

sapele (*Entandrophragma cylindricum*) a medium-brown modestly-grained hardwood. Sapele is similar in appearance to mahogany and weighs 39 pounds per cubic foot. It machines well and can be used for guitar backboards and sides. Sapele comes from West, Central, and East Africa.

sapwood the youngest wood in a tree that still functions to store nutrients, transport them to some other part of the tree or carry sap up the tree. Sapwood is the active or live part of the tree as compared to the heartwood, which consists of non-functioning cells.

scalloped brace a supporting member inside the soundboard of a guitar, mandolin, violin- or viol-family instrument. Scalloped braces have one or two peaks and are shaped low in the center (between the peaks) and low at the extremities (between the peaks and the ends of the braces). Scalloped braces offer strength with reduced mass and provide stiffness in the peaked area, tapering off to more supple (thinner) regions away from the peaks.

SCALLOPED
BRACES

scalloped fretboard a fretboard with a fretless portion nearest the bridge that has been shaped lower than the main part of the fretboard to allow clearance for playing over that area. Scalloped fretboards can be prepared for any instrument and are common on banjos used for frailing. (see frailing)

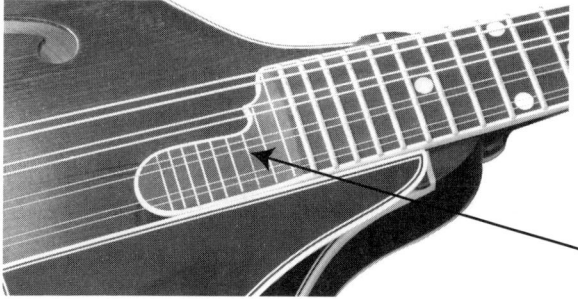

SCALLOPED FRETBOARD

COURTESY LYNN DUDENBOSTEL

scarfed joint an overlapping, angular connection of two pieces of wood such that they are glued mostly side-grain to side-grain. Scarfed joints provide better strength than joints that are glued side-grain to end-grain or end-grain to end-grain. Some scarfed joints have some end grain connecting to side grain.

SCARFED JOINTS

scooped fretboard (see scalloped fretboard)

scraper a hardened steel blade used to shave away layers of wood. The edge of a scraper is ground square as opposed to being sharpened to a razor edge. Scrapers are available in many sizes and shapes. Also known as "cabinet scrapers."

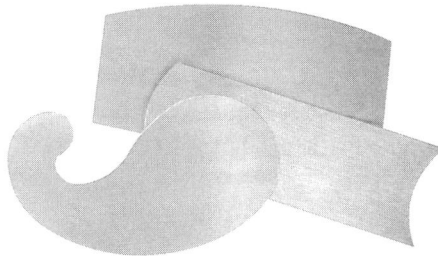

SCRAPERS

scraping a method of removing thin shavings of woods to leave a surface clean, smooth, and flat. In scraping, the blade is drawn across the work rather than gouged into the work as with a plane or chisel. The use of a flat (i.e., square) scraper is an ideal way to work small areas of a fretboard or peghead veneer. Curved

scrapers are used for working neck wood as well as other concave and convex shapes.

scrimshaw 1) the art of engraving bone or tusks and back filling the recesses with a black pigment to enhance the appearance of the image. 2) a piece of bone or tusk that has been engraved.

scroll a rounded part of a musical instrument's body or peghead. Scrolls are most common on Florentine, violin- and viol-family instruments.

scroll saw a tool for cutting small or delicate shapes from wood, plastics, and thin metals. Scroll saws have deep throats for ample turning room, and use a single fixed blade that is attached at the top and bottom. Scroll saw blades move up and down as compared to the continuous blade of a band saw. Sometimes referred to as a "jig saw."

scroll strengthener a plug installed cross grain in the crotch of an F-style mandolin's peghead scroll opening to provide additional support to the scroll's protrusion.

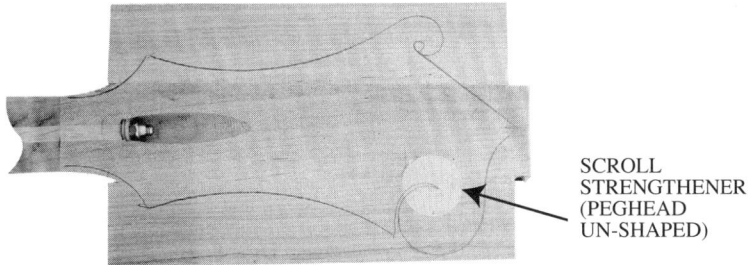

SCROLL STRENGTHENER (PEGHEAD UN-SHAPED)

sealer a first coating used over the staining medium to cover the filler and the stain to prevent them from running or bleeding into the subsequent finishing coats. Sealers prepare the wood to accept the finishing medium. Wood sealers seal the grain, fill small pores, encapsulate any stain or dye, and generally trap anything on the surface of the wood so that the finishing coat can be applied with even coverage and adhesion. (see filler)

seasoning (see air dried, kiln drying)

sectioning (see wood sectioning)

semi-gloss a finish or surface in which the reflections of shapes and highlights are somewhat diffused. The higher the gloss, the better the definition of the reflected shapes and highlights. If the gloss is reduced, the definition of reflected shapes and highlights is diminished and the finish becomes "semi-matte." (see gloss, high-gloss, matte, semi-matte)

semi-matte a finish or surface in which the reflections of shapes and highlights are barely perceptible. The higher the gloss, the better the definition of the reflected shapes and highlights. If the sheen of the semi-matte finish is reduced further, the barely perceptible reflected shapes and highlights disappear and the finish becomes "matte." (see gloss, high-gloss, matte, semi-gloss)

sense of hearing the human system for capturing sound and transmitting it to the brain for interpretation is one of the five human senses. The sense of hearing uses the mechanisms of the external and internal ear, the transmissive nerves to the brain, and the brain's ability to interpret and recognize the sounds that are heard.

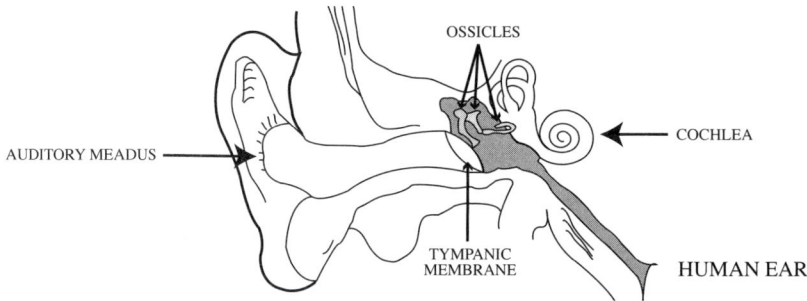

OSSICLES

COCHLEA

AUDITORY MEADUS

TYMPANIC
MEMBRANE

HUMAN EAR

Sequoia sempervirens the botanical name for redwood. (see redwood)

shaded finish a coloring technique that runs from a darker tone of a color to a lighter tone of the same or similar color. Typically, a shaded finish is darker along edges and lighter in the center to emphasize the shape of the instrument or part being colored. Some shaded finishes are taken to an almost black color near the edges. Recesses such as indents on the side of a peghead are commonly shaded darker to emphasize the depth. Shaded finishes can be subtle as in the violin family or dramatic as on Florentine-style instruments. (see sunburst)

shading the process of adding dyes by hand or spray to enhance the visual appearance of an instrument. Most shading processes are used to make parts of the instrument darker or to alter their overall color, but shading can also be used to create a multi-colored sunburst effect. In Florentine-style instruments, shading is used to accentuate the shapes of the instruments, especially at the edges and in concave areas. (see sunburst)

shading gun a spray gun used for applying dyes, stains or finishes that have been tinted. A shading gun is basically the same as a small spray gun except that it is used only for the purpose of shading (so as to not accidentally mix shading residue with clear finish). (see spray gun)

shake a split of the wood's fibers that runs between and parallel to the annular rings. Shakes range from hairline fractures to 1/8″ wide. (Shakes wider than 1/8″ are called "open shakes.") Wood that contains shakes should not be used for musical instrument parts. (see check)

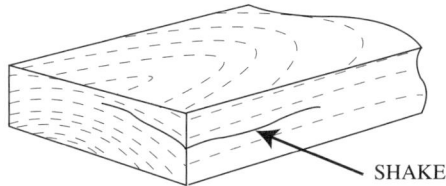

SHAKE

shaper, shaper table a heavy-duty, table-mounted device with a vertical shaft to which cutters are fitted for various machining and routing procedures. To follow patterns, bearings and collars can be mounted on the shaper's spindle under the cutter. Because of the size of the cutters, shapers run at a slower speed (about 9,000 RPM) than routers (approximately 20,000 RPM) and are more powerful than conventional table-mounted routers. Shapers can be used for roughing out neck blanks.

shaping in luthierie, altering the physical form of a piece of wood.

shellac a finishing medium consisting of flakes of *coccus lacca* (a scale insect from India and Southern Asia that feeds on trees), which is dissolved in ethanol (alcohol). Shellac dries quickly and becomes medium hard with a semi-gloss luster and good water resistance. Shellac has a short shelf life once it is prepared and should be used within six months of when the flakes are dissolved to prevent esterfication (reduction in ability to dry to hard finish).

shielding in an electric instrument, the covering around the electrical components that inhibits noise to or from surrounding electronics.

shoe an attachment to the side of some banjo rims to secure the bracket hooks in place and provide a shoulder against which the hooks can be tightened. (see bracket hook)

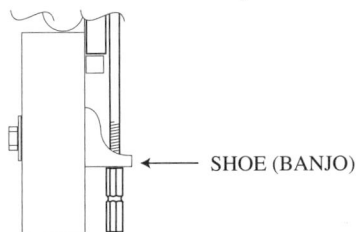

SHOE (BANJO)

shoulder on a violin, the curved heel end of the instrument's neck.

shrinkage a contraction of the cells in wood that occurs when the moisture content of the wood falls below the fiber saturation point (FSP). Wood shrinks in three directions: longitudinal (parallel to the length of the board – the direction of least shrinkage); tangential (at right angles to or across the annular rings – the direction of greatest shrinkage); and radial (in an arc with the annular rings – the direction of minimal shrinkage). The differential between radial and tangential shrinkage is dependent on the species. Uneven shrinkage can cause cupping and case hardening. (see case hardening, cupping, fiber saturation point, moisture content)

side reinforcement a tape, gauze or wooden strut used to strengthen the rims of an acoustic string instrument. The side reinforcement is used to ensure that the wood will not check or crack and to maintain the straight or curved attributes of the side wood.

sides the part of the body of an acoustic string instrument to which the soundboard and backboard are attached. The sides determine the depth of the instrument's air chamber. The word "sides" is commonly used by guitar luthiers. Mandolin and violin makers use the word "ribs," and banjo makers speak of "rims," but the words are often used interchangeably. (see rib, rim)

silk in spruce, the name given to the miniscule medullary rays that appear as cross-grain wisps. The cross-grain nature of the silk adds stiffness and stability to spruce and provides a pleasant iridescent appearance.

Sitka spruce (*Picea sitchensis*) a light, strong wood used for making soundboards. Sitka spruce has the greatest weight-to-strength ratio of commercially available woods. The harvesting of Sitka spruce became popular in the late-1930s when the material was used for building airplane wings and fuselage parts, and later as the inner core of helicopter blades. Sitka spruce is excellent for soundboards, provides a brighter, "harder" tone than Adirondack red spruce, and has an average weight of 27 pounds per cubic foot. (see red spruce)

slab-sawn a method of cutting logs in which the log is run through the saw sequentially without being rotated. The slab-sawn method yields wide, flat planks of various widths (limited by the diameter of the tree) and is the common method for sawing hardwoods. The grain direction through slab-sawn woods differs greatly from board to board. However, while the boards differ from each other, all boards have similarly angled grain through their cross section with the outer boards having flatter grain than the inner boards. (see pie-cut, quarter-sawn)

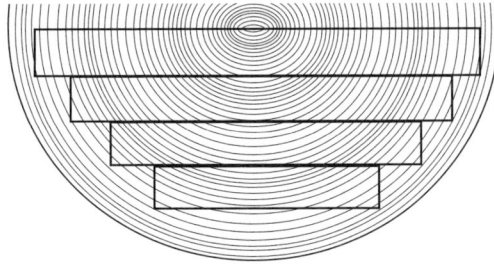

SLAB-SAWN

slanted saddle a saddle on a string musical instrument that is positioned at a counterclockwise angle to the center axis of the instrument. Saddles are typically slanted to provide an *average* correction for intonation problems on those instruments where intonation-corrected saddles are not used. (see intonation correction)

slotted neck joint a neck connection that uses a male and female mating connection. A slotted joint usually has parallel sides but can be either V-shaped or dovetailed. (see V-joint)

SLOTTED NECK JOINT (V-JOINT)

slotted peghead the string-anchoring end of a neck that is designed so the tuning machines attach to the side of the neck with their string posts accessible through elongated openings. Slotted pegheads are traditional on classical and resophonic guitars.

snake peghead a wedge-shaped design in which the end of the neck (peghead) is narrower than the area closer to the nut.

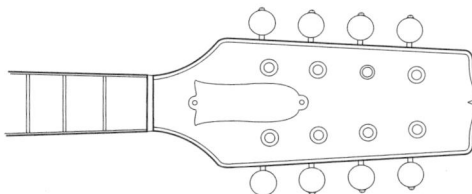

SNAKE PEGHEAD

snipe an unintentional, deep cut in wood caused by a brief, improper down pressure of the tensioning rollers or improper vertical alignment of the wood on a thickness sander or thickness planer. A snipe appears as a shallow recess in the wood's surface and usually occurs at the very beginning or end of a board.

solvent any compound or chemical used to dissolve or thin a finish, paint or adhesive.

soprano ukulele (see ukulele)

sound a disturbance in the air as a result of an object in motion that causes waves of compression and rarefaction, which are then realized and interpreted by the human sense of hearing.

sound pressure the amount of energy generated by a sound-emitting device and propagated through the air. Sound pressure is measured in decibels (dB). (see decibel, decibelometer)

soundboard a membrane attached to, near or under the bridge of a string musical instrument for the purpose of distributing and amplifying the energy transmitted to it from the strings via the bridge. With the exception of the banjo that has a soundboard (head) made of either Mylar® or animal skin, the soundboard of string acoustic instruments is made of a light, strong wood with the most common being spruce or cedar.

soundboard loading the result of the string's force pressing down upon or exerting a twisting force to the instrument's top plate. The soundboard of an instrument with a *movable bridge* is loaded in a downward force as a result of the string's lateral force against the bridge saddle. The downward force is met with a force of equal resistance from the soundboard and they reach a stasis. The soundboard of a *fixed-bridge* instrument is loaded from a lengthwise force as a result of the string's longitudinal tension against the bridge saddle, bridge base, and bridgeplate. The lengthwise tension torques (twists) the bridge forward, and the load

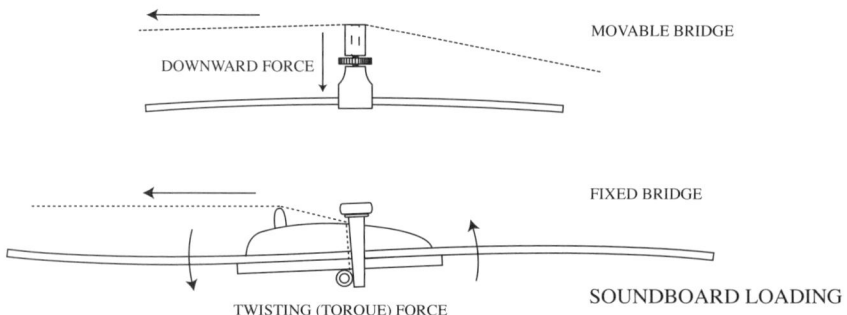

MOVABLE BRIDGE

DOWNWARD FORCE

FIXED BRIDGE

TWISTING (TORQUE) FORCE

SOUNDBOARD LOADING

is met by a force of equal resistance from the soundboard and they reach a stasis. This torque force results in the typical depression in front of, and bulge behind, the bridge on fixed-bridge guitars. In both movable-bridge and fixed-bridge systems, the soundboard is loaded and ready to be responsive to any movement of the strings. (see down pressure, X-bracing, *Reference Tables: Soundboard Loading - Fixed Bridges* and *Soundboard Loading - Movable Bridges*)

soundhole, sound hole an opening in the soundboard of a musical instrument whose purpose is to connect the air within the instrument to the air surrounding the instrument. Soundholes can be oval, round, triangular or "f" shaped, and they can be singular, paired or multiple. The size of the soundhole is one of the factors that determines the tuning of the air chamber to which it is attached. As the size of the soundhole is enlarged, the resonant frequency of the air chamber is raised. As the size of the soundhole is decreased, the resonant frequency of the air chamber is lowered. The soundhole can be used to tune the air chamber to an optimal resonance. (see Helmholtz)

sounding board (see soundboard)

soundpost, sound post a vertical support used in violin-family instruments to drive energy to the bass bar and partially damp the soundboard and backboard. With the treble foot of the bridge resting close to, but not on, the soundpost, the sideways motion of the bridge drives energy to the bass bar using the soundpost as a fulcrum. The soundpost also serves to stiffen the soundboard and backboard and damp unwanted overtones. The damping effects of the soundpost would be detrimental to most picked or plucked instruments, but the powerful, continuous energy of the bow overrides the sound-damping attributes of the soundpost. [Some *false* notions about the soundpost are it transfers energy from the soundboard to the backboard, it reinforces the soundboard, it transfers vibrations from the bridge directly into the air chamber, and it couples the soundboard and backboard so they vibrate as a unit.] (see bass bar)

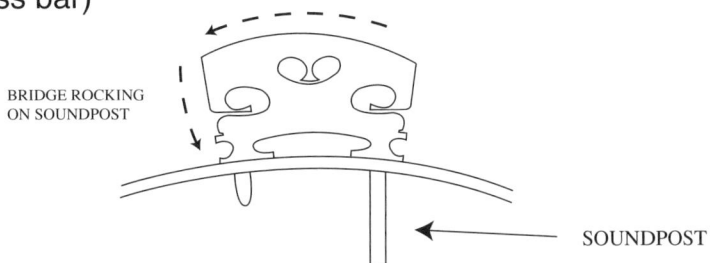

BRIDGE ROCKING ON SOUNDPOST

SOUNDPOST

spalted, spalting an elaborate and varigated figure caused by insects, rot, infection, trunk or limb bifurcation or a combination of these conditions. Spalting often occurs in rotted wood and appears as a black line running randomly through the wood. Spalted wood, while attractive, is not structurally sound and, therefore, not recommended for necks or structural parts of an instrument. While some degree of spalting occurs in all maples, it is most pronounced in big leaf maple.

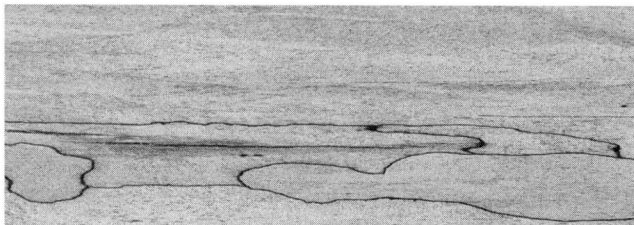

SPALTED (MAPLE)

Spanish construction a method of building instruments in which the neck is attached directly to the sides early in the production cycle. In Spanish construction, the headblock is part of the neck, and the sides fit into a notch in the side of the neck/headblock. In conventional construction techniques, the headblock is a separate part that is attached to the sides, and the neck is attached after the body is assembled. Conventional construction techniques enable the neck to be finished apart from the body.

Spanish guitar (see classical guitar)

speed of set the rate at which an adhesive or finish can build strength and maintain structural integrity.

spider an aluminum frame to which the bridge is attached on a resophonic guitar. The spider supports the load of the bridge and directs the strings' energy to a metal disk with a peaked center called a "cone" that is fitted directly beneath the spider. (see resophonic guitar)

spider-web, spider-webbing naturally occurring dark lines in rosewood that run across the annular rings in a lacy pattern.

spindle sander a heavy-duty, table-mounted device with a vertical shaft to which sanding drums are mounted for various shaping and finishing procedures. While some spindle sanders feature a tilting table, having the sanding drum set at a right angle to the table is an advantage for many sanding procedures. (see oscillating spindle sander)

spoke shave a cutting blade set in a two-handle frame for shaping wood. Spoke shaves are handy tools for rough shaping necks and curved shapes. Since the tool is pulled towards the body, it offers great cutting power. As the name implies, the tool was originally designed for shaping the spokes on wooden wheels. (A similar tool called a "draw knife" has two handles and an open blade, and can be used for removing larger quantities of wood.) [Be sure that the work is held or clamped securely.]

SPOKE SHAVE

spool clamp a threaded rod fitted with small dowels or disks and wing nuts on each end. Spool clamps are easy to fabricate and are used to apply a clamping pressure when gluing soundboards and backboards in place.

SPOOL CLAMPS

spray booth a chamber with a controlled environment used when applying finishes. Most spray booths are equipped to provide proper ventilation and a means of collecting the overspray in a filter or in an aqueous scrubber (a water bath that removes particulate from the air and traps it in water). Some spray booths feature inlet filters to keep dust from entering the spray area. [It is important that spray booths contain explosion-proof fan motors.]

spray gun a device for controlling the release of a finishing medium under air pressure from a container or canister. Most spray guns are designed to control the pattern, the amount of spray, and the proportional blending of air to finishing medium. (see shading gun)

springwood the circumferential area of rapid growth within a tree that is comprised of large cells. In most woods, springwood is recognized as the lighter colored, wider cells between the dark annular rings. In Europe, springwood is often referred to as earlywood. (see summerwood)

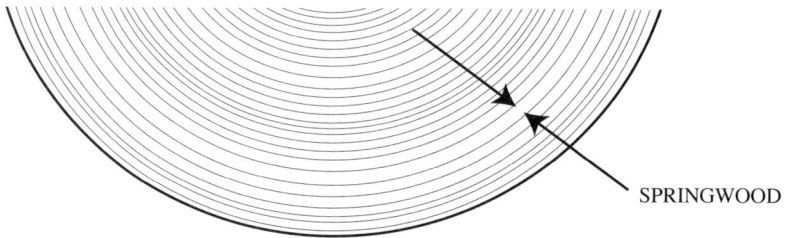

SPRINGWOOD

spruce (*Picea* spp.) a member of the Pineaceae family, spruce is an evergreen that features great strength for its weight. Sitka spruce is known to have the greatest weight-to-strength ratio of wood. Both Englemann and Sitka spruce are widely used for soundboards and generally provide a somewhat brighter, "harder" tone than red spruce. There are about 20 species of spruce. (see Englemann spruce, red spruce, Sitka spruce)

square 1) a piece of wood that has 90° corners. 2) a plane or surface that is perfectly flat and smooth. 3) a tool to measure right angles (90°).

square tube (neck support) a hollow steel component used in the neck of guitars to act as a non-adjustable strengthening member. The square tube neck support was developed by the CF Martin Organisation in 1967. (see steel-reinforced neck)

SQUARE TUBE
NECK SUPPORT
(MARTIN)

squeeze out adhesive that is forced out of a joint when clamping pressure is applied.

starved joint a joint that does not have enough adhesive to enable a proper bond to occur.

steam bending the process of using steam to soften wood during the bending process. The steam permeates the wood and softens the cells, which facilitates bending and re-shaping the wood. The cells of steam-bent wood are re-formed to their new shape without being fractured. The wood can be either enclosed in a steam-pressure chamber until it softens or steam-under-pressure can be applied directly to wetted wood.

steel-reinforced neck an instrument neck with a structural center component to help stiffen the wood. Steel reinforcements can be T-bars, square hollow tubes or any similar structure. Typically, the reinforcements are glued into a channel in the neck. The T-bar was introduced by the CF Martin Organisation in 1934, and the company introduced the square tube in 1967. In the late-1970s, Ovation Guitars (Kaman Music Corp.) developed an adjustable steel and aluminum support that can exert a powerful corrective force independent of the neck wood. (see truss rod)

STEEL-REINFORCED NECK BAR, ADJUSTABLE (KAMAN)

steel-string acoustic guitar a general description of a six-course instrument with a hollow-body. A steel-string acoustic guitar can have either a flat or arched soundboard and backboard, and the aperture(s) can be round, oval or *f*-hole(s). Although designed as an acoustic instrument, the steel-string acoustic guitar can have integral electronic amplification. (see guitar)

stepped joint a joint whose adjacent surface is higher than the neighboring wood due to additional moisture in the glued seam (usually caused by water in the adhesive or wetting the wood prior to the applying the adhesive). (see sunken joint).

sticker, stick a slat placed between boards to enable air circulation. A stack of wood with stickers between the boards is said to be stickered. (see stickering)

stickered lumber cut wood that is stacked for drying with slats (called sticks or stickers) placed between the boards.

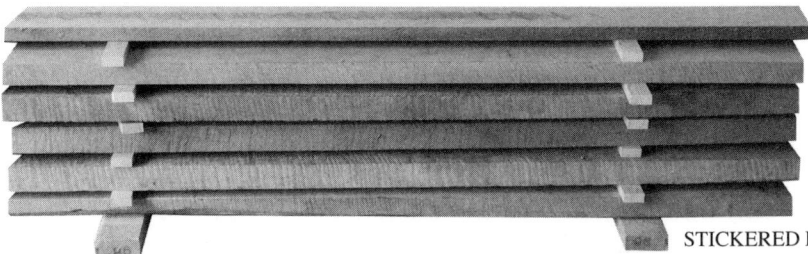

STICKERED LUMBER

stickering the process of placing wooden slats (stickers) between dried or undried boards of lumber to allow air to circulate around them for drying or seasoning. Stickers should be the same size and placed directly above each other to keep the boards from sagging in unwanted places.

Stradivari, Antonio (1644-1737) one of the most respected and prolific luthiers. Stradivari brought many refinements to the construction of the violin-family instruments including a refined *f*-hole, a graduated soundboard and backboard, a voiced air chamber, and unique finishes. He produced more than a 1,000 instruments during his lifetime including violins, violas, cellos, guitars, harps, and mandolins. Stradivari's shop was in the Piazza San Domenico, Cremona, Italy, and he used the Latin genitive declension "Stradivarius" on his labels to indicate "of [the] man." Most historians believe Stradivari was a student of Nicolo Amati.

Stradivarius arching a term given to the tortoise-shell shape imparted to the soundboard and backboard of violins and similar curved-body instruments. The name was derived from the work of Antonio Stradivari who introduced the exaggerated arching.

strength of attack (see intensity of attack)

stretcher band a steel or brass ring fitted around the outside of a banjo head to which the bracket hooks are attached to draw the head tightly and evenly into position. The stretcher band pulls down on the support ring of a Mylar® head or on the flesh hoop of a skin head to tighten it to the proper tension.

string a linear element made of wire, gut or synthetic fiber that is set into motion to impart its energy to the soundboard via the bridge. The string's energy is transmitted though both lateral and longitudinal vibrations. The earliest versions of musical strings were horsehair, braided silk, plant fibers, and sheep intestines ("gut"). Strings can be plain or wound with an outer wire to make the string heavier so that it can produce low notes at tensions similar to the plain strings. (see lateral vibrations, longitudinal vibrations, wound string)

string action (see action)

string break angle the angle a string makes where it bends over a nut or bridge. The string break angle is a factor of bridge height, neck pitch, tailpiece height, action or a combination of these. (see *Reference Table: Soundboard Loading - Movable Bridges*)

string load (see string tension)

string pin (see bridge pin)

string scale the active vibrating length of the strings from the strings' contact points at the nut to the strings' contact points at the bridge. Traditionally, the string scale is based on the length of the first string since the length of the other strings may have to be compensated for intonation. (see intonation)

string tension the amount of compressive force placed on an instrument from tailpiece to peghead. The total string load is the result of the string tension of all strings. Many string manufacturers today provide the tension information for each string when it is tuned to pitch. String tension should be considered when selecting the gauges for a set of strings with the goal of using similar tensions for each string on fixed-bridge instruments. On movable-bridge instruments, lighter gauges should be selected for strings that rest over posts or feet, and heavier gauges for strings over the spaces or arches to improve the string-to-string balance. (see soundboard loading, string break angle, *Reference Tables: Soundboard Loading - Movable Bridges* and *Soundboard Loading - Fixed Bridges*)

string tension ratio the relationship between the effective string load (tension) of two consecutive notes (with the string fixed at the same scale length). The string tension ratio can be determined by using an algebraic formula known as the "twelfth root of two." To calculate the tension of the next lower note, divide the known tension (in pounds) by 17.817. To calculate the tension of the next higher note, multiply the known tension (in pounds) by 1.05946. (see twelfth root of two)

string winding the process of mechanically wrapping an outer wire around a center core wire. String winding machines resembling small lathes are used to tension and rotate the core wire so that a wrap wire can be tightly tensioned around the core. The wrap wire adds weight to the string so that it can produce lower notes at the tension of the core wire. (see wound string)

stripper 1) a chemical compound used to remove old finish. [Care should be taken to first test the stripper on binding material to ensure the stripper does not attack or destroy the instrument's binding.] 2) a tool for removing the outer covering of wire when working on electric instruments.

strobe tuner, strobetuner an electronic frequency-measuring device that uses a light that flashes in cadence with a musical or rhythmic sound. The flashing light is positioned behind a wheel that is turning at a known speed, the combination of which makes the image on the wheel appear to stop when the frequency of the light (which is the same as the frequency of the sound) and speed of the wheel are in unison. Strobe tuners are used for tuning strings as well as tuning parts of an instrument. (see tap tuning)

STROBE TUNERS

strut a supporting member on an acoustic guitar's soundboard. One of the braces of a X-bracing system used to stiffen or strengthen a section of the soundboard. Struts are typically positioned either across or at an angle to the grain.

sugar maple (*Acer saccharum*) a species of maple that typically has the highest density of members of this species (40 pounds per cubic foot). Sugar maple is an excellent choice for banjo necks and banjo rims. Often referred to as "hard maple," "rock maple" or "sweet maple." The sugar maple tree is the source of maple syrup. (see red maple, big leaf maple)

summerwood the circumferential area of slow growth within a tree that is comprised of small, dark cells. In most woods, summerwood is recognized as the thin darker-colored part of the annular rings. In Europe, summerwood is often referred to as latewood. (see springwood)

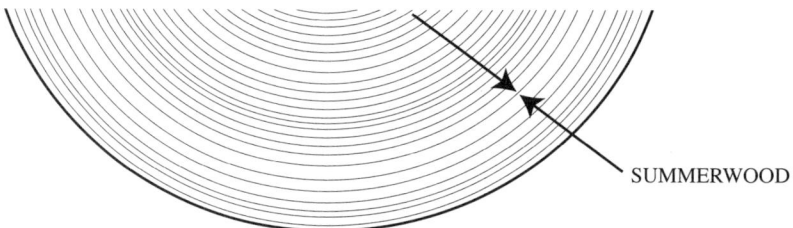

SUMMERWOOD

sunburst a coloring and shading technique in which the outer portions of the instrument are made darker than the centermost portion. Typically, a sunburst goes from light yellowish colors in the center to dark reddish brown colors along the perimeter of the instrument. Finishes that merely go from light to dark shades of the *same* color are referred to as a "shaded finish." (see shaded finish)

sunken joint a joint whose adjacent surface is lower than the neighboring wood, usually caused by machining a joint before the adhesive has fully cured and not all of the moisture in the adhesive has evaporated. (see stepped joint)

Superglue® (see cyanoacrylate)

surface filler (see filler)

surface sealer (see sealer)

sweet maple (see sugar maple)

Swietenia macrophylla the botanical name for Honduras mahogany. (see Honduras mahogany)

sycamore (*Acer pseudoplantanus*) a light blond-colored wood of moderate hardness. Sycamore and maple are both of the genus *Acer* and have similar physical attributes. Sycamore machines, sands, and bends similar to maple and is found in both plain and curly figure (although sycamore is often found with tighter curls). Sycamore is ideal for guitar sides and backboards and weighs 38 pounds per cubic foot.

sympathetic vibration the movement of a soundboard, backboard, string or other component that is set into motion by the energy it absorbs from some other part of the instrument or from some other stimulus. Sympathetic vibrations are greatest when the resonant frequency of the recipient part is identical to the frequency of the donor part. For example, picking one string of a pair of strings on a 12-string guitar will send the adjacent string of the same note into vibration through sympathetic vibration.

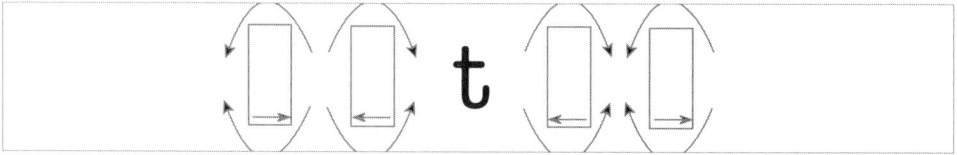

T-bar a steel or aluminum reinforcement in an instrument's neck with a cross section shaped like the letter "T." The T-bar was first used by the CF Martin Organisation as a neck reinforcement device in 1934. (see steel-reinforced neck)

T-BAR REINFORCEMENT

table the term used by some European luthiers when referring to a soundboard.

tack coat in finishing, a light primary coating allowed to partially dry so that the sealer or any staining coats are set before the final finish coats are applied.

tack rag a cloth that is saturated with shellac or varnish, allowed to dry about 50% and then used as a wipe to pick up sawdust and other debris from the surface of a part to be finished.

tail pin a wooden or metal plug that fits into the tailblock of an instrument to act as an attachment location for a strap. More properly known as an "end pin."

tailblock, tail block a piece of wood at the butt end of an instrument whose purpose is to support a joint, a tailpiece, an end pin or a combination of these. Sometimes referred to as an "end block" or "butt block."

tailpiece, tail piece a device used to anchor one end of the strings on movable-bridge instruments. Tailpieces are also used on resophonic guitars, and are needed on some inexpensive fixed-bridge guitars whose structure necessitates a tailpiece.

tambura an instrument made with numerous stringings and tunings (according to region) including three double strings, two double strings plus two single strings (four notes), four single strings, and two double strings with one single string (three notes). The instrument features a pear-shaped body, a round soundhole, a movable bridge, and a tailpiece. The backboard is either flat or bowl-shaped. Known in Northern India as a tanpura.

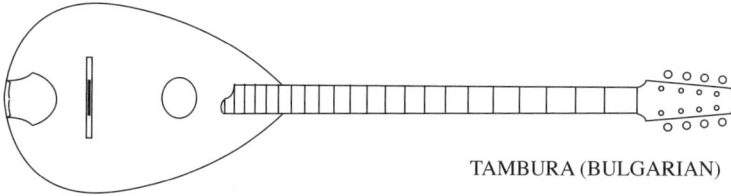

TAMBURA (BULGARIAN)

tang the lower extension on the bottom of fretwire. The tang is the part that is forced into the fretboard slots. The sides of the tang usually have small bumps called "beads" that help secure the fretwire in place. Most fretwire tangs are .023″ thick. (see bead)

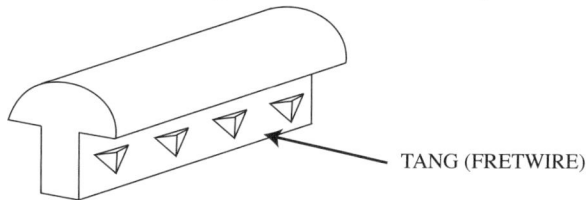

TANG (FRETWIRE)

tangential as it relates to the preparation of wood, the direction parallel to the core of the log and in a plane across the annular rings. Boards that are cut tangentially are often referred to as being "flat sawn." (see annular rings, radial, transverse)

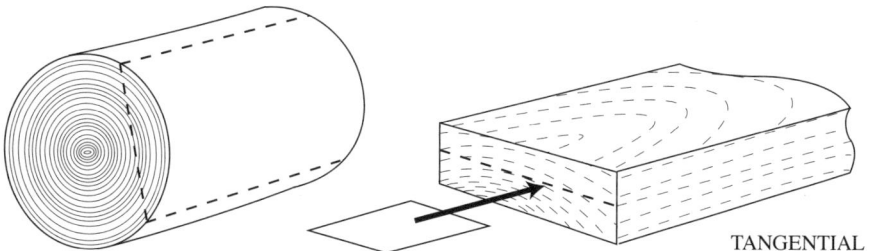

TANGENTIAL

tap a long thin tool used to cut threads into a bore or hole. Standard taps used in the United States are referred to as either NF (National Fine) or NC (National Coarse) threads and are measured by the screw or diameter size and the number of threads per inch. For example, a 10-32 tap is an NF #10 screw size with 32 threads to the inch. Other common types of threads are NEF (National Extra Fine), NPS (National Pipe Straight), NPT (National Pipe Taper), and NS (National Special). Taps are prepared in three basic shapes: taper (used for beginning threads in hard materials); plug (for most standard threading); and bottoming (for threading a hole as close to the end of the bore as possible). (see *Reference Table: Drills and Taps*)

tap plate a thin plastic guard on classical and flamenco guitars to protect the guitar's surface under the picking area. The tap plate also serves the purpose of providing a hard surface for the rhythmical tapping of the guitarist's fingers.

tap tune hammer a light-weight tool with a padded face used to excite an object's fundamental frequency during the tap tuning process. The soft face of a tap tune hammer promotes the production of the fundamental and inhibits the production of upper partials. (see tap tuning)

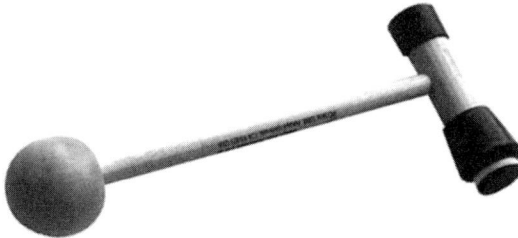

TAP TUNE HAMMER

tap tuning the art of exciting a part of a musical instrument to determine its resonant frequency. In the process of tap tuning, the stiffness of the part (a factor of its resonant frequency) is adjusted by removing wood until the desired frequency is reached. Additionally, the resonant frequency of the air chamber is adjusted by altering the size of its aperture(s). (see aperture)

target tuning the specific value a luthier strives to achieve when tap tuning. (see tap tuning)

TB a model designation for a tenor banjo. (see tenor banjo)

template a form or pattern used to reproduce a known shape. Templates are typically made from aluminum, brass or plastic.

tenon (see mortise and tenon)

tenon joint a connection of two parts made by the mating of a straight-sided male component into a female component. (see mortise and tenon)

tenor banjo an instrument with four strings, featuring a round body, a movable bridge, a tailpiece, geared machines, and a membrane-like soundboard (head) of animal skin or plastic. The tenor banjo is tuned *A, D, G, C* (high to low) and has a string scale of 19″ to 21″.

The body (rim) is constructed of either laminated strips or blocks of wood. The sound-producing, neck-connecting, and head-attaching hardware varies with the make and model of the instrument.
The back of most models of the tenor banjo is fitted with a tone-projecting shell called a "resonator." (see folk banjo, frailing banjo, guitar banjo, mandolin banjo, plectrum banjo, regular banjo, ukulele banjo)

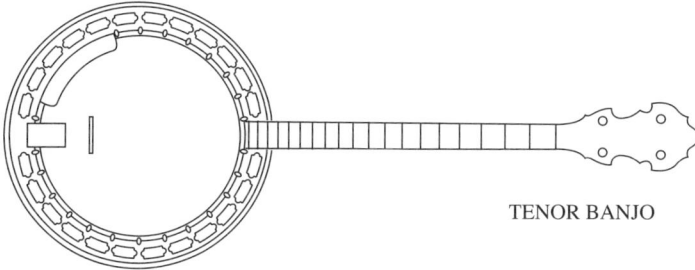

TENOR BANJO

tenor ukulele (see ukulele)

tensile strength the attribute of a material or compound that describes the load required to rupture the material or compound when a force is applied to pull them apart in a lengthwise direction.

tension a measurement of the energy exerted at two points being pulled together.

tension hoop (see stretcher band)

tension rod (see truss rod)

thickness planer a machine used to cut and square the surface of wood to a smooth, even height. Thickness planers utilize feed rollers that pull the work under a set of revolving planer blades. Thickness planers are used to remove significant quantities of wood as compared to thickness sanders that are used to dress the surface. (see thickness sander)

thickness sander a machine into which wood is fed to sand and shape its surface to a smooth, even height. Thickness sanders utilize a continuous-feed belt with pressure rollers to pull the work through the sander. The sanding mechanism is either a sanding belt tensioned between two rollers or a sanding strip wrapped diagonally around a single roller. Thickness sanders are used to dress the surface of the wood, compared to thickness planers that are used to reduce the wood's thickness by a significant amount. (see thickness planer)

three course a reference to the number of sets of strings on an instrument. On a three-course instrument, there are three sets of strings with each course containing one to four strings.

three-ply rim a banjo rim constructed from three plies of ¼″ maple. A Gibson-style banjo with a one-piece flange requires a three-ply rim. (Because of the additional lip needed to support the tube, a tube-and-plate flange assembly requires a four-ply rim.)

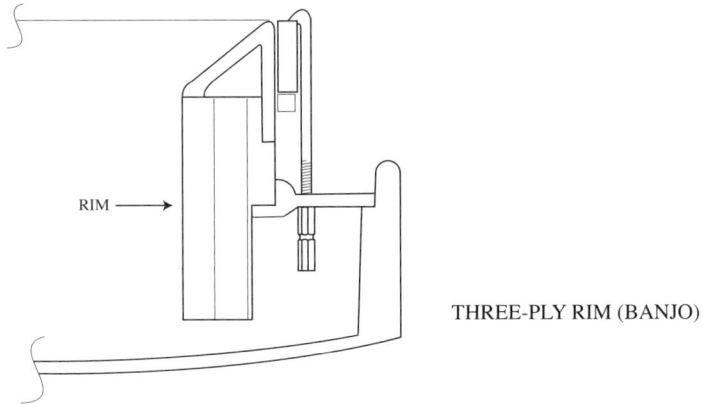

RIM →

THREE-PLY RIM (BANJO)

threshold of pain in the human sense of hearing, the point of excessive sound pressure at which discomfort is felt. In an adult, the threshold of pain is typically about 135dB.

Thuja plicata the botanical name for Western red cedar. (see Western red cedar)

thumb plane (see finger plane)

tiger maple a lay term used to describe the tiger-like stripe figure of curly maple. (see curly maple, fiddle maple)

tiger stripes an informal reference to the ribbon-like figure in wood, more properly referred to as curly figure. Curly figure is most prominent in maple and sycamore but can occur in many other hardwoods and softwoods. (see curly figure)

Tilia americana the botanical name for basswood. (see basswood)

timber logs that are freshly cut or fallen.

timbre in musical acoustics, the quality of sound described by its richness and sonorous qualities rather than its pitch or amplitude. The quality of tone produced by an instrument or voice. Also referred to as "color" or "tone color."

Timeless Timber™ a trademarked industry name for lumber that has been recovered after lying for many years on the bottom of lakes and rivers, which is then dried and used for furniture and similar trade purposes. While some luthiers use this wood for instrument building, its partially decomposed nature makes it more brittle than newly cured wood of the same species, and the wood is often prone to edge chipping and cracking on the delicate corners and sides of instrument pegheads, etc. (Timeless Timber™ is the registered name of Timeless Timber, Ashland, WI.)

tine one blade of a tuning fork.

tiple a treble or soprano instrument found with numerous stringings and body formats. The Columbian tiple (tiple Colombiano) features 12 strings arranged in four courses. The instrument uses steel strings, and the four courses are tuned *E, A, B, D* (high to low) with the center string of the *B* and *D* set tuned one octave lower than their neighboring strings. In 1950, CF Martin developed a 10-string tiple with four courses of strings tuned *B, F#, D, A* (high to low). The courses are arranged with two *B* strings, three *F#* strings, three *D* strings, and two *A* strings. The middle *F#*, middle *D*, and bottom *A* strings are tuned one octave lower than the neighboring strings of their sets. The tiple originated in South America.

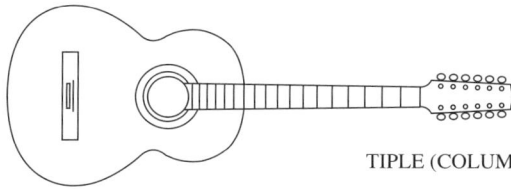

TIPLE (COLUMBIAN)

Titebond® Original Wood Glue a general purpose wood glue with great setting and bonding characteristics. Titebond Original Wood Glue is an aliphatic resin emulsion that requires a clamping pressure of 100-150 psi for softwoods, 125-175 psi for medium-hard woods, and 175-200 psi for hardwoods. Titebond has a fast speed-of-set time, and glued joints can be worked in 15 minutes if properly clamped. Titebond can be softened with water and heat, is easily sanded, accepts finishes well, and is generally resistant to solvents. The dried film is an opaque cream color. A product of Franklin International.

Titebond® II (Premium) Cement an adhesive intended for exterior use. Titebond II is a cross-linking polyvinyl acetate and is both waterproof and heat resistant. Because Titebond II doesn't cure as hard as Titebond Original Wood Glue, it is not recommended for luthierie. The dried film is a translucent yellow. (Some luthiers mistakenly believe that Titebond II is a superior product for luthierie because "II" suggests it is better than Titebond Original Wood Glue.) A product of Franklin International.

Titebond® III Cement an adhesive intended for exterior use with water clean-up capabilities. Titebond III is an advanced polymer product that is proprietary to Franklin International. Because Titebond III does not cure as hard as Titebond Original Wood Glue, it is not recommended for luthierie. The dried film is a light brown and may show a dark line if used for gluing the seams of soundboards and backboards. (Some luthiers mistakenly believe that Titebond III is a superior product for luthierie because "III" suggests it is better than Titebond Original Wood Glue.)

tone bar a wood strut attached to the inside of a soundboard to adjust the soundboard's stiffness. By adjusting the size of a tone bar, a soundboard can be "tuned." Changing its size results in an adjustment to the tone bar's stiffness that, in turn, affects the stiffness of the soundboard. The larger the tone bar, the higher the resonant frequency (pitch) of the soundboard. As the tone bar is made smaller, the resonant frequency of the soundboard decreases. (This is opposite to the bars on a xylophone. As xylophone bars get larger, their frequency is lowered.)

tone chamber a hard, supporting ring in a banjo upon which the head rests. The tone chamber is fitted to a wood rim. Most cast tone chambers are made of bronze (rather than brass). Some early banjo makers used tone rings (a piece of round rod bent into a circle), but the tone rings did not provide the sustain and amplitude of the denser cast tone chamber. Two designs developed by Gibson were popular: the arch-top tone chamber and the flat-head tone chamber. (see arch-top tone chamber, bell bronze, brass, bronze, flat-head tone chamber)

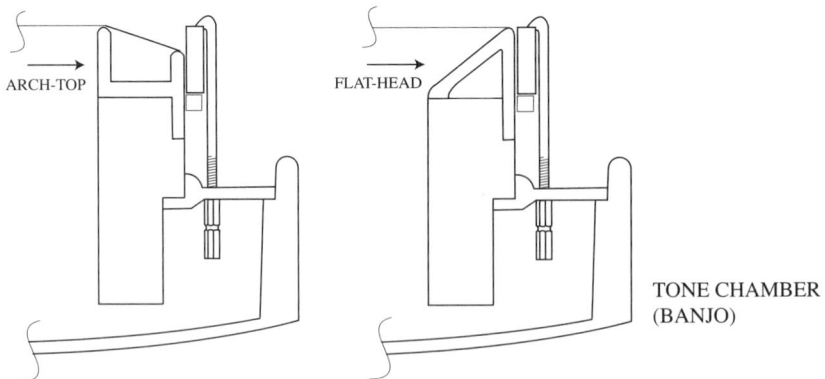

ARCH-TOP

FLAT-HEAD

TONE CHAMBER (BANJO)

tone color in musical acoustics, the quality of sound described by its richness and sonorous qualities rather than its pitch or amplitude. The quality of tone produced by an instrument or voice. More formally referred to as "timbre."

tone ring a round rod (usually brass) shaped in a circle and used on some early banjos to provide a hard contact surface for the banjo's head. The tone ring sits on top of the banjo's rim. Tone rings are not commonly used today because they do not provide as much amplitude and sustain as cast tone chambers.

tonewood a name given to a grading selection of wood used for musical instruments. Tonewood is not a species or a type of wood grown in a specific geography; the name refers to the wood's quality, consistency of grain, tightness of grain, color, and visual appearance. The four gradings are A, AA, AAA, and Master.

top (see soundboard)

top plate (see plate, soundboard)

top tension a banjo hardware design developed by Gibson in the mid-1930s as an attachment and tightening means for a banjo's head. The top-tension banjo has the feature of allowing the head to be tightened or adjusted from the top of the instrument without removing the resonator to tighten the nuts from inside. This was especially important for the early skin heads that were so susceptible to changes in humidity and required constant adjustment.

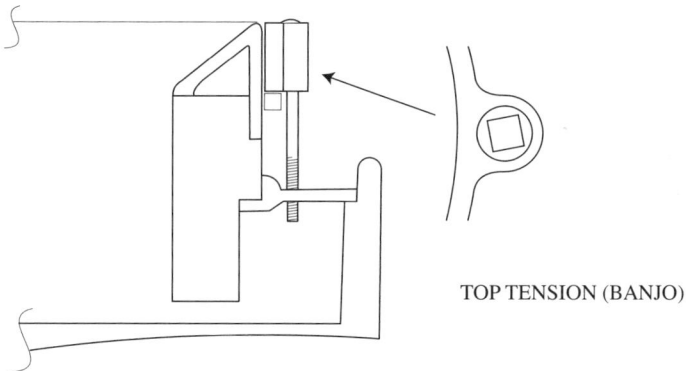

TOP TENSION (BANJO)

torque load as it relates to soundboards, a twisting force exerted at the bridge of a fixed-bridge instrument caused by the longitudinal load of the strings. (see soundboard loading)

tortoise shell the decorative material taken from the shell of the hawksbill turtle. Natural shell is multi-colored, easily machined and polished, very durable, and was used for many products until the trade of natural shell was banned by the 1973 CITES embargo. (see CITES)

tortoise shell plastic variegated and multi-colored synthetic materials used for fingerrests and pickguards, the earliest versions of which were made of cellulose nitrate (celluloid). The name is derived from the similar appearance to natural tortoise shell from the hawksbill turtle.

total assembly time the elapsed time between when glue is first applied to a joint and when the joint is closed.

transducer a device that changes energy from one form to another. (see piezo transducer)

transverse a method of cutting wood by sawing across the log or board. While transverse cuts display the annular rings and are attractive in some figured woods, the wood produced is not very strong or dimensionally stable and is prone to checking and cracking. (see radial, tangential)

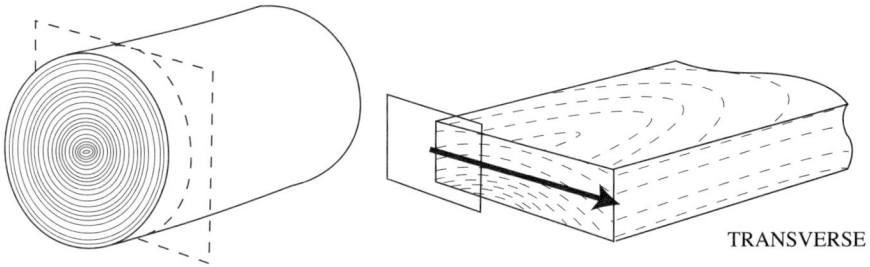

TRANSVERSE

transverse brace a supporting member used for strength and stability that runs across the width of an instrument (perpendicular to its length) and across the grain of the part to which it is attached.

trap-door banjo the name given to the earliest design of Gibson banjos that had resonators. A segment of the resonator's lid was hinged (thus the name "trap door") so that it could be partially opened to improve the banjo's tone projection and amplitude.

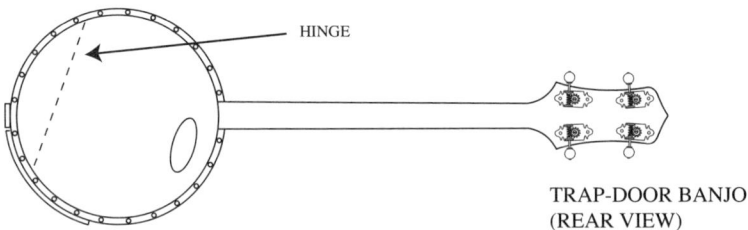

HINGE

TRAP-DOOR BANJO
(REAR VIEW)

trapeze tailpiece an anchoring point for strings on movable-bridge instruments (typically arch-top guitars). Trapeze tailpieces are made of two long stems or rods that attach with some hinge or swivel means to the tailpiece's back plate at one end and to a solid cross bar to which the strings are attached at the other end. The hinged mechanism permits the tailpiece to attain a natural angle to the bridge when the strings are brought up to tension. The trapeze tailpiece derives its name from both its appearance and how it is hinged to its back plate.

treble bout (see bout)

triangular file a steel tool whose three-sided cutting surfaces are covered with numerous teeth of various configurations. Triangular files come in many shapes and sizes and are available in fine, medium, and coarse teeth. Tiny versions of the triangular file that are used for intricate work are called "flat needle files," and they are ideal for cutting the V-shaped string notches in bridges and saddles.

triple-O guitar (see OOO guitar)

truss rod a steel bar placed in the neck of a musical instrument to counteract the bending force exerted on the neck by the compressive load of the strings. The earliest adjustable truss rod was designed by Gibson engineer Thaddeus McHugh in 1921 and featured a curved rod positioned higher in the center and lower at both ends. The idea behind the patent was that the low positioning of the anchor points would pull the bottom of the peghead toward the bottom of the neck heel. This worked to a point, but when the rod got very tight, it tended to straighten, which forced the neck into a hollow rather than a bow. In the early-1930s, Gibson inverted the rod so that it was lower in the center and higher at both ends to exert a post-tensioning effect and raise the center of the fretboard when the rod was tightened. Truss rods are typically adjustable, and numerous mechanical systems exist. T-bars, composite rods, and square tubes are not true "truss rods" and fall into their own non-adjustable category of structural neck beams. (see carbon fiber, double-acting truss rod, post-tensioning, square tube, T-bar)

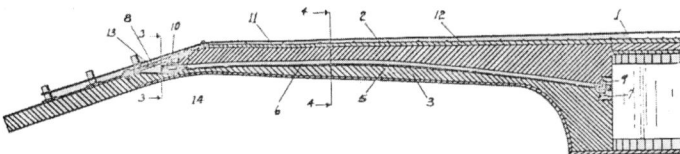

TRUSS ROD
(McHUGH'S PATENT DRAWING)

truss rod cover a small plate used to conceal the access opening to the truss rod. Truss rod covers can be made of any material, and the design of the cover is either subdued or made prominent.

truss rod pocket the opening in the peghead that provides access to the truss rod adjustment nut.

tube-and-plate flange a hardware design for banjo rims developed by Gibson in the early-1920s. The assembly consists of a tubular ring that fits snugly up to a wood lip on the rim, beneath which is attached a stamped brass plate. The tube and the plate are pulled together by threaded rods called "bracket hooks" that draw the stretcher band down to the tube-and-plate flange to tighten the banjo's head. The plate acts as a decorative cover for the space between the open edge of the resonator and the banjo's rim. The tube-and-plate system was later replaced by a one-piece flange casting of similar appearance. The one-piece flange requires only a three-ply rim instead of the four-ply rim of the tube-and-plate system. (see one-piece flange)

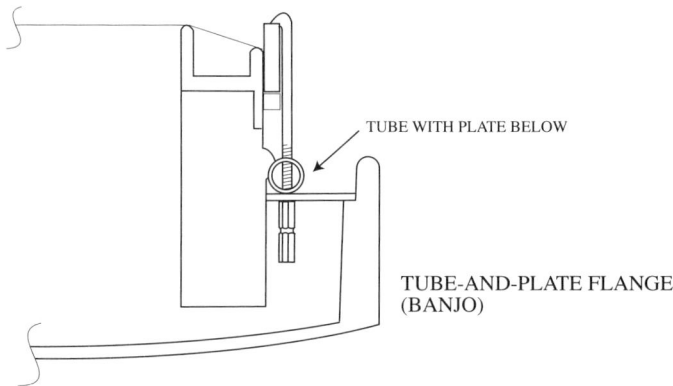

TUBE WITH PLATE BELOW

TUBE-AND-PLATE FLANGE
(BANJO)

tuners (see strobe tuner, tuning machine)

tuning fork a metal device with two parallel blades (tines) connected at one end. The excitation of either or both of the blades makes the tuning fork produce a note that can be used as a tuning reference. The connection of the blades enhances the transference of energy from one blade to the other, which acts as a restoring force to keep them both in motion. Tuning forks are available in several notes and frequencies. [Tuning forks used for neurological testing are still manufactured using the early concert pitch of $C=256Hz$ and should not be used for tuning musical instruments for today's $A=440Hz$. Medical forks are made in both $C=128Hz$ and $C=256Hz$.] (see concert pitch, restoring force)

tuning machine a geared device attached to one end of a string musical instrument for the purpose of providing a tensioning means for the strings. The strings are tuned to pitch by tightening the geared mechanism.

tuning peg an adjustable post used to tension a string and bring it up to pitch. Tuning pegs can be friction or geared. The reference to a tuning peg is typically for a single device and not for a set as on a strip of connected geared tuning machines. (see geared machine)

twelfth root of two an algebraic formula that represents the ratio of the frequency, string tension or scale length of any two consecutive intervals of a musical string. The formula, predicated on the divisor 17.817 or multiplier 1.059, is used to calculate a fretting scale or string tension. To find the next lower interval, divide the frequency (in Hz), the tension or the scale length by 17.817. To find the next higher interval, multiply the frequency (in Hz), the tension or the scale length by 1.059. (For further accuracy: use divisor of 17.81715375 or multiplier of 1.05946309.) The twelfth root of two was devised by Chinese mathematician Chu Tsai-Yu in 1596.

12-fret neck 1) a description of an instrument whose neck joins the body at the 12th fret. 2) the point at which the 12th fret on an instrument is aligned to the body binding. (see joins the body)

two-way non-disclosure agreement (see non-disclosure agreement)

tympanic membrane a small disk at the end of the ear canal. The first sensory mechanism of the human sense of hearing, followed by the ossicles and the cochlea. (see sense of hearing)

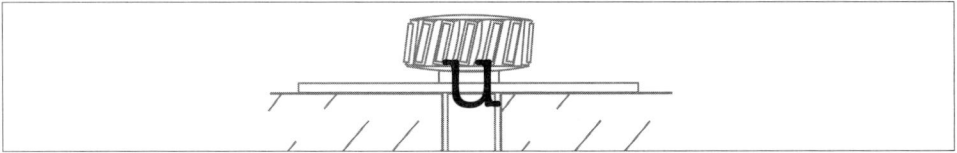

ukulele, uke a small instrument shaped like a guitar, with four strings of either gut or nylon tuned (high to low) *A, C, E, A* (tenor uke), *E, B, G, D* (baritone uke), and either *B, F#, D, A* or *A, E, C, G* (soprano uke). The instrument has its roots in Hawaii and is traditionally made with Hawaiian koa backs and sides. The instrument has one round soundhole, and the spruce soundboard is braced with three lateral "ladder strutting" braces. The fixed bridge features a saddle and an integral harness around which the ends of the strings are tied. (see ladder strutting)

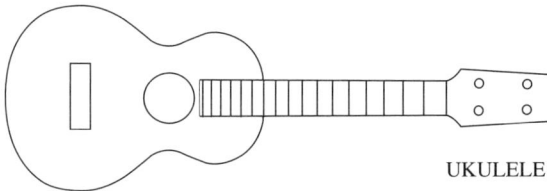

UKULELE

ukulele banjo an instrument with four strings, a round body, a movable bridge, and a membrane-like soundboard (head). The ukulele banjo is tuned *E, B, G, D* (high to low). The instrument features a 6″ or 8″ diameter skin or Mylar® head, a tailpiece, friction pegs, and a movable bridge. The body (rim) is constructed of either laminated strips or blocks of wood. The sound-producing, neck-connecting, and head-attaching hardware varies with the make and model of the instrument. (see folk banjo, frailing banjo, guitar banjo, mandolin banjo, plectrum banjo, regular banjo, tenor banjo)

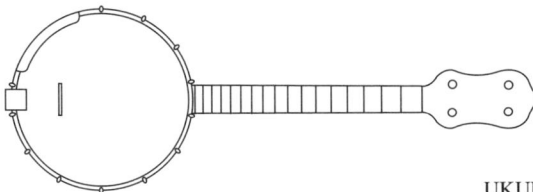

UKULELE BANJO

unkerfed lining a thin, solid wood strip used at the intersection of the rib and soundboard or backboard to add sufficient material to secure the parts together. The lining in violin- and viol-family instruments is solid wood absent of kerfs (small saw cuts to aid in bending the wood). (see kerfed lining)

upholsterer's tape a heavy gauge, non-sticky strip of fabric ranging from 1″ to 2″ wide used as a means to hold binding in place during the gluing process. The upholsterer's tape is wrapped around the instrument to draw and hold the newly glued binding to the instrument's body. The upholsterer's tape does not lift the wood's fibers or leave a residue as would regular masking tape or other sticky tape.

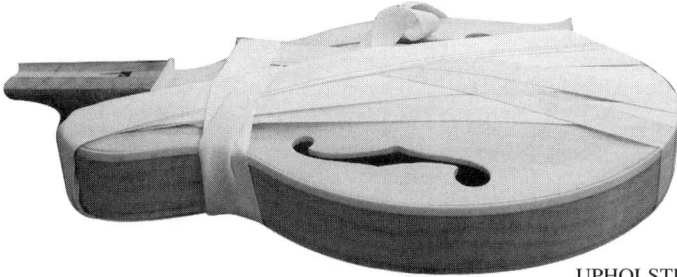

UPHOLSTERER'S TAPE

upper bout (see bout)

upright bass (see bass viol)

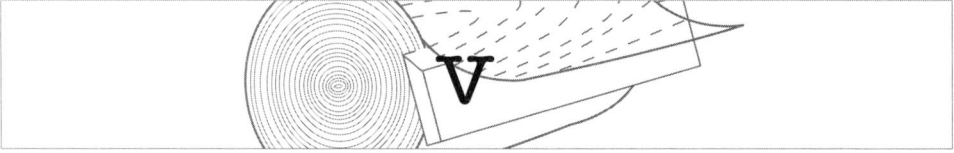

V-joint a connection system for securing the neck to an instrument's body. In the V-joint system, there are only three mating surfaces – the two sides of the neck heel and the back of the neck (compared to five mating surfaces of a dovetail joint). The V-joint has been used in viol- and violin-family instruments for centuries. In 1970, Roger Siminoff modified the V-joint system for use on mandolins by using two dowels to lock the neck to the headblock from the bottom of the heel. When finished, the external appearance of an instrument with a V-joint is identical to one with a dovetail joint. (see slotted neck joint)

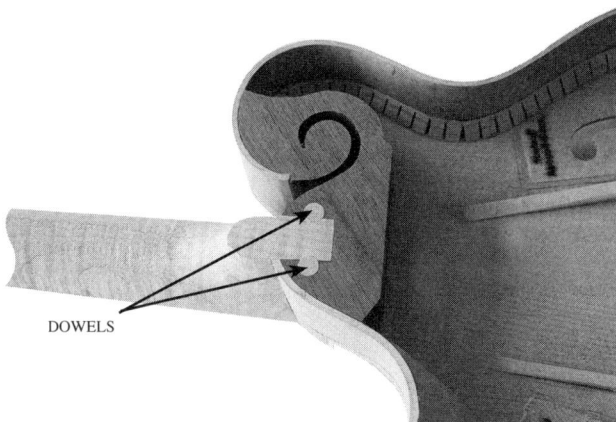

DOWELS

V-JOINT (SIMINOFF)

varnish a finishing medium consisting of particles of dammer, mastic, lac or sandarac dissolved in a volatile solvent such as ethanol (alcohol), benzene, acetone or turpentine. There are two main groups of varnish – oil and spirit. As the name implies, the finishing particles of oil varnish are dissolved in a fast-drying *oil* such as linseed or walnut oil. In spirit varnish, the particles are dissolved in a spirit such as ethanol. (see shellac)

veneer a thin sheet of wood that is either sawn from a flat board or shaved from a round core or square slabs of wood by forcing the wood against a sharp blade. Since shaved veneers are taken from the circumference of the log, they typically show grain figure with minimal or no annular rings. Shaved veneers are very thin and are used for decorative and structural plywoods. Sawn veneers are used for peghead coverings and heel caps. Sawn veneers taken tangentially or radially will show more annular rings than shaved veneers. (see radial, tangential)

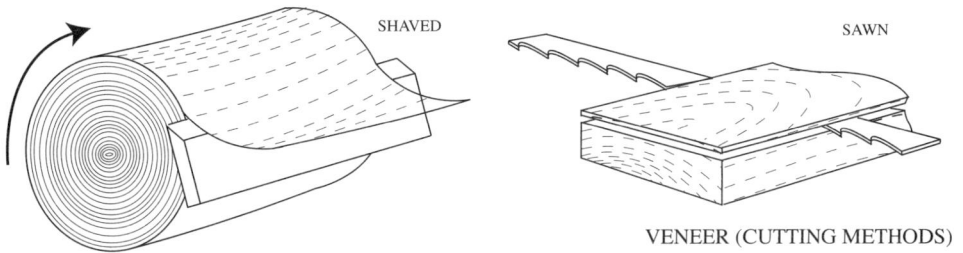

VENEER (CUTTING METHODS)

viol family a group of fretted instruments that are somewhat similar in shape to the violin and constructed in several sizes, tunings, and voicings. Viol-family instruments feature tied-on frets and are played with a bow. Viols are typified by their C-shaped soundholes and the absence of a soundpost, and they are strung with gut strings unlike the steel strings of the modern violin-family instruments. A major distinction between viol- and violin-family instruments is that violin-family instruments have a fretless fingerboard and *f*-shaped soundholes. While "viola da gamba" is broadly used to describe the viol family, the viola da gamba is a specific member of this family. (see viola da gamba, violin family)

viola a four-string instrument, and the alto or middle-size member of the violin family with strings tuned *A, D, G, C* (high to low). The viola is structurally identical to the violin, although slightly larger to enhance the alto range of the instrument's voice. The viola features a carved and graduated belly (soundboard) and backboard, a single longitudinal bass bar, a soundpost, two *f*-holes, and a pegbox fitted with friction pegs. In the 15th Century, the word "viola" referred to any bowed instrument. The viola was developed as a violin-family instrument of a specific size in the 16th Century with the greatest developments attributed to the Amati family. Major improvements, including voicing of the instrument's body, came from former Amati apprentice Antonio Stradivari. The viola is most often played with a bow but occasionally played in a pizzicato style (plucked by the fingers). (see Amati[s], Stradivari)

VIOLA

viola da gamba a fretted and bowed instrument of the viol family played in an upright (a gamba) position. The viola da gamba is about the size of a cello and has a similar range. The viola da gamba and other members of the viol family do not have soundposts. The translation of the Italian *viola da gamba* is "viol of [by] the leg."

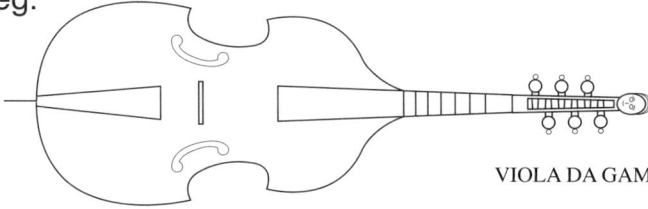

VIOLA DA GAMBA

violin a four-string instrument and the smallest of the violin family with strings tuned *E, A, D, G* (high to low). The most popular of orchestral instruments, the violin features a carved and graduated belly (soundboard) and backboard, one longitudinal bass bar, a soundpost, two *f*-holes, and a pegbox fitted with friction pegs. The violin was developed in the 16th Century with its greatest foundation coming from the artistic hands of the Amati family (ca. 1520-1684) and more specifically under the watchful eyes and hands of Nicolo Amati (1596-1684). Major improvements, including voicing of the instrument's body, came from former Amati apprentice Antonio Stradivari. The violin is mostly played with a bow but occasionally played in a pizzicato style (plucked by the fingers). The word "fiddle" is often used to refer to a violin played in grassroots or traditional musical styles (e.g., bluegrass, country, old-time) although the true fiddle is a smaller forerunner of the violin. (see Amati[s], Stradivari)

VIOLIN

violin family a series of wood-bodied string musical instruments developed in the 16th Century. Violin-family instruments have un-fretted fingerboards, a carved and graduated soundboard and backboard, one longitudinal bass bar, a soundpost, two *f*-holes, and a pegbox fitted with either friction or geared pegs depending on the size of the instrument. Standard body sizes, from smallest to largest, are the violin, viola, cello, and double bass.

Virzi, John and Joseph the sons of violin maker Giuseppi Virzi, John and Joseph were born in Palermo, Italy, and moved to the United States in the early-1900s to set up a distribution point for their family's line of bowed instruments.

Virzi Tone Producer a thin wood disk suspended by two feet inside the air chamber of an acoustic string instrument to enhance the overtone series. The Virzi Tone Producer was the design of John and Joseph Virzi and patented in 1922. The disk was commonly fitted in violins, guitars, mandolas, and mandolins. The Virzi Tone Producer was offered by the Gibson Mandolin-Guitar Company as an optional accessory for its wood-bodied instruments from 1922 until 1925.

VIRZI TONE PRODUCER
(FROM 1924 GIBSON F5
MANDOLIN)

voice in luthierie, a reference to the tonal characteristics of an instrument. More commonly known as "timbre." (see timbre)

voicing 1) the process of making final adjustments to the size of the instrument's aperture(s) to change the tuning of the air chamber. 2) the process of adjusting the parts of an acoustic string instrument to tune them to specific notes. Also known as "tap tuning." (see tap tuning)

volatile organic compound (VOC) a group of chemical elements that are commonly found in luthierie supplies such as adhesives, solvents, and finishes. These chemicals are emitted into the air as gases during the drying process. VOC concentrations are up to ten times higher indoors than outdoors. [Luthiers should be aware of the VOC content of all chemicals used, and should avoid prolonged or unfiltered breathing of vapors to avoid short-term and long-term health problems. All manufacturer recommendations and warnings should be carefully followed.]

volume 1) a measurement of the cubic space within the body of an instrument. 2) a lay term for the measurement of amplitude as perceived by the human ear. (see loudness)

volute a carved spiral decoration on some early instruments. The use of volutes was influenced by the Florentine design style. On the Florentine mandolin, the volute is the peak on the soundboard and backboard that runs through the center of the scroll. (see Florentine)

w/b/w (see white/black/white)

waist on guitars and members of the violin and viol families, the narrowest region in the center of the instrument's body (measured across the soundboard or backboard).

walnut (*Juglans spp.*) a dark brown wood of moderate density with attractive grain. There are about 20 species of walnut, ranging in weight from 40 to 48 pounds per cubic foot. Walnut has large pores that require filling prior applying finish. (see European walnut)

walnut oil an extract from walnuts, used by luthiers as a lubricant while applying French polish. Walnut oil is a common food item and can be found at most supermarkets.

warp 1) an unintended bend in wood caused by improper storage, moisture, curing or a combination of these. A warp is usually a permanent change in the shape of wood and may not be correctable. Warped wood is often an indication of case hardening. 2) a low spot in a neck caused by excessive string load or improper truss rod tension. Also referred to as a "hollow." (see case hardening)

waxed wood whose end grain has been sealed by dipping it in hot wax. Sealing the end grain retards the drying process, enabling moisture to escape from only the side grain, which results in the wood drying more evenly throughout its width and length. Waxing reduces the tendency for checking. (see checking)

wedge 1) a small triangular-shaped piece of wood used to secure the horsehair into the tip and frog of a violin bow. 2) a triangular piece of wood or metal used to secure parts or pry them apart.

Western red cedar (*Thuja plicata*) a coffee-colored wood, light in weight and brittle in structure. Western red cedar is often chosen for flamenco guitar soundboards and works well for arched-top mandolin soundboards. It weighs 22 pounds per cubic foot.

wet-or-dry sandpaper a water-resistant, paper-based material used to smooth out a surface between coats of finish. As the name implies, wet-or-dry sandpaper can be used with or without a wetting agent. For leveling a finish coat between spray applications, wet-or-dry sandpaper is used with a wetting agent such as water. (see wet sanding)

wet sanding the process of using water as a lubricating agent when leveling the finish of a surface. The water helps to flow the particles away from the sanded area, keeps the sandpaper from clogging, and reduces surface heat caused by sanding. Wet-or-dry sandpaper is placed in a dish of water just prior to use (rather than applying water to the work). (see wet-or-dry sandpaper)

white/black/white the name given to laminated binding comprised of three layers. Named for the colors of each layer, white/black/white binding ("w/b/w") comes in many thicknesses and many laminate-thickness combinations. If ivoroid is used as the outer layer, the material is usually referred to as "ivoroid/black/white" or "i/b/w." (see ivoroid)

white spruce (*Picea glauca*) a light-weight, strong wood used for soundboards. White spruce, a wood sometimes inadvertently sold as "Adirondack red spruce," comes from Canada and Northeastern United States and is often referred to as "skunk wood" because of the pungent odor that is released when its needles are crushed.

whitewood, white-wood the stage in building a string musical instrument when the instrument is fully sanded, but not yet colored and finished.

wolf note a howling or warbling sound caused by the continuous exchange of energy from the strings of a bowed instrument and the response of either the air chamber, soundboard or backboard or a combination of these. A wolf note is the dramatic result of an intense restoring force. For example, if the resonant frequency of some component of a violin's body (i.e., backboard, soundboard or air chamber) is excited by a continuous note drawn on the strings with the violin's bow, the energy of that component is transmitted back to the strings as a restoring force. The strings are then excited by both the restoring force and the continuous drawing of the bow, and the instrument begins to produce a pulsing or warbling sound known as a wolf note. The effect stops when either the bowing action ceases or the frequency of the played note changes (which no longer excites the resonant frequency of the component that was previously excited). (see restoring force)

wolf tone (see wolf note)

wood filler (see filler)

wood screw threaded stud a fastener with wood threads on one end and machine threads on the other end. Contemporary banjo makers use wood screw threaded studs to secure banjo necks in place. The earliest Gibson banjos used a #8 screw (both machine and wood), and the company's banjos made after the ball-bearing models used a #10 screw. Also called a "hanger bolt."

wood sealer (see sealer)

wood sectioning a description of the various directions wood can be cut. A board can be cut across its end grain (transverse), perpendicular to its heartwood and through the annular rings (radial) or parallel to the heartwood and across the annular rings (tangential). The appearance of the wood's grain is quite different in each of the three sectioning methods. (see radial, tangential, transverse)

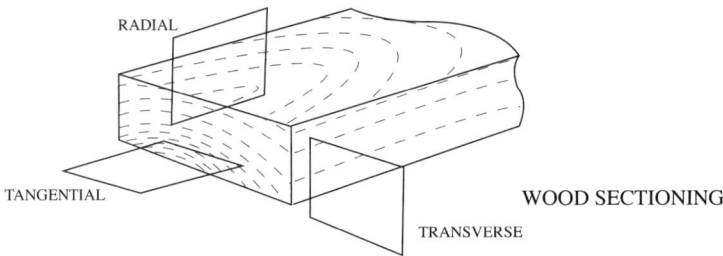

RADIAL

TANGENTIAL

TRANSVERSE

WOOD SECTIONING

wood shrinkage (see shrinkage)

worm and round gear an assembly of two gears in which one has screw-like threads and the other has more conventional gear-like teeth. Worm and round gears are aligned at right angles. The turning effort is applied to the worm gear, which applies a threading motion to the round gear causing it to turn. Worm and round gears have a high mechanical advantage. Since the round gear locks into the worm gear and cannot turn it, the assembly has a positive locking action and cannot slip. In a worm and round gear assembly, the mechanical advantage or gear ratio is calculated by simply counting the number of teeth on the round gear (e.g., a system with 10 teeth on the round gear has a gear ratio of 10:1). Most guitar and mandolin tuning machines feature worm and round gears. The round gear is also known as a "worm wheel" or "spur gear." (see planetary gears)

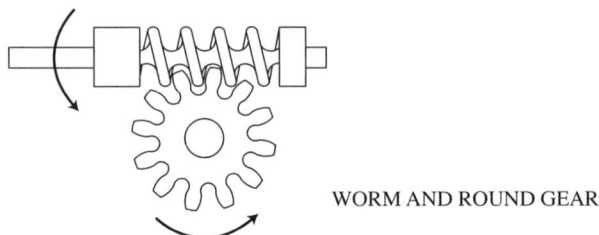

WORM AND ROUND GEAR

worm gear (see worm and round gear)

wound string a musical string that has an outer covering or wrap wire over a core wire. The winding provides the core wire with additional mass to lower its frequency. The additional weight added to the string lowers its frequency but does not affect its tension. Adding a winding to the strings of lower notes enables all of the strings of a set to have similar tension. (see core wire, string tension)

wrap, wrap wire in musical strings, the outermost wire of wound strings. On these strings, the wrap wire is wound around a core wire. (see core wire, wound string)

wrapped string (see wound string)

wriggle work an engraving style in which the graver is rocked back and forth as it is pushed forward to make a fine zigzag line. To get wriggle work to follow a line, the graver can be worked against a straight edge or pattern. (see graver)

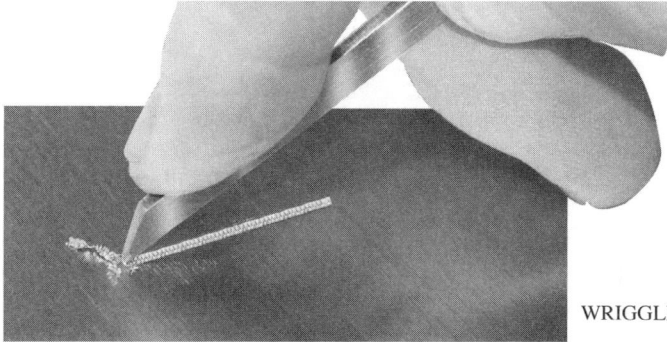

WRIGGLE WORK

xyz

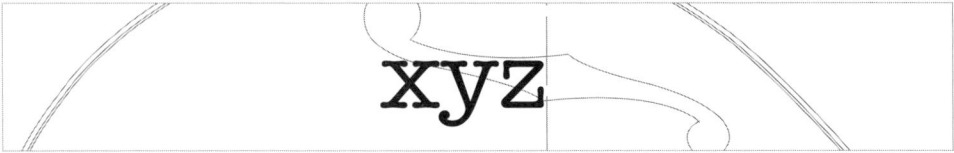

X-bracing a method of strengthening the soundboard of an acoustic guitar. X-bracing was developed by Christian Frederick Martin, Sr. in the mid-1800s as a means of adding strength and stability to the guitar's soundboard. In the X-bracing system, two long braces intersect just below the soundhole. Smaller braces and tone bars are added to the unbraced portions of the soundboard to inhibit harsh overtones.

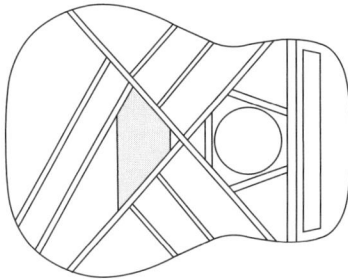

X-BRACING

X-strutting (see X-bracing)

XY axis machine (see CNC)

XYZ axis machine (see CNC)

zebrano (*Microberlinia brazzavillensis*) a hardwood with pronounced dark and light stripes. A bold looking wood for soundboards and sides. Zebrano weighs 46 pounds per cubic foot, comes from Africa and is also known as "zebrawood," named for the stripes is bears.

zero-fret a string-stop positioned just in front of the nut to provide better intonation and action. In a zero-fret installation, the nut only serves the purpose of maintaining proper string-to-string spacing. The zero-fret (a fret installed where the edge of the nut would be) provides a calculated intonation point for where the strings should be terminated as well as a perfect playing action at the first fret because the strings are resting on the zero-fret. However, zero-frets are generally frowned upon by luthiers of better quality instruments. (see action)

ziricote (*Cordia dodecandra*) a blackish hardwood with tan wisps. Ziricote weighs 48 pounds per cubic foot and is used for backboards, sides, fretboards, and peghead veneers.

Reference Tables

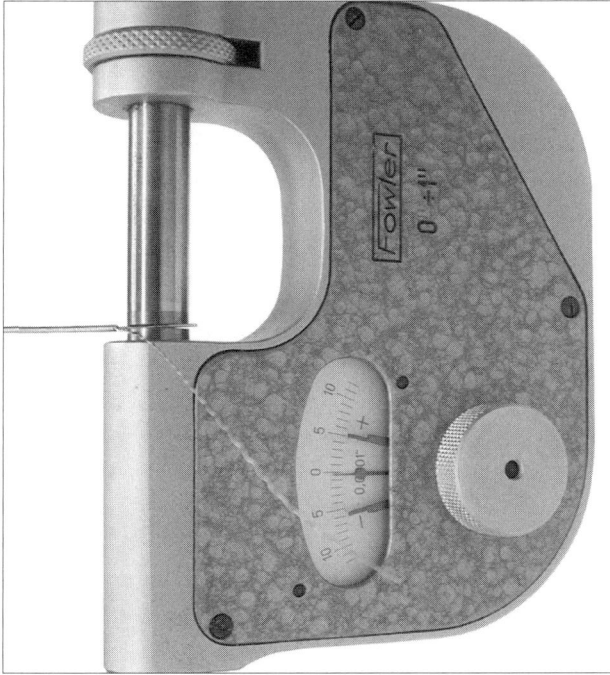

This section includes several tables that may be helpful to your work. Here you will find a decimal/fraction equivalent chart (with corresponding metric values) and a chart showing the amplitudes of instruments, shop tools, common sounds, and OSHA limits for noise levels over a period of time. Two frequency charts are included, one for tuning strings and the other for tap tuning instrument parts one-quarter tone off concert pitch. There is a listing of tunings for more than 45 instruments along with a listing of suggested string gauges for these instruments. Two charts are provided to show the string tensions on a 26″ scale for both steel and nylon strings. There are two interesting tests; one describes the down pressure at various string break angles for movable-bridge instruments, and the other describes the torque load for fixed-bridge instruments with the saddle set at different heights. And, there is a chart showing the weights and common usages for more than 40 woods.

Fraction / mm	Decimal	Fraction / mm	Decimal
1/64	.015625	33/64	.515625
1/32	.03125	17/32	.53125
1mm	.03937	35/64	.546875
3/64	.046875	14mm	.55118
1/16	.0625	9/16	.5625
5/64	.078125	37/64	.578125
2mm	.07874	15mm	.59055
3/32	.09375	19/32	.59375
7/64	.109375	39/64	.609375
3mm	.11811	5/8	.625
1/8	.125	16mm	.62992
9/64	.140625	41/64	.640625
5/32	.15625	21/32	.65625
4mm	.15748	17mm	.66929
11/64	.171875	43/64	.671875
3/16	.1875	11/16	.6875
5mm	.19685	45/64	.703125
13/64	.203125	18mm	.70866
7/32	.21875	23/32	.71875
15/64	.234375	47/64	.734375
6mm	.23622	19mm	.74803
1/4	.250	3/4	.750
17/64	.265625	49/64	.765625
7mm	.27559	25/32	.78125
9/32	.28125	20mm	.78740
19/64	.296875	51/64	.796875
5/16	.3125	13/16	.8125
8mm	.31496	21mm	.82677
21/64	.328125	53/64	.828125
11/32	.34375	27/32	.84375
9mm	.35433	55/64	.859375
23/64	.359375	22mm	.86614
3/8	.375	7/8	.875
25/64	.390625	57/64	.890625
10mm	.39370	23mm	.90551
13/32	.40625	29/32	.90625
27/64	.421875	59/64	.921875
11mm	.43307	15/16	.9375
7/16	.4375	24mm	.94488
29/64	.453125	61/64	.953125
15/32	.46875	31/32	.96875
12mm	.47244	25mm	.98425
31/64	.484375	63/64	.984375
1/2	.500	1	1.000
13mm	.51181	26mm	1.02362

Relative sound pressures in decibels (dB)

Musical instruments and voice	Amplitude
Piano, non-amplified, 8'	60-70dB
Singer, strong voice, 5'	70dB
Mandolin, F5, non-amplified, 4'	80dB
Guitar, flat-top acoustic, non-amplified, 4'	82-83dB
Dobro, non-amplified, 4'	84dB
Violin, fiddle, 4'	82-92dB
Rock music, loud, concert hall	150dB
Shop sounds	
Drill press, twist drill, maple, 4'	64dB
Drill press, Forstner bit, maple, 4'	68dB
Electric table sander, maple peghead, 4'	80-81dB
Bandsaw, cutting 1"ebony, 4'	84-85dB
Jointer, planing fretboard plane, maple neck, 4'	86dB
3/4 horsepower table router, maple, 4'	91dB
Common sounds	
Still quiet, no perceived sounds	0-5dB
Whisper, 4'	30dB
Few people talking, 4'	60-70dB
Normal office noise, several people	70dB
Traffic, busy city sounds	90dB
Jet engine, 100'	145dB
Thresholds	
Threshold of hearing (low point)	5dB
Threshold of pain (high point)	135dB
Hearing damage (potential)	175dB+
Loudest sound measurable	194dB
Maximum amplitude permitted by OSHA:	
8 hrs/day	90dB
6 hrs/day	92dB
4 hrs/day	95dB
3 hrs/day	97dB
2 hrs/day	100dB
Perceptions of loudness	
Imperceptible change	1dB
Perceptible change	3dB
Noticeable change	5dB
Twice as loud	10dB
Four times as loud	20dB

A=440Hz

Concert pitch: A=440Hz

Octave	C	C#	D	D#	E	F	F#	G	G#	A	A#	B
1 (Frequency)	32.70	34.65	36.71	38.89	41.20	43.65	46.25	49.00	51.91	55.00	58.27	61.74
2 (Frequency)	65.41	69.30	73.42	77.78	82.41	87.31	92.50	98.00	103.83	110.00	116.54	123.47
3 (Frequency)	130.81	138.59	146.83	155.56	164.81	174.61	185.00	196.00	207.65	220.00	233.08	246.94
4 (Frequency)	261.62	277.18	293.66	311.13	329.63	349.23	369.99	392.00	415.30	440.00	466.16	493.88
5 (Frequency)	523.25	554.36	587.33	622.25	659.25	698.46	739.99	783.99	830.61	880.00	932.32	987.76
6 (Frequency)	1046.50	1108.73	1174.65	1244.50	1318.51	1396.91	1479.98	1567.98	1661.22	1760.00	1864.65	1975.52
7 (Frequency)	2092.99	2217.45	2349.31	2489.01	2637.01	2793.82	2959.95	3135.96	3322.44	3520.00	3729.30	3951.04

Two frequency charts are provided. This A=440 table is for concert pitch as of 2008. The C=256 (A=431) table (facing page) is for tap tuning parts of an instrument one-quarter tone off and should not be used for tuning strings. To determine the frequencies for any other concert pitch, you can download a free user-definable Musical Frequency Calculator (Excel® spreadsheet) from the "Instruction Sheets (downloads)" page of our web site at www.siminoff.net/pages/siminoff_downloads.html. For more information on tap tuning and the history of concert pitch read *The Art of Tap Tuning.**

* Published by Hal Leonard Corporation, Milwaukee, WI.

THIS TABLE <u>NOT</u> TO BE USED FOR TUNING STRINGS

Concert pitch: *C*=256Hz (*A*=431Hz*)
For use when tap-tuning to notes that are one quarter-tone off.

	C	C#	D	D#	E	F	F#	G	G#	A	A#	B
Octave 1 Frequency	32.00	33.90	35.92	38.05	40.32	42.71	45.25	47.95	50.80	53.82	57.02	60.41
Octave 2 Frequency	64.00	67.81	71.84	76.11	80.63	85.43	90.51	95.89	101.59	107.64	114.03	120.82
Octave 3 Frequency	128.00	135.61	143.67	152.22	161.27	170.86	181.02	191.78	203.19	215.27	228.07	241.63
Octave 4 Frequency	256.00	271.22	287.35	304.44	322.54	341.72	362.04	383.57	406.38	430.54	456.14	483.26
Octave 5 Frequency	512.00	542.44	574.70	608.87	645.08	683.44	724.08	767.13	812.75	861.08	912.28	966.52
Octave 6 Frequency	1024.00	1084.89	1149.40	1217.75	1290.16	1366.88	1448.16	1534.27	1625.50	1722.16	1824.56	1933.05
Octave 7 Frequency	2048.00	2169.78	2298.80	2435.49	2580.32	2733.75	2896.31	3068.54	3251.00	3444.32	3649.12	3866.10

* Precise pitch for A is set to 430.54Hz to arrive at C=256Hz.

THIS TABLE <u>NOT</u> TO BE USED FOR TUNING STRINGS

Instrument Tunings

Instrument	1st	2nd	3rd	4th	5th	6th	7th	8th	9th	10th	11th	12th
bajo sexto	F	F	C	C	G	G	D	D"	A	A"	E	E"
balalaika	A	E	E									
bandurria (a)	A	A	E	E	B	B	F#	F#	C#	C#"	G#	G#"
bandurria (b)	A	A	E	E	B	B	F#	F#	C#	C#	G#	G#
banjo												
5-string (*G*-tuning)	D	B	G	D	G							
5-string (*C*-tuning)	D	B	G	C	G							
plectrum	D	B	G	C								
tenor	A	D	G	C								
guitar (banjo)	E	B	G	D	A	E						
mandolin (banjo)	E	E	A	A	D	D	G	D				
ukulele (banjo)	E	B	G	D								
bass viol, acoustic	G	D	A	E								
bouzouki												
3-course (a)	D	D	A	A	D	D"						
3-course (b)	E	E	B	B	E	E						
4-course	D	D	A	A	F	F	C	C				
Irish bouzouki	D	D	A	A	D	D	G	G				
cavaguhino	D	B	G	D								
cello	A	D	G	C								
charango	E	E	A	A	E	E"	C	C	G	G		
cittern	D	D	A	A	D	D	G	G	A	A		
cuatro*	B	F#	D	A								
dulcimer (mountain)	C	C	G									
fiddle (violin)	E	A	D	G								
guitar												
steel string	E	B	G	D	A	E						
classical	E	B	G	D	A	E						
flamenco	E	B	G	D	A	E						
resophonic (Dobro®)	D	B	G	D	G	D						
12-string	E	E	B	B	G	G"	D	D"	A	A"	E	E"
acoustic bass (guitar)	G	D	A	E								
tenor guitar	A	D	G	C								
guitarrone	E	B	G	D	A	E						
harp guitar												
bass course (drones)	G#	G	F#	F	D#	D	C#	C	B	A#		
fretted course	E	B	G	D	A	E						
laud	A	A	E	E	B	B	F#	F#	C#	C#	G#	G#
mando-bass	G	D	A	E								
mando-cello	A	A	D	D	G	G	C	C				
mandola	A	A	D	D	G	G	C	C				
mandolin	E	E	A	A	D	D	G	G				
octave mandolin	E	E	A	A	D	D	G	G				
oud	G	G	D	D	A	A	E	E	B	B	F#	
tiple, Columbian	E	E	E	A	A	A	B	B'	B'	D	D'	D
tiple, Martin	B	B	F#	F#'	F#	D	D'	D	A	A'		
ukulele												
baritone	E	B	G	D								
soprano (a)	B	F#	D	A								
soprano (b)	A	E	C	G								
tenor	A	C	E	A								
viola	A	D	G	C								
violin (fiddle)	E	A	D	G								

1) ′=one octave lower than neighboring strings. 2) ″=one octave higher than neighboring strings.

Instrument	1st	2nd	3rd	4th	5th	6th	7th	8th	9th	10th	11th	12th
bajo sexto	.026"w	.026"w	.036"w	.036"w	.046"w	.046"w	.062"w	.032"w	.078"w	.034"w	.092"w	.046"w
balalaika	.008"	.010"	.012"									
bandurria (a)	.014"	.014"	.026"w	.026"w	.036"w	.036"w	.046"w	.046"w	.060"	.030"w	.076"w	.036"w
bandurria (b)	.010"	.010"	.014"	.014"	.019"w	.019"w	.023"w	.023"w	.030"	.030"w	.035"w	.035"w
banjo												
5-string (*G*-tuning)	.010"	.012"	.016"	.023"w	.010"							
5-string (*C*-tuning)	.010"	.012"	.016"	.023"w	.010"							
plectrum	.010"	.012"	.016"	.023"w								
tenor	.009"	.016"	.023"w	.030"w								
guitar (banjo)	.012"	.016"	.024"w	.032"w	.042"w	.053"w						
mandolin (banjo)	.011"	.011"	.015"	.015"	.026"w	.026"w	.040"w	.040"w				
ukulele (banjo)	.011"	.014"	.024"w	.011"								
bass viol, acoustic	.045"w	.065"w	.085"w	.105"w								
bouzouki												
3-course (a)	.010"	.010"	.013"	.013"	.021"w	.010"						
3-course (b)	.009"	.009"	.012"	.012"	.018"w	.018"w						
4-course	.010"	.010"	.013"	.013"	.022"w	.010"	.028"w	.013"				
Irish bouzouki	.011"	.011"	.016"	.016"	.028"w	.028"w	.038"w	.038"w				
cavaguhino	.011"	.013"	.023"w	.028"w								
cello	.022"w	.032"w	.042"w	.064"w								
charango*	.019"	.019"	.028"	.028"	.033"	.020"	.024"	.024"	.030"	.030"		
cittern	.014"	.014"	.022"	.022"	.032"	.032"	.046"	.046"	.054"	.054"		
cuatro*	.033"	.022"	.028"	.033"								
dulcimer (mountain)	.012"	.012"	.014"									
fiddle (violin)	.010"w	.014"w	.022"w	.032"w								
guitar												
steel string	.013"	.017"	.026"	.035"w	.045"w	.056"w						
classical*	.028"	.032"	.040"	.030"w	.040"w	.043"w						
flamenco*	.028"	.032"	.042"	.030"w	.040"w	.046"w						
resophonic (Dobro®)	.016"	.018"w	.026"w	.035"w	.045"w	.056"w						
12-string	.009"	.009"	.013"	.013"	.021"w	.008"	.029"w	.011"	.036"w	.016"	.045"w	.026"w
acoustic bass (guitar)	.045"w	.065"w	.080"w	.100"w								
tenor	.010"	.014"	.022"w	.032"w								
guitarrone**	.033"	.046"	.078"	.068"w	.078"w	.102"w						
harp guitar												
bass course (drones)	.038"w	.044"w	.048"w	.050"w	.052"w	.054"w	.056"w	.058"w	.060"w	.062"w		
fretted course	.013"	.017"	.026"w	.035"w	.045"w	.056"w						
laud	.012"	.012"	.017"	.017"	.021"w	.021"w	.027"w	.027"w	.033"w	.033"w	.042"w	.042"w
mando-bass	.049"w	.063"w	.097"w	.130"w								
mando-cello	.022"w	.022"w	.034"w	.034"w	.048"w	.048"w	.074"w	.074"w				
mandola	.015"	.015"	.025"w	.025"w	.035"w	.035"w	.050"w	.050"w				
mandolin	.011"	.011"	.015"	.015"	.026"w	.026"w	.040"w	.040"w				
octave mandolin	.012"	.012"	.022"w	.022"w	.032"w	.032"w	.046"w	.046"w				
oud*	.022"w	.022"w	.028"w	.028"w	.025"w	.025"w	.029"w	.029"w	.033"w	.033"w	.041"w	
tiple, Columbian	.009"	.009"	.009"	.007"	.007"	.018"w	.008"	.008"	.020"w	.010"	.010"	.025"w
tiple, Martin	.010"	.010"	.012"	.026"w	.012"	.015"	.034"w	.015"	.010"	.022"w		
ukulele												
baritone*	.028"	.034"	.038"	.035"								
soprano (a)*	.024"	.030"	.034"	.022"								
soprano (b)*	.028"	.032"	.040"	.028"								
tenor*	.024"	.032"	.036"	.028"								
viola	.012"w	.020"w	.030"w	.040"w								
violin (fiddle)	.010"w	.014"w	.022"w	.032"w								

1) Measurements are for medium gauge strings. Gauges may vary based on instrument construction, string manufacturer, and luthier or artist preference. 2) *=nylon or gut strings. 3) **Guitarrone has nylon *E, B, G* strings and steel/wound strings for *D, A, E.* 4) w=wound strings.

String Tensions - Nylon Strings, 26" String Scale

gauge	C3	D3	E3	F3	G3	A3	B3	C4	D4	E4	F4	G4	A4	B4	C5	D5	E5	F5	core/wrap
.026"															11.50	12.90	14.50	15.40	
.028"															11.90	13.30	15.00	15.80	
.030"														10.70	11.30				
.031"														11.00	11.60				
.032"													11.00	11.70	12.40				.017"/.006"
.033"													11.14	12.50	13.30				.018"/.006"
.035"												10.90	12.20						.016"/.008"
.037"											10.02	11.25	12.60						.018"/.008"
.039"											10.40	11.70	13.13						.020"/.008"
.040"											10.85	12.20	13.70						.016"/.010"
.041"											11.10	12.40	13.90						.020"/.010"
.028"W								13.30	15.00	16.80	17.80								.019"/.012"
.030"W								14.30	16.10	18.00	19.20								.020"/.012"
.032"W								15.15	17.00	19.00	20.20								.021"/.012"
.034"W					11.35	12.70	14.25	15.95											.023"/.012"
.036"W					13.00	14.60	16.30	17.30											
.038"W					13.45	15.10	16.95												
.040"W				12.60	14.10	15.90	17.80												
.042"W		11.75	13.20	13.90	15.65														
.044"W		12.90	14.50	15.35	17.25														
.045"W		13.90	15.70	16.60	18.60														
.046"W		14.25	16.00	16.90	19.00														

Loads are for strings at pitch on a 26" string scale. To calculate loads for the same string gauges at longer or shorter string scales, use the "twelfth root of two" formula.

Core/wrap wire combinations for a particular nylon string gauge will vary according to manufacturer and the precise sizing and quantity of filament strands.

String Tensions - Steel Strings, 26" String Scale

gauge	C3	D3	E3	F3	G3	A3	B3	C4	D4	E4	F4	G4	A4	B4	C5	D5	E5	F5	core/wrap
.009"																9.25	11.50	13.50	
.010"															9.25	11.25	14.50	16.10	
.011"															11.15	14.50	18.00	20.00	
.012"															14.50	17.00	21.50	24.00	
.013"														11.75	14.75	19.25	24.75		
.014"													12.50	15.50	18.00	24.50			
.015"												11.50	15.00	19.10	21.20				
.016"												13.00	17.25	20.50	23.00				
.017"											11.50	15.00	19.75	24.75					
.018"											15.75	18.60	21.00						
.018"W									10.00	14.10	15.50	18.40	20.75						.010"/.004"
.020"W										13.00	15.00	18.50	23.75						.012"/.0035"
.022"W									13.25	17.00	19.25	24.00							.013"/.0045"
.024"W									17.50	22.00	25.00	30.00							.015"/.0045"
.026"W								15.75	21.20	23.50	28.25								.016"/.005"
.028"W							14.00	16.00	20.50	26.00									.014"/.007"
.030"W							18.00	20.25	26.00	30.50									.017"/.0065"
.032"W						16.50	21.00	24.00	29.00										.017"/.0075"
.034"W					12.25	15.50	19.50	21.50											.014"/.010"
.036"W				12.50	16.00	20.00	25.25												.015"/.010"
.038"W				13.75	17.10	21.00	27.00												.017"/.010"
.040"W				17.20	19.75	23.00	29.00												.017"/.011"
.042"W			15.75	18.25	23.25	29.00													.016"/.013"
.044"W			16.75	18.75	24.00	30.00													.015"/.014"
.046"W		14.20	16.00	20.00	25.50														.017"/.0145"
.048"W		14.20	16.00	20.00	25.50														.019"/.014"
.050"W		16.25	21.00	23.50															.020"/.015"
.052"W		17.00	21.50	23.75															.020"/.016"
.054"W	16.10	19.50	25.00																.016"/.019"
.056"W	16.00	20.75	25.50																.018"/.019"
.058"W	16.50	21.25	26.50																.020"/.019"

Loads are for strings at pitch on a 26" string scale. To calculate loads for the same string gauges at longer or shorter string scales, use the "twelfth root of two" formula.

Movable Bridges

As the height of the bridge saddle increases on movable-bridge instruments, the down pressure on the soundboard increases disproportionately. Setting up an instrument with excessive saddle height could lead to damage to the bridge, structural failure of the soundboard or both.

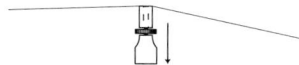

For movable-bridge instruments, the string break angle is the result of neck pitch, soundboard contours, and bridge height.

This graph shows the loads on a soundboard for an F5-style mandolin using D'Addario® J-73 mandolin strings at 22 different string break angles. The results show that string break angles above 16° approach the threshold of the soundboard's strength and should not be used.

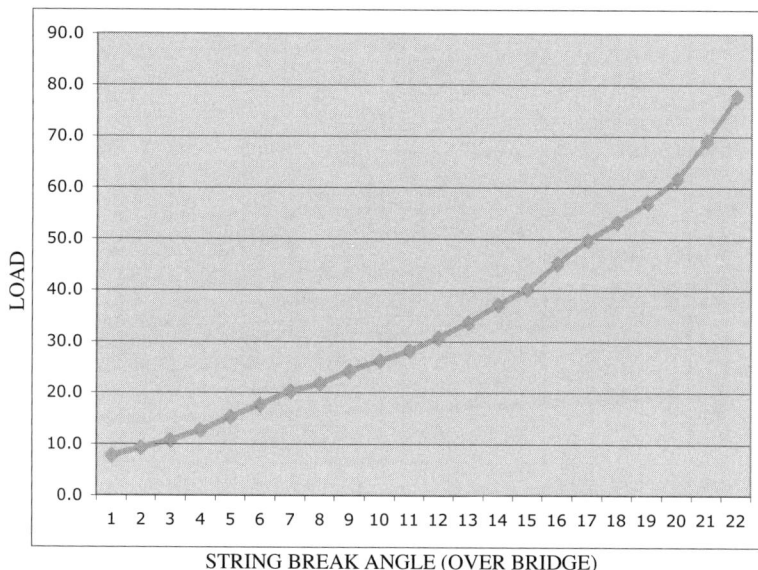

LOAD vs. STRING BREAK ANGLE (OVER BRIDGE) — graph, LOAD axis 0.0 to 90.0, string break angle 1 to 22

String break angle:																					
1°	2°	3°	4°	5°	6°	7°	8°	9°	10°	11°	12°	13°	14°	15°	16°	17°	18°	19°	20°	21°	22°
Corresponding loads:																					
8.0	9.5	11.0	13.0	15.5	18.0	20.5	22.0	24.5	26.5	28.5	31.0	34.0	37.5	40.5	45.5	50.0	53.5	57.5	62.0	69.5	78.0

1) The optimum string break angle is 16° at which point the down pressure is 45.5 pounds on the soundboard or about 58% of an F5 soundboard's capacity. (An F5 mandolin soundboard made of Adirondack red spruce, properly graduated, with two tone bars can withstand a downward force of about 78 pounds before rupturing.)

2) An F5 mandolin with a 6° neck pitch, a soundboard that measures .640″ above its baseline at the crown, and a "normal" action will deliver a 16.5° string break angle.

3) Slight irregularities in the chart are caused by friction points in the test fixture's saddle, the inability to read degrees to greater precision than one degree (1°), and the inability to read the analog Dillon® Force Gauge to greater precison than 1/2 pound.

4) Loads will vary for other gauges of strings.

As the height of the bridge saddle increases on fixed-bridge instruments, the torque load on the soundboard increases disproportionately. Setting up an instrument with excessive saddle height could lead to damage to the bridge, bridgeplate or structural failure of the soundboard.

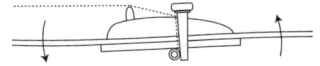

The height of the saddle over the soundboard determines the amount of leverage on the soundboard and is a more important issue to consider than the string break angle from the saddle to the bridge pins.

This graph shows the loads on a soundboard of a flat-top acoustic guitar using D'Addario® EJ16 strings at 19 different saddle heights above the soundboard, at intervals of .025″ measured at the center of the saddle.

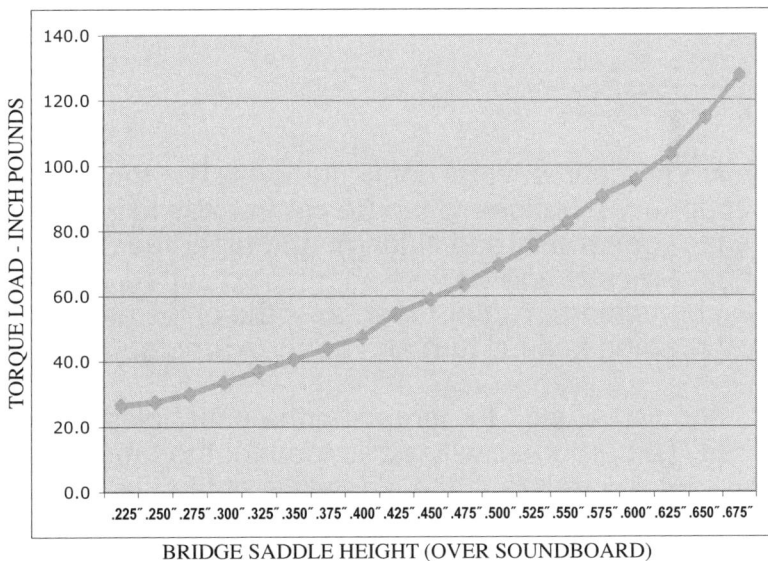

BRIDGE SADDLE HEIGHT (OVER SOUNDBOARD)

Height of top of saddle above soundboard (thousandths of an inch):																		
.225	.250	.275	.300	.325	.350	.375	.400	.425	.450	.475	.500	.525	.550	.575	.600	.625	.650	.675
Corresponding torque loads (inch pounds):																		
27.0	28.0	30.5	34.0	37.5	41.0	44.5	48.0	55.0	59.5	64.0	70.0	76.0	83.0	91.0	96.0	104.0	115.0	128.0

1) An optimum saddle height is difficult to determine since a failure is not limited to just one stress point. On a test instrument, a saddle height of .625″ (104 inch pounds of torque) caused a crack in the lead edge of the bridge base.

2) Regardless of the saddle height on fixed-bridge instruments, the down pressure through the vertical center axis of the bridge will remain zero.

3) At .450″ (the average height of a saddle on a Martin D18), the torque load was 59.5 inch pounds.

4) Slight irregularities in the chart are caused by friction points in the test fixture's bridge/saddle mechanism and the inability to read foot pounds to greater precision than 1/2 pound on the fixture's torque wrench.

5) Loads will vary for other gauges of strings.

The following list shows thread sizes, thread types, and the corresponding number-drill size to use when drilling the hole to be tapped. Cutting oil should be used when tapping holes in most metals; kerosene or WD-40® may be used when tapping holes in aluminum; and brass parts may be tapped without a cutting agent.

1-64 NC	53	4-40 NC	43	8-32 NC	29	14-20 NS	10
1-72 NF	53	4-48 NF	42	8-36 NF	29	14-24 NS	7
2-56 NC	50	5-40 NC	38	10-24 NC	25	1/4-20 NC	7
2-64 NF	50	5-44 NF	37	10-32 NF	21	1/4-28 NF	3
3-48 NC	47	6-32 NC	36	12-24 NC	16		
3-56 NF	45	6-40 NF	33	12-28 NF	14		

(Larger sizes not typical in luthierie. Consult other tap/drill tables.)

NC = National Coarse Thread
NF = National Fine Thread
NS = National Special Thread

Hand taps are made in several configurations. The three common end shapes are bottoming tap (to cut threads to bottom of hole), plug tap (general thread cutting), and taper tap (for starting threads in hard metals and for less aggressive cutting of threads). When using bottoming, plug or taper taps, the chips need to be broken by threading in a full turn and then backing out a half turn.

Taper taps should be used for threading the post holes into ebony bridge bases. The progressively-sized teeth of the tapered cutting edge applies less pressure to the side walls of the ebony and reduces the chance of wood breakage. And, the longer taper helps to guide the tap into the hole.

Spiral-point taps can be fed continuously (without reversing to break chips) and should be used for high-speed cutting (e.g., threading brass truss rod nuts with an electric hand drill) where fast and efficient chip removal is required.

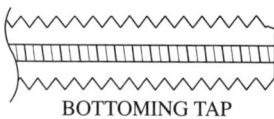
BOTTOMING TAP

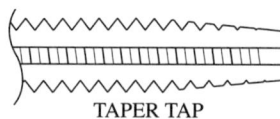
TAPER TAP

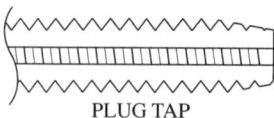
PLUG TAP

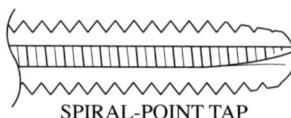
SPIRAL-POINT TAP

Band saw blades are measured by their width, number of teeth per inch, tooth configuration, and circumference (example: 1/2", 14-tooth, variable tooth, 80"). Standard widths of band saw blades for the typical shop-size band saw are 1/8", 1/4", 3/8", 1/2", and 5/8". Most better blades are available in .024" thickness with some blades available in .018" thickness. (The thicker blades provide a straighter cut and less chatter when cutting heavy stock.) Wide blades cannot cut as small a radius as narrow blades. Here are the standard configurations used for cutting wood and aluminum.

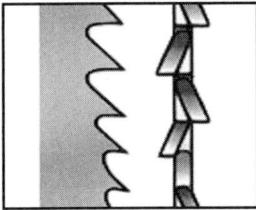

variable tooth, variable-set teeth are of different sizes and depths and are set in an alternating left/right pattern. Ideal for cutting hard, dense woods like ebony and rosewood. Can be used to cut aluminum for making fixtures, templates, and patterns.

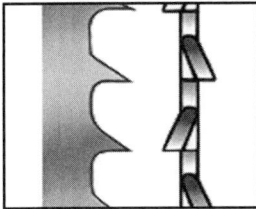

skip tooth, raker-set teeth are deep and of the same size, with open space between them and are set in an alternating left/right pattern. Deep teeth help to remove chips when cutting or re-sawing fibrous woods (e.g., spruce). Ideal for general re-sawing and heavy cutting.

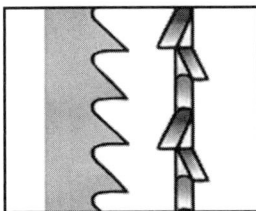

regular tooth, raker-set teeth are of different sizes and depths and are set in a wavy pattern to help reduce chatter and prolong blade life. Deep, straight teeth help clear chips from the blade. Ideal for most general wood-cutting situations.

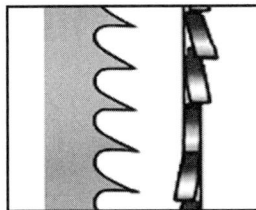

regular tooth, wavy-set teeth are the same size and depth and are set in a wavy pattern. Ideal for cutting thin metals. Not recommended for cutting hardwoods as teeth may clog and chatter.

Common name	Botanical name	lbs/ft³	kg/m³	Common uses	Appearance	Origin
Basswood	Tilia americana	26	416	lining, marquetry, purfling	medium beige, tight grain	Eastern Canada, Great Lakes region of U.S.
Blackwood, African	Dalbergia melanoxylon	75	1201	backboards, fretboards, ribs, veneers	black with beige and brown streaks	Eastern Africa
Bocote	Cordia gerascanthus	55	881	backboards, binding, fretboards, ribs, veneers	reddish brown w/ black swirly stripes	Central America, Mexico
Bubinga	Guibourtia tessmannii	55	881	backboards, ribs, veneers	rich brown, mildly figured	Africa
Cedar, Western Red	Thuja plicata	22	352	soundboards	light tan	British Columbia, Northwestern U.S.
Cocobolo	Dalbergia retusa	65	1041	backboards, fretboards, ribs, veneers	orange-brown, heavily figured	Mexico, Nicaragua, Western Costa Rica
Cypress	Cupressus sempervirens	40	641	backboards, ribs, veneers	blonde	Italy
Ebony, African	Diospyros mespiliformis	75	1201	bridges, fretboards, veneers	black with some wisps of beige	Africa, Burma
Ebony, Gabon (Gaboon)	Diospyros crassiflora hiern	65	1041	bridges, fretboards, veneers	black	Africa, Madagascar
Ebony, Macassar	Diospyros macassar	69	1105	bridges, fretboards, veneers	black with beige and brown streaks	Burma, Ceylon, Indonesia, Southern India
Fir, Douglas	Pseudotsuga taxifolia	33	528	soundboards	medium beige, dark summerwood	British Columbia, Western U.S.
Holly	Ilex opaca	50	801	marquetry, purfling	very light tan (whitish)	Europe, Western Asia
Koa	Acacia koa	41	657	backboards, ribs, veneers	medium to dark brown, figured	Hawaiian Islands
Lignum Vitae	Guaiacum officinale	77	1234	chisel handles, mallet heads	medium brown with tan streaks	Central America, Columbia, Venezuela
Mahogany, African	Khaya ivorensis	33	528	backboards, blocks, necks, patterns, ribs	dark tan	Africa
Mahogany, Honduras	Swietenia macrophylla	36	577	backboards, blocks, necks, patterns, ribs	light golden brown	Central America, Northern South America
Maple, Big Leaf	Acer macrophyllum	36	577	backboards, ribs	blonde, plain/quilted/curly	Canada, Northwestern U.S.
Maple, Red	Acer rubrum	37	593	backboards, banjo rims, necks, ribs	pinkish, plain/curly	Canada, Europe, Northeastern U.S.
Maple, Sugar	Acer saccharum	40	641	backboards, banjo rims, necks, ribs	beige, plain/curly/bird's eye	Canada, Northeastern U.S.
Oak	Quercus spp.	48	769	fixtures, truss rod filler strips	medium-coffee color	Eastern Canada, U.S.
Ovangkol	Guibourtia ehie	50	801	backboards, ribs, veneers	rich tan, dark wavy grain	Ghana, Ivory Coast, Nigeria
Padouk, African (1)	Pterocarpus soyauxii	48	769	backboards, ribs, veneers	reddish brown	Africa
Pearwood	Pyrus communis	44	705	marquetry, purfling	very light beige, subdued grain	Europe, U.S., Western Asia
Poplar	Liriodendron tulipifera	28	449	marquetry, purfling	yellowish tan	Canada, U.S.
Purple Heart	Peltogyne porphyrocardia	54	865	binding, marquetry, purfling	bluish-magenta	Central America, Northern South America
Redwood (California)	Sequoia sempervirens	25	400	soundboards	reddish tan	California, Oregon
Rosewood, Amazon	Dalbergia spruceana	68	1089	backboards, bridges, fretboards, ribs, veneers	dark brown, rich figure	Brazil
Rosewood, Brazilian	Dalbergia nigra	63	1009	backboards, bridges, fretboards, ribs, veneers	reddish brown with purple and black	Brazil
Rosewood, Honduras	Dalbergia stevensonii	60	961	backboards, bridges, fretboards, ribs, veneers	dark reddish brown, mild figure	Belize, Guatemala
Rosewood, Indian	Dalbergia latifolia	53	849	backboards, bridges, fretboards, ribs, veneers	blackish brown with light wisps	India
Rosewood, Madagascar	Dalbergia baronii	40	641	backboards, bridges, fretboards, ribs, veneers	deep reddish brown, figured	Madagascar
Rosewood, Santos	Caesalpinia ferrea	59	945	backboards, bridges, fretboards, ribs, veneers	deep reddish brown, figured	Brazil

Common name	Botanical name	lbs/ft³	kg/m³	Common uses	Appearance	Origin
Sapele	Entandrophragma cylindricum	39	625	backboards, ribs, veneers	medium brown	Africa
Spruce, Black (2)	Picea mariana	28	449	dulcimer soundboards, bracing, tone bars	light beige, some silk	Alaska, Northwestern U.S., Western Canada
Spruce, Englemann	Picea engelmannii	27	432	bracing, soundboards	light beige, some silk	Alaska, Canada, Oregon, Washington
Spruce, German Silver	Picea abies	27	432	bracing, soundboards	light color, some silk, tight grain	Central and Northern Europe
Spruce, Red (3)	Picea rubens sarg.	28	449	bracing, soundboards	beige, some silk	Canada, Northeastern U.S.
Spruce, Sitka	Picea sitchensis	27	432	bracing, soundboards	beige, some silk	Alaska, Northwestern U.S., Western Canada
Spruce, White (4)	Picea glauca	28	448	bracing, soundboards	beige, some silk	Canada, Northeastern U.S.
Sycamore	Acer pseudoplantanus	38	609	backboards, necks, ribs, veneers	blonde, plain/curly	Central and Southern Europe, Eastern U.S.
Walnut, (American) Black	Juglans nigra	40	641	backboards, necks, ribs, veneers	rich brown, figured	Canada, U.S.
Walnut, European (5)	Juglans regia	40	641	backboards, necks, ribs, veneers	rich brown, heavily figured	England, France, Italy, Spain
Zebrano	Microberlinia brazzavillensis	46	737	backboards, ribs, veneers	medium tan, dark stripes	West Africa
Ziricote	Cordia dodecandra	48	769	bridges, fretboards, peghead veneers	blackish tan, wavy stripes	Belize, Guatemala, Mexico

1) Several varieties of Padouk exist.

2) Black Spruce is provided in this list as reference only. While very similar in appearance to Red Spruce, Black Spruce trees are typically much smaller, and it is difficult to yield wood of sufficient size for guitar soundboards.

3) Red Spruce is commonly known to luthiers as "Adirondack Red Spruce" referring to the Adirondack Mountain region from which it was originally taken for use as instrument soundboards.

4) White Spruce is sometimes inadvertently cut and sold as Adirondack Red Spruce. (Black Spruce, Red Spruce, and White Spruce trees have very similar features that are difficult to distinguish, with the exception of Black Spruce that is smaller than Red and White Spruce.)

5) European Walnut (Juglans regia) is named for its region of origin and includes Carpathian Walnut, Circassian Walnut, English Walnut, French Walnut, and Persian Walnut. Some variations in figure, grain, and color exist due to geographical and climatic differences.

6) Due to space constraints, "blocks" refers to headblocks, corner blocks, and tailblocks; "bracing" refers to braces and tone bars; "ribs" refers to ribs and sides; and "veneers" refers to peghead veneers.

VIOLIN

VIOLA

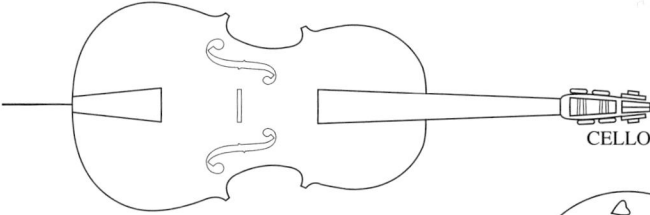
CELLO

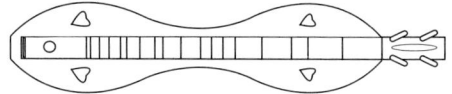
DULCIMER (MOUNTAIN)

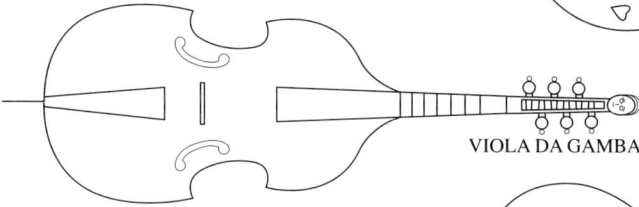
VIOLA DA GAMBA

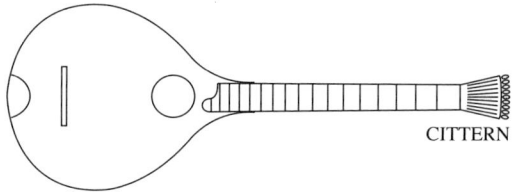
CITTERN

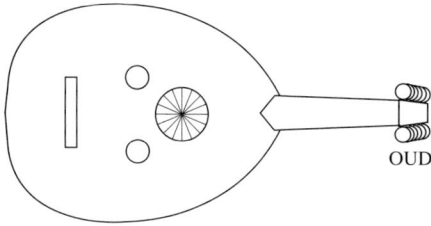
OUD

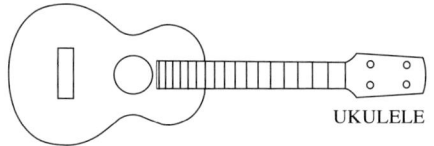
UKULELE

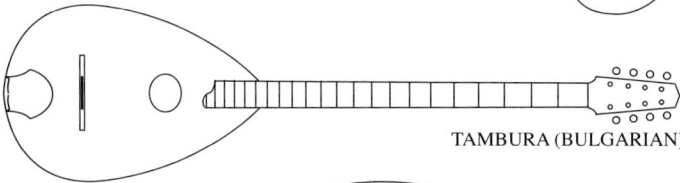
TAMBURA (BULGARIAN)

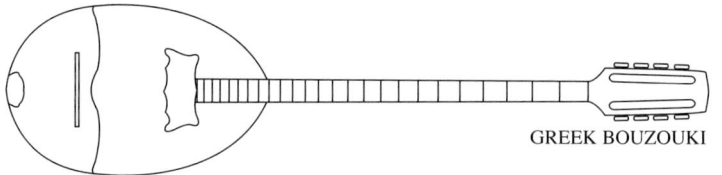
GREEK BOUZOUKI

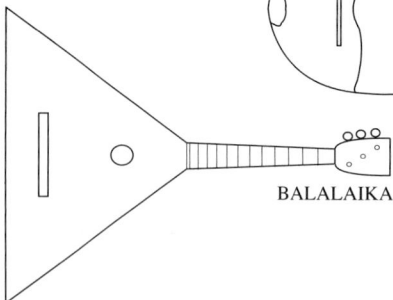
BALALAIKA

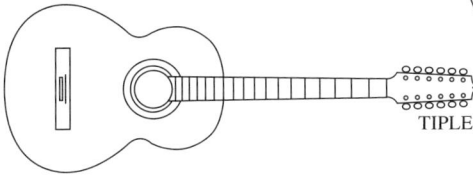

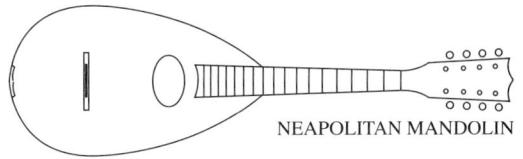

NEAPOLITAN MANDOLIN

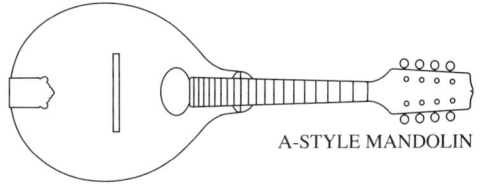

TIPLE

A-STYLE MANDOLIN

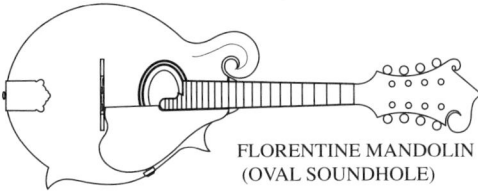

FLORENTINE MANDOLIN
(OVAL SOUNDHOLE)

FLORENTINE MANDOLIN
("*f*" HOLES)

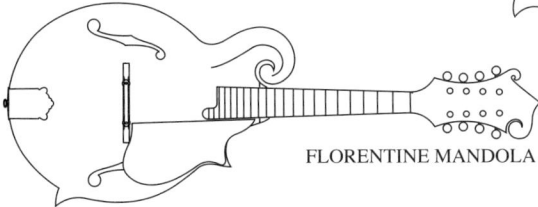

FLORENTINE MANDOLA

OCTAVE MANDOLIN

MANDO-CELLO

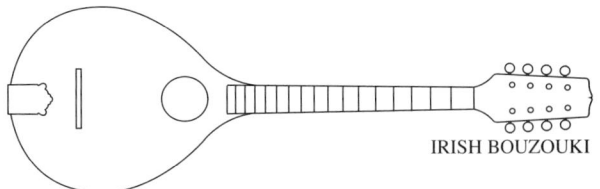

IRISH BOUZOUKI

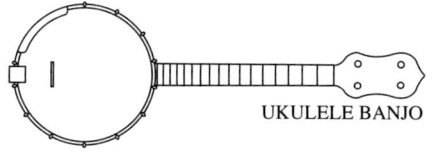

UKULELE BANJO

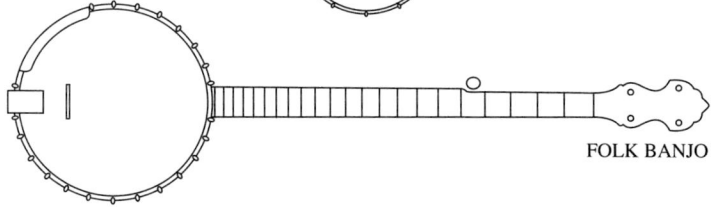

FOLK BANJO

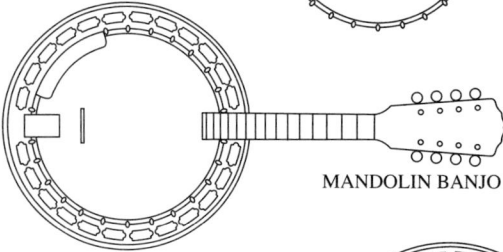

MANDOLIN BANJO

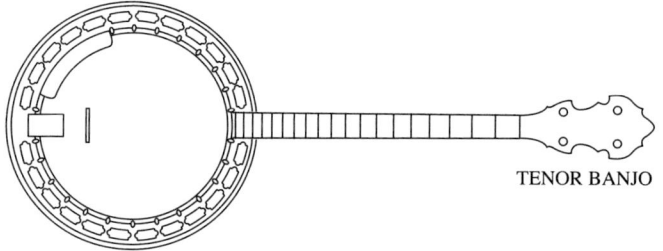

TENOR BANJO

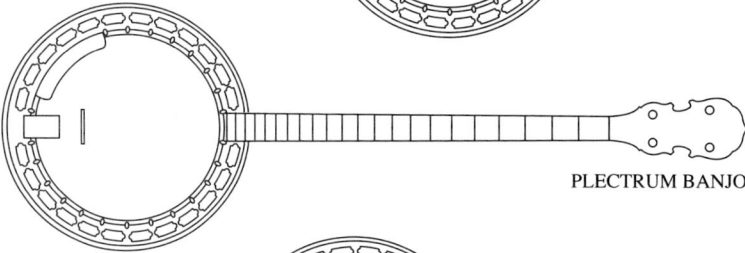

PLECTRUM BANJO

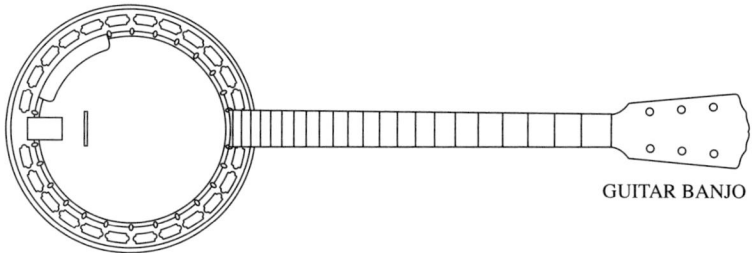

GUITAR BANJO

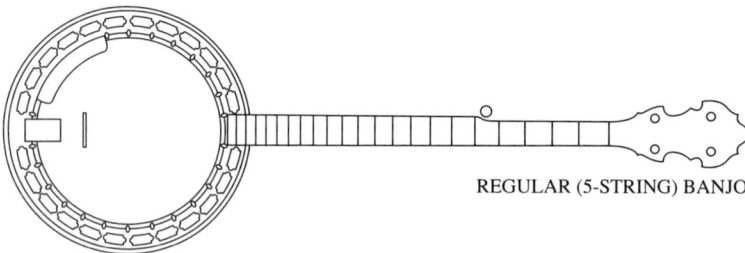

REGULAR (5-STRING) BANJO

RESOPHONIC GUITAR

CLASSICAL GUITAR

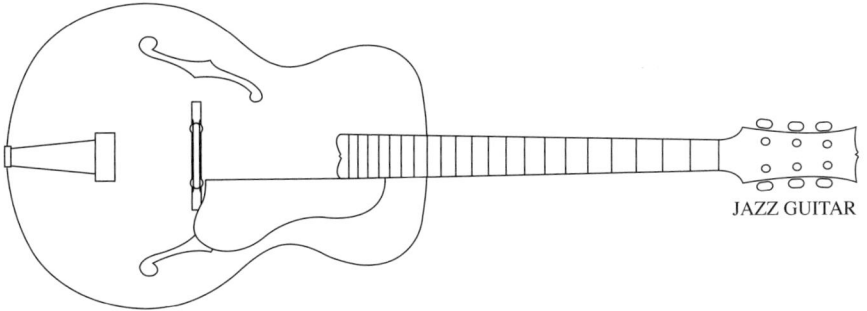

JAZZ GUITAR

FLAMENCO GUITAR

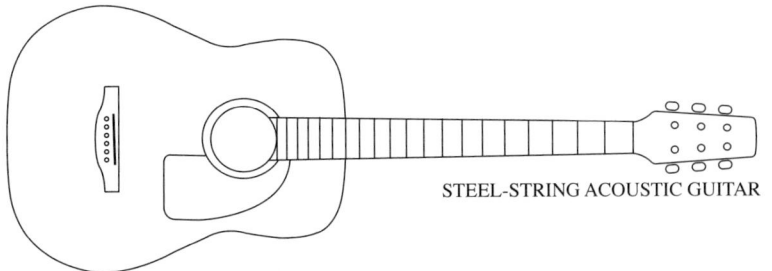

STEEL-STRING ACOUSTIC GUITAR

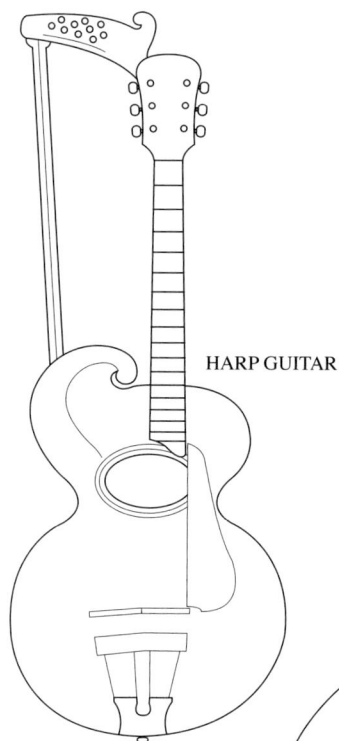

HARP GUITAR

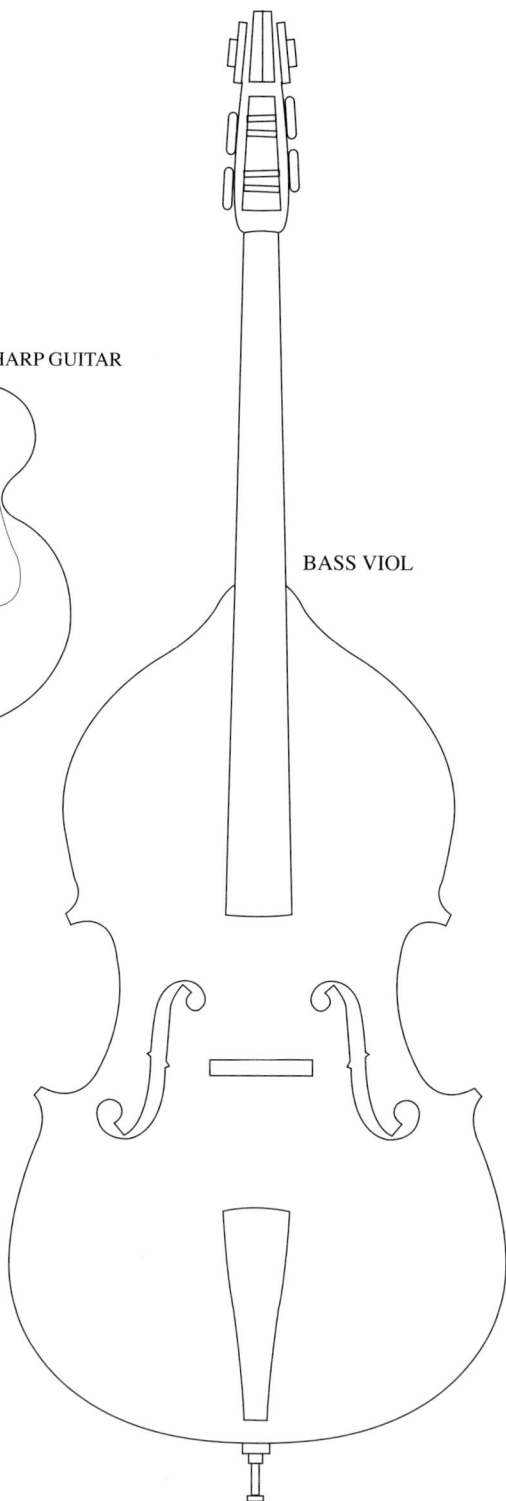

BASS VIOL

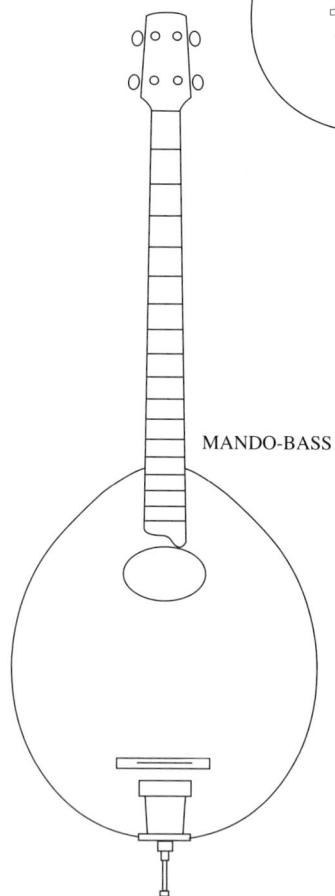

MANDO-BASS

References

Acoustic Guitar Forum, The. http://www.acousticguitarforum.com.

APC International Ltd. http://www.americanpiezo.com.

Bachmann, Alberto. 1975. *An encyclopedia of the violin.* New York: Da Capo Press, Inc.

Brenton Arboretum, The. http://www.thebrentonarboretum.org.

Brough, J. C. S. 1969. *Timbers for woodwork.* New York: Drake Publishers.

Ceolas. http://www.ceolas.org.

C. F. Martin & Co. http://www.mguitar.com.

Chasteen, Stephanie. 2007. Inside mother-of-pearl. *Physical review focus,* July 2. http://focus.aps.org/story/v20/st1.

Constantine, Albert J., Jr. 2005. *Know your woods.* Guilford, CT: The Lyons Press.

Cornwall Wildlife Trust, The. http://www.cornwallwildlifetrust.org.uk.

Cozio.com. http://www.cozio.com.

D'Addario & Company, Inc. http://www.daddario.com.

D'Addario, Jim. E-mail message to author. July 1, 2008.

Dudenbostel, Lynn. E-mail message to author. April 10, 2008.

E.&O. Mari, Inc. http://www.labella.com.

Edlin, Herbert L. 1969. *What wood is that?* New York: Penguin Putnam Inc.

Environmental Protection Agency. http:/www.epa.gov/laq/voc.html.

Exotic Wood Group. http://www.exoticwoodgroup.com.

Fiebing Company, The. http://www.fiebing.com.

Franklin International. http://www.titebond.com.

Friends of the Earth. http://www.foe.co.uk.

Grimm, William Carey. 1962. *Trees for positive identification.* New York: Hawthorn Books, Inc.

Guarnieri Home Web Page, The. http://www.guarnieri.com.

Helmholtz, Hermann. 1954. *On the sensations of tone as a physiological basis for the theory of music.* New York: Dover Publications, Inc.

Hough, Romeyn Beck. 1928. *The wood book.* London: Taschen.

Institute for Learning Technologies, Columbia University. http://www.ilt.columbia.edu.

Johnson, Hugh. 1973. *The international book of trees.* New York: Simon & Schuster.

JustStrings.com. http://www.juststrings.com.

Larson, Daniel. http://www.daniellarson.com.

Legal Information Institute, Cornell University Law School. http://topics.law.cornell.edu.

Longworth, Mike. 1975. *Martin guitars, a history.* Cedar Knolls, NJ: Colonial Press.

Luscombe Violins. http://www.violins.ca.

Luthiers Mercantile International, Inc. http://www.lmii.com.

McDonald, Graham. http://www.mcdonaldstrings.com.

Maderas Barber S.L. http://www.maderasbarber.com.

Mandozine. http://www.mandozine.com.

Massachusetts Maple Producers Association. http://www.massmaple.org/treeID.html.

Mechanical Woods Digest. http://www.mmdigest.com.

Minnesota Historical Society. http://www.mnhs.org.

Monteleone, John. E-mail message to author. March 15, 2008.

Norris, John. E-mail message to author. January 25, 2007.

North Carolina Forestry Association. http://www.ncforestry.org.

Occupational Safety and Health Administration. http://www.osha.gov.

Peterson Electro-Musical Products, Inc. http://www.petersontuners.com.

Porter, Terry. 2004. *Wood identification & use.* East Sussex, England: Guild of Master Craftsman Publications Ltd.

Protea Timber & Building Materials International (Pty) Limited. http://www.protea-timbers.co.za.

Saul, Ron. Personal conversation with author. July 31, 2008.

Siminoff, Andrew. Personal conversation with author. August 2, 2008.

Siminoff, Mark. Personal conversation with author. June 12, 2008 and July 27, 2008.

Smithsonian Encyclopedia. http://www.si.edu/Encyclopedia%5FSI/.

Strings Magazine. http://www.stringsmagazine.com.

Tamarit, Laura. E-mail message to author. February 12, 2008.

U.S. Forest Service, Northeastern area. http://na.fs.fed.us.

Viola da Gamba Society of America. http://vdgsa.org/pgs/stuff.html.

Woodfinder. http://www.woodfinder.com.

Woodworkers Source. http://www.exotichardwoods-africa.com.

My Data

Space is provided here to keep notes of your custom sizes, thicknesses, mixing proportions, part numbers, tools, supplies you order frequently, tuning records, vendor's names, and more.

Adding a word to your Glossary? Please e-mail it to siminoff@siminoff.net for consideration in the next edition.

continued

continued

Wood Identifier

COURTESY MADERAS BARBER S.L.

These wood samples are only suggestive of the species and many variations occur in wood color, grain, and figure. The characteristic of the grain and figure is entirely dependent on the individual board as well as the method of log segmentation.

Each wood sample is provided in its natural state (left image) and finished state (right image). The finished example suggests one coat of clear lacquer, but variations should be expected with other finishing materials, tinted finishes, as well as the number of coats applied.

This section shows nearly 30 woods that are commonly used for instrument construction and is not all inclusive. Woods such as lignum vitae and oak are not shown since they are used for tools and fixtures.

The color of images in this section may differ from the color of natural woods due to variations in photography, printing technologies, and viewing conditions. For accurate evaluation of color, view these plates in the same light source you use to view the natural wood.

WOOD SAMPLE COURTESY MADERAS BARBER S.L.

Bubinga (*Guibourtia tessmannii*)

Origin: Africa

Weight, average (dried): 55 lb/ft^3 (881 kg/m^3)

Typical usage: backboards, ribs/sides, peghead veneers (guitar)

Physical attributes: naturally resistant to decay, difficult on cutting tools, test adhesives on scrap first. Sample shown is plain bubinga; also available in curly figure (inset photo)

Finishing: finishes well, wood filler not needed, accepts all finishing mediums

Also known as: Akume, Bingbinba, Kevazingo

WOOD SAMPLE COURTESY SIMINOFF BANJO & MANDOLIN PARTS

Cedar, Western Red (*Thuja plicata*)

Origin: British Columbia, California to Alaska

Weight, average (dried): 22 lb/ft^3 (352 kg/m^3)

Typical usage: soundboards (classical, flamenco, mandolin)

Physical attributes: light weight, durable, sands well, glues well

Finishing: finishes well, wood filler not needed, accepts all finishing mediums

Also known as: Canoe cedar, Giant arbor vitae, Idaho cedar, Pacific red cedar

WOOD SAMPLE COURTESY MADERAS BARBER S.L.

Cocobolo (*Dalbergia retusa*)

Origin: Mexico, Nicaragua, Western Costa Rica

Weight, average (dried): 65 lb/ft^3 (1041 kg/m^3)

Typical usage: backboards, ribs/sides (guitar), fretboards, peghead veneers, decoratives

Physical attributes: moderate steam and heat bending properties, difficult on cutting tools, difficult to glue, dust is hazardous. The oil it contains can cause problems when gluing.

Finishing: clean with acetone first, finishes well, wood filler not needed, accepts all finishing mediums

Also known as: Nicaraguan rosewood

Cypress (*Cupressus sempervirens*)

Origin: Italy

Weight, average (dried): 40 lb/ft^3 (641 kg/m^3)

Typical usage: backboards, ribs/sides (guitar), veneers

Physical attributes: moderate steam and heat bending properties, glues well

Finishing: finishes well, wood filler not needed, accepts all finishing mediums

Also known as: n/a

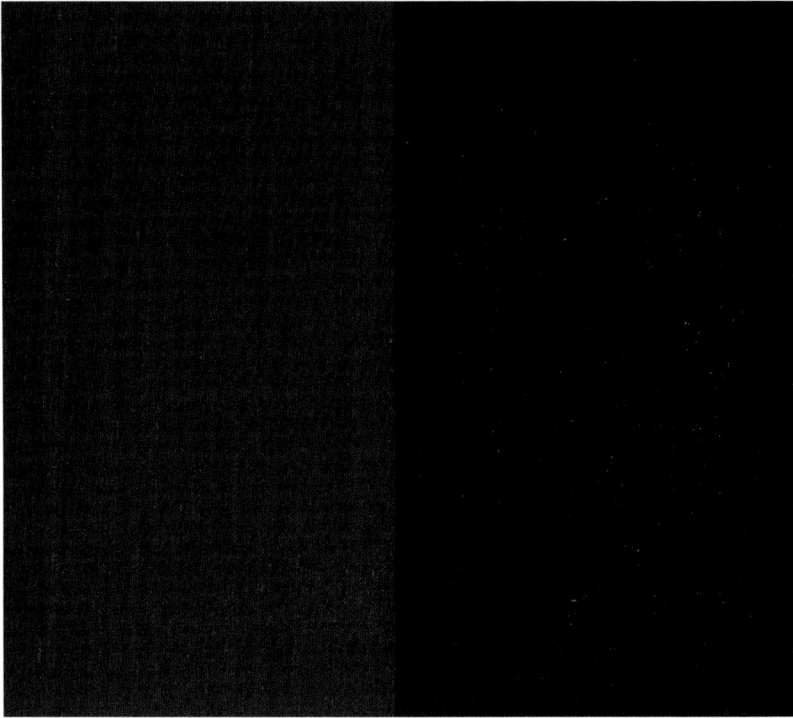

Ebony, Gaboon (*Diospyros crassiflora hiern*)

Origin: Africa (Cameroun, Gabon, Nigeria), Madagascar

Weight, average (dried): 65 lb/ft^3 (1041 kg/m^3)

Typical usage: fretboards, fingerboards, peghead veneers, end pins, bridges, decoratives, violin- and viol-family tailpieces, chin rests, and tuning pegs, woodwinds

Physical attributes: durable, wear resistant, difficult on cutting tools, poor bending properties, polishes well. Can crack easily when atmospheric conditions change.

Finishing: finishes well, wood filler not needed, accepts all finishing mediums, can be waxed and polished

Also known as: Cameroon ebony, Cameroun ebony, Gabon ebony, Madagascar ebony (not to be confused with Macassar ebony)

Ebony, Macassar (*Diospyros macassar*)

Origin: Burma, Ceylon, Indonesia, Southern India

Weight, average (dried): 69 lb/ft^3 (1106 kg/m^3)

Typical usage: peghead veneers, as replacement for Gaboon Ebony where some light coloration is desired

Physical attributes: durable, wear resistant, difficult on cutting tools, poor bending properties, polishes well

Finishing: finishes well, wood filler not needed, accepts all finishing mediums

Also known as: Calamander wood, Golden ebony, Indian ebony, Marblewood, Tendu ebony

Fir, Douglas (*Pseudotsuga taxifolia*)

Origin: British Columbia, Western U.S.

Weight, average (dried): 33 lb/ft^3 (528 kg/m^3)

Typical usage: soundboards (mandolin)

Physical attributes: denser and stiffer than traditional spruce soundboard materials, frequent sap pockets

Finishing: finishes well, wood filler not needed, accepts all finishing mediums

Also known as: Columbian pine, Oregon pine, Red fir, Red spruce (not to be confused with Adirondack red spruce), Yellow Fir

WOOD SAMPLE COURTESY MADERAS BARBER S.L.

Koa (*Acacia koa*)

Origin: Hawaiian Islands

Weight, average (dried): 41 lb/ft^3 (657 kg/m^3)

Typical usage: backboards, ribs/sides, peghead veneers, decoratives (guitar)

Physical attributes: good steam and heat bending properties, glues well

Finishing: finishes well, wood filler not needed, accepts all finishing mediums

Also known as: Hawaiian mahogany, Koa-ka

Mahogany, African (*Khaya ivorensis*)

Origin: Africa

Weight, average (dried): 33 lb/ft³ (528 kg/m³)

Typical usage: backboards, ribs/sides (guitar), headblocks, tailblocks, point blocks, fixtures, patterns

Physical attributes: moderate steam and heat bending properties, dimensionally stable, glues well, hazardous dust, very similar to genuine mahogany

Finishing: finishes well, wood filler required, accepts all finishing mediums

Also known as: Akuk, Bandoro, Bisselon, Ogwango

Mahogany, Honduras (*Swietenia macrophylla*)

Origin: Central America, South America (northern regions)

Weight, average (dried): 36 lb/ft^3 (577 kg/m^3)

Typical usage: backboards, ribs/sides (guitar), headblocks, tailblocks, point blocks, necks, fixtures, patterns

Physical attributes: moderate steam and heat bending properties, dimensionally stable, glues well, machines well, hazardous dust

Finishing: finishes well, wood filler required, accepts all finishing mediums

Also known as: Aguano, American mahogany, Baywood, Big-leaf mahogany, Black mahogany, Black-veined mahogany, Brazilian mahogany, Guatemala mahogany, Mexican mahogany

WOOD SAMPLE COURTESY SIMINOFF BANJO & MANDOLIN PARTS

Maple, Big Leaf (*Acer macrophyllum*), curly figure

Origin: Canada, Northwestern U.S.

Weight, average (dried): 36 lb/ft³ (577 kg/m³)

Typical usage: backboards, ribs/sides, necks (guitar, mandolin, violin)

Physical attributes: excellent steam and heat bending properties, glues well, machines well but some chipping may occur; this wood also available in plain or quilted figure

Finishing: finishes well, wood filler not needed, accepts all finishing mediums

Also known as: Big-leaved maple, Broad-leaf maple, Oregon maple, Soft maple

WOOD SAMPLE COURTESY SIMINOFF BANJO & MANDOLIN PARTS

Maple, Big Leaf (*Acer macrophyllum*), quilted figure

Origin: Canada, Northwestern U.S.

Weight, average (dried): 36 lb/ft^3 (577 kg/m^3)

Typical usage: backboards, ribs/sides (mandolin)

Physical attributes: poor steam and heat bending properties, glues well, machines well; this wood also available in plain, curly and spalted (inset photo) figure

Finishing: finishes well, wood filler not needed, accepts all finishing mediums

Also known as: Big-leaved maple, Broad-leaf maple, Oregon maple, Soft maple

Maple, Sugar (*Acer Saccharum*), bird's eye figure

Origin: Canada, Northeastern U.S.

Weight, average (dried): 40 lb/ft³ (641 kg/m³)

Typical usage: backboards, ribs/sides, necks, peghead veneers

Physical attributes: moderate steam and heat bending properties, machines well, glues well; this wood is also available in plain figure

Finishing: finishes well, wood filler not needed, accepts all finishing mediums

Also known as: Hard maple, Rock maple, White maple

Maple, Sugar (*Acer saccharum*), curly figure

Origin: Canada, Northeastern U.S.

Weight, average (dried): 40 lb/ft³ (641 kg/m³)

Typical usage: backboards, ribs/sides (plain sugar maple is used for banjo rims), peghead veneers, necks

Physical attributes: excellent steam and heat bending properties, glues well, machines well but some chipping may occur; this wood also available in plain figure

Finishing: finishes well, wood filler not needed, accepts all finishing mediums

Also known as: Hard maple, Rock maple, White maple

WOOD SAMPLE COURTESY MADERAS BARBER S.L.

Ovangkol (*Guibourtia ehie*)

Origin: Ghana, Ivory Coast, Nigeria

Weight, average (dried): 50 lb/ft³ (801 kg/m³)

Typical usage: backboards, ribs/sides, fretboards, peghead veneers

Physical attributes: moderate steam and heat bending properties, naturally resistant to decay, difficult on cutting tools, test adhesives on scrap first

Finishing: clean with acetone first, finishes well, wood filler not needed, accepts all finishing mediums

Also known as: Amazakoue, Anokye, Hyeduanini

Padouk, African (*Pterocarpus soyauxii*)

Origin: Africa

Weight, average (dried): 48 lb/ft³ (769 kg/m³)

Typical usage: backboards, ribs/sides

Physical attributes: moderate steam and heat bending properties, moderately difficult on cutting tools, test adhesives on scrap first

Finishing: finishes well, wood filler not needed, accepts all finishing mediums

Also known as: Barwood, Bosulu, Camwood

WOOD SAMPLE COURTESY SIMINOFF BANJO & MANDOLIN PARTS

Redwood (California) (*Sequoia sempervirens*)

Origin: California, Oregon

Weight, average (dried): 25 lb/ft³ (400 kg/m³)

Typical usage: soundboards (mandolin)

Physical attributes: naturally resistant to decay, soft, light, easy to sand and cut, glues well, must be well braced

Finishing: finishes well, wood filler not needed, accepts all finishing mediums

Also known as: Californian redwood, Coast redwood, Sequoia

WOOD SAMPLE COURTESY MADERAS BARBER S.L.

Rosewood, Amazon (*Dalbergia spruceana*)

Origin: Brazil

Weight, average (dried): 68 lb/ft^3 (1089 kg/m^3)

Typical usage: backboards, ribs/sides (guitar), fretboards, peghead veneers, bridges, decoratives

Physical attributes: good steam and heat bending properties, naturally resistant to decay, difficult on cutting tools, test adhesives on scrap first

Finishing: clean with acetone first, finishes well, wood filler not needed, accepts all finishing mediums

Also known as: Amazonian rosewood

WOOD SAMPLE COURTESY MADERAS BARBER S.L.

Rosewood, Honduras (*Dalbergia stevensonii*)

Origin: Belize, Guatemala

Weight, average (dried): 60 lb/ft^3 (961 kg/m^3)

Typical usage: backboards, ribs/sides (guitar), fretboards, peghead veneers, bridges, decoratives

Physical attributes: good steam and heat bending properties, naturally resistant to decay, difficult on cutting tools, test adhesives on scrap first

Finishing: clean with acetone first, finishes well, wood filler not needed, accepts all finishing mediums

Also known as: Nogaed, Hoduras palisander

WOOD SAMPLE COURTESY MADERAS BARBER S.L.

Rosewood, Indian (*Dalbergia latifolia*)

Origin: India

Weight, average (dried): 53 lb/ft³ (849 kg/m³)

Typical usage: backboards, ribs/sides (guitar), fretboards, peghead veneers, bridges, decoratives

Physical attributes: good steam and heat bending properties, naturally resistant to decay, difficult on cutting tools, test adhesives on scrap first

Finishing: clean with acetone first, finishes well, wood filler not needed, accepts all finishing mediums

Also known as: Biti, Bombay blackwood, Indian palisander, Kalaruk, Malabar

WOOD SAMPLE COURTESY MADERAS BARBER S.L.

Rosewood, Madagascar (*Dalbergia baronii)*

Origin: Madagascar

Weight, average (dried): 40 lb/ft^3 (641 kg/m^3)

Typical usage: backboards, ribs/sides (guitar), fretboards, peghead veneers, bridges, decoratives

Physical attributes: good steam and heat bending properties, naturally resistant to decay, moderately difficult on cutting tools, test adhesives on scrap first, available in a wide array of dramatic figure (inset photo). Most similar wood to Brazilian rosewood. Dark to light coloration with spider webbing and dark grain.

Finishing: clean with acetone first, finishes well, wood filler not needed, accepts all finishing mediums

Also known as: African rosewood

WOOD SAMPLE COURTESY MADERAS BARBER S.L.

Rosewood, Santos (*Caesalpinia ferrea*)

Origin: Brazil

Weight, average (dried): 59 lb/ft^3 (945 kg/m^3)

Typical usage: backboards, ribs/sides (guitar), fretboards, peghead veneers, bridges, decoratives

Physical attributes: good steam and heat bending properties, naturally resistant to decay, difficult on cutting tools, test adhesives on scrap first, less expensive substitute for other rosewoods

Finishing: clean with acetone first, finishes well, wood filler not needed, accepts all finishing mediums

Also known as: Pau ferro

WOOD SAMPLE COURTESY MADERAS BARBER S.L.

Sapele (*Entandrophragma cylindricum*)

Origin: Africa

Weight, average (dried): 39 lb/ft³ (625 kg/m³)

Typical usage: backboards, ribs/sides (guitar)

Physical attributes: poor-to-moderate steam and heat bending properties, test adhesives on scrap first. Good substitute for genuine mahogany.

Finishing: finishes well, wood filler not needed, accepts all finishing mediums

Also known as: Aboudikro, Penkra, Sapelewood, Scented mahogany

WOOD SAMPLE COURTESY SIMINOFF BANJO & MANDOLIN PARTS

Spruce, Englemann (*Picea engelmannii*)

Origin: Canada, Western U.S.

Weight, average (dried): 27 lb/ft³ (432 kg/m³)

Typical usage: bracings and tone bars, soundboards

Physical attributes: straight moderately-even grain with some silk, machines and glues well. Can stain (blemish) easily. [Do not store in humid place.]

Finishing: finishes well, wood filler not needed, accepts all finishing mediums

Also known as: Canadian spruce

WOOD SAMPLE COURTESY SIMINOFF BANJO & MANDOLIN PARTS

Spruce, German Silver (*Picea abies*)

Origin: Central and Northern Europe

Weight, average (dried): 27 lb/ft^3 (432 kg/m^3)

Typical usage: bracings and tone bars, soundboards

Physical attributes: straight tight grain with silk, machines and glues well

Finishing: finishes well, wood filler not needed, accepts all finishing mediums

Also known as: European spruce

Spruce, Red (*Picea rubens sarg.*)

Origin: Canada, Northeastern U.S.

Weight, average (dried): 28 lb/ft^3 (448 kg/m^3)

Typical usage: bracings and tone bars, soundboards

Physical attributes: straight tight grain with some silk, machines and glues well

Finishing: finishes well, wood filler not needed, accepts all finishing mediums

Also known as: Adirondack red spruce. (Not to be confused with the "Red spruce" reference to Douglas fir.)

WOOD SAMPLE COURTESY SIMINOFF BANJO & MANDOLIN PARTS

Spruce, Sitka (*Picea sitchensis*)

Origin: Alaska, Northwestern U.S., Western Canada

Weight, average (dried): 27 lb/ft^3 (432 kg/m^3)

Typical usage: soundboards

Physical attributes: straight grain, machines and glues well

Finishing: finishes well, wood filler not needed, accepts all finishing mediums

Also known as: Menzies spruce, Tideland spruce

Sycamore (*Acer pseudoplantanus*)

Origin: Central and Southern Europe, U.S.

Weight, average (dried): 38 lb/ft^3 (609 kg/m^3)

Typical usage: figured variety used for backboards, ribs/sides (guitar)

Physical attributes: good steam and heat bending properties, glues well, often used as substitute for maple, similar physical and acoustical attributes as maple, available in curly figure (inset photo)

Finishing: finishes well, wood filler not needed, accepts all finishing mediums

Also known as: Bergahorn, Great maple

WOOD SAMPLE COURTESY MADERAS BARBER S.L.

Walnut, (American) Black (*Juglans nigra*)

Origin: Canada and U.S.

Weight, average (dried): 40 lb/ft³ (641 kg/m³)

Typical usage: backboards, necks, ribs/sides (guitar), veneers

Physical attributes: moderate steam and heat bending properties, glues well, good on cutting tools

Finishing: finishes well, wood filler needed, accepts all finishing mediums

Also known as: Eastern black walnut, Gunwood, Virginia walnut

WOOD SAMPLE COURTESY MADERAS BARBER S.L.

Zebrano (*Microberlinia brazzavillensis*)

Origin: West Africa

Weight, average (dried): 46 lb/ft³ (737 kg/m³)

Typical usage: backboards, ribs/sides (guitar)

Physical attributes: good steam and heat bending properties, naturally resistant to decay, difficult on cutting tools, test adhesives on scrap first

Finishing: clean with acetone first, finishes well, wood filler not needed, accepts all finishing mediums

Also known as: Ele, Okwen, Singana, Zebrawood

WOOD SAMPLE COURTESY MADERAS BARBER S.L.

Ziricote (*Cordia dodecandra*)

Origin: Belize, Guatemala, Mexico

Weight, average (dried): 48lb/ft^3 (769kg/m^3)

Typical usage: backboards, fretboards, ribs/sides, veneers

Physical attributes: good steam and heat bending properties, naturally resistant to decay, difficult on cutting tools, test adhesives on scrap first. Cracks easily.

Finishing: clean with acetone first, finishes well, wood filler not needed, accepts all finishing mediums

Also known as: Canalete, Peterebi, Sericote